MEDIA, FEMINISM, CULTURAL STUDIES

The Sacred Cinema of Andrei Tarkovsky
by Jeremy Mark Robinson

Liv Tyler
by Thomas A. Christie

The Cinema of Hayao Miyazaki
Jeremy Mark Robinson

Stepping Forward: Essays, Lectures and Interviews
by Wolfgang Iser

The Christmas Movie Book
by Thomas A. Christie

Wild Zones: Pornography, Art and Feminism
by Kelly Ives

'Cosmo Woman': The World of Women's Magazines
by Oliver Whitehorne

The Cinema of Richard Linklater
by Thomas A. Christie

Andrea Dworkin
by Jeremy Mark Robinson

Cixous, Irigaray, Kristeva: The Jouissance of French Feminism
by Kelly Ives

The Erotic Object: Sexuality in Sculpture From Prehistory to the Present Day
by Susan Quinnell

Women in Pop Music
by Helen Challis

Sex in Art: Pornography and Pleasure in Painting and Sculpture
by Cassidy Hughes

Erotic Art
by Cassidy Hughes

John Hughes
by Thomas A. Christie

THE GOSPEL
ACCORDING
TO MATTHEW

THE GOSPEL ACCORDING TO MATTHEW

PIER PAOLO PASOLINI

POCKET MOVIE GUIDE

Jeremy Mark Robinson

CRESCENT MOON

Crescent Moon Publishing
P.O. Box 1312, Maidstone
Kent, ME14 5XU, Great Britain
www.crmoon.com

First published 2022.
© Jeremy Mark Robinson 2022.

Set in Times New Roman 9 on 12pt.
Designed by Radiance Graphics.

The right of Jeremy Mark Robinson to be identified
as the author of this book has been asserted generally in
accordance with sections 77 and 78 of the Copyright,
Designs and Patents Act 1988.

British Library Cataloguing in Publication data
available for this title.

ISBN-13 9781861718518

CONTENTS

ACKNOWLEDGEMENTS

To the authors and publishers quoted.
To the copyright holders of the illustrations.

ABBREVIATIONS

ES   Enzo Siciliano, *Pier Paolo Pasolini*
PP   *Pasolini On Pasolini*

ALFREDO BINI
PRESENTA

UN FILM DI
PIER PAOLO PASOLINI

IL
VANGELO
SECONDO
MATTEO

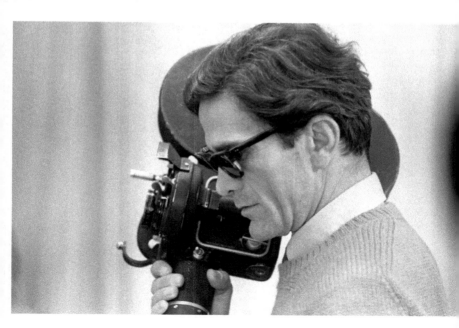

PART ONE
✤
PIER PAOLO PASOLINI

Oso alzare gli occhi
sulle cime secche degli alberi:
non vedo il Signore, ma il suo lume
che brilla sempre immenso.

(Daring to lift my eyes
towards the dry treetops,
I don't see God, but his light
is immensely shining.)

Pier Pasolo Pasolini, 'Mystery' (1945)[1]

---

1 Trans. A.P. Nicolai, C.U.N.Y., Brooklyn.

1

INTRODUCTION

This study focusses on *The Gospel According To Matthew* (1964), directed by Pier Paolo Pasolini. It should be remembered that he was also a poet, novelist, essayist and playwright. Indeed, there is still a huge interest in Pasolini as a poet and writer, and there are as many articles and books about Pasolini's writing as there are about his cinema. (For many, it is Pasolini the poet who is more valuable culturally than Pasolini the filmmaker – which's a *very* unusual situation for a film director who's regarded as a major player in Italian and European cinema). But Pasolini is one of those filmmakers, like Orson Welles or Jean-Luc Godard, who is so enormously talented and full of life, they produced major works in a number of areas, not only in cinema.

There are plenty of approaches to the work of Pier Paolo Pasolini – I have focussed on the cinema, and Pasolini as a filmmaker. Another obvious approach is to consider the gay, queer and homosexual elements in Pasolini's work (as I have done so much of this elsewhere, I have left that approach aside).

I began my study of Pasolini's cinema (*Pasolini: Il Cinema di Poesia/ The Cinema of Poetry*) in the early 2000s, and added to it over the years, including in 2011, 2015 and 2017 (when it was nearly complete). It has been difficult to finish – partly because Pasolini is a fascinating filmmaker and artist, and there always seems to be more to say about his work. This book is an off-shoot of my main study of Pasolini, which has been rewritten and expanded numerous times, and has demanded an enormous amount of work to complete.

2

PIER PAOLO PASOLINI:
BIOGRAPHY

LIFE.

Pier Paolo Pasolini was born on March 5, 1922, in
Bologna, Italy. He died on November 2, 1975, in Ostia,
Rome (he was buried in Casarsa, in his beloved Friuli).
Italy, by the way, has a population of 57 million (in
1997), and a land mass of 116,341 square miles. The
country was re-unified in 1870.

Pier Paolo Pasolini looks like one of the characters
in his movies: the suave, chiselled, sometimes gaunt
features (beautiful cheekbones!), the short, dark hair,
and those beady eyes that don't miss a thing. Pasolini
comes across in interviews (and in his films) as an
aristocrat – an artist, surely, but debonair, sophisticated
and clever. He appears highly educated, intellectual, out-
spoken, but also mischievous and very individual
(people compared him to a priest – and of course he
played priests in his movies).

He was a slim, rangy guy, 5' 6" (with those
prominent cheekbones and piercing dark eyes, he was
often compared to actor Jack Palance: the street kids of
Roma called him *Giacche Palànce*).[2] He prided himself
on keeping active into middle-age, and being able to

---

2 Jack Palance in his red Alfa Romeo in *Contempt* (1963) is strikingly
reminiscent of Pier Paolo Pasolini.

play soccer.[3]

Later, when he was a film director (starting late, at age 39), Pier Paolo Pasolini was certainly an intimidating presence, with a formidable reputation – like Cecil B. DeMille, Erich von Stroheim or Akira Kurosawa. Very confident, very smart, a great talker and interviewee, a leader on set, with no doubts from anyone about who was the primary creator and author.

It's clear, if you know anything about Pier Paolo Pasolini, that he was a very bright guy from an early age. He doesn't seem to have been afflicted by a lack of self-confidence – certainly with regard to his own work (which affects writers almost as a matter of course). Pasolini happily, in his twenties, takes on any big subject he likes.

Pasolini's background was bourgeois – ironic, considering how passionately he detested the bourgeoisie. His mother, Susanna Colussi, was born in 1891 and died in 1981. His father Carlo Alberto Pasolini (1892-1958) was a lieutenant in the Italian Army[4] (consequently, like many military families, they moved around a good deal). They married in 1921. For Pasolini, his father was 'overbearing, egoistic, egocentric, tyrannical and authoritarian' (PP, 13).

Pier Paolo Pasolini's relationship with his mother Susanna Colussi, and hers with him, has been described as unhealthily eroticized: according to Enzo Siciliano, Susanna invested far too much in her son emotionally: she gave Pasolini what she withheld from her husband Carlo Alberto (ES, 33). The theme of (hints of) incestuous relations between mothers and sons crop up in Pasolini's work (in *Mamma Roma*, obviously; some Pasolini movies, such as *Theorem*, play the incestuous fantasy literally and explicitly).

Pier Paolo Pasolini's brother Guidalberto (b. 1925) died in WWII (in 1945), when he was part of the Resistance. In the war, Pasolini was taken prisoner by the Germans, but escaped back to Friuli. WWII looms

3 Tho', like everybody, he also disliked ageing (the bad teeth, the thinning hair), and dressed younger than his years.
4 His father had once prevented an assassination attempt on Benito Mussolini.

very large over all of Pasolini's work.

Pier Paolo Pasolini described himself as a child as stubborn, capricious, naïve, credulous, easily enthusiastic, and also shy and awkward (ES, 45). As a boy, Pasolini lived in Bologna, Belluno, Conegliano, Casarsa della Delizia (in Friuli), Cremona, Scandiano and Reggio Emilia.[5] From 1950, Pasolini made Rome[6] his home (PP, 19).

Apart from literature[7] (he formed a literature club at high school), Pier Paolo Pasolini enjoyed football. As a child Pasolini studied music (piano and violin) briefly.

Pier Paolo Pasolini worked as a teacher in the late 1940s and early 1950s. Pasolini had a number of teaching posts, and the teacher in him never left – it was always a part of his movies, for instance (indeed, a character such as the talking bird in *The Hawks and the Sparrows* was entirely a teacher figure). And in interviews, Pasolini can't help coming across at times like an instructor.

That Pier Paolo Pasolini was a highly, passionately politicized artist is obvious: his passion for political issues runs throughout his movies and his poetry, his interviews, his essays, and pretty much everything he did or said publicly. Pasolini is always talking about Italian society, Italian culture, about Communism in Italy, about how Italy is becoming modernized, about Italy losing something when it embraces new technologies, etc. If there's an opportunity for rumin-ating on contemporary, Italian culture and society, Pasolini will take it.

Among the important friends in Pier Paolo Pasolini's life were:

Laura Betti (1927-2004).

Alberto Moravia (1907-1990).[8]

5 As a youth, Pier Paolo Pasolini said he grew up in Bologna, Parma, Conigilano, Belluno, Sacile, Idria, Cremona and other towns in Northern Italy (PP, 11).

6 Pasolini bought a country retreat at Chai, near Viterbo, which Dante Ferretti had re-modelled for him.

7 Pasolini's early literary idols included Rimbaud, Dostoievsky, Tolstoy, Shakespeare, Novalis and Coleridge.

8 The *dolce vita* set included Federico Fellini, Pier Paolo Pasolini, Luchino Visconti, Alberto Moravia *et al.*

Elsa Morante (1912-1985).

Franco Citti (1938-2016).

Sergio Citti (1933-2005).

Susanna Colussi, mother (1891-1981).

Ninetto Davoli (b. 1948).

One of Pier Paolo Pasolini's first lovers was the fourteen year-old Tonuti Spagnol, whom Pasolini had met in Versuta (where he and his mom Susanna Colussi had retreated during the bombings of WW2). Pasolini tended to go for much younger lovers (like Ninetto Davoli later, 26 years younger than him).

Way before Pier Paolo Pasolini began to write for movies and then to direct them, he was deeply into poetry, into writing, and into literature. Way back in the 1940s, when Pasolini was in his twenties (and during WWII), he was already publishing poetry, writing essays,[9] reviews, and memorials (such as for his brother Guido who died in the war at the hands of Communists).

Another of Pier Paolo Pasolini's passions, long before he became enamoured of cinema, was Friuli: Friuli the place, the landscape, and the local people (and, later, the Friulian dialect). Pasolini moved away from Bologna (which he associated with his father) to Friuli.

Pier Paolo Pasolini had grown up around Casarsa, near Pordenone, in the Friuli-Venezia Giulia region, right up in the Northern corner of Italy. Yugoslavia is not far off to the East, with the Alps to the North; Venice isn't too far away (the Venice Film Festival looms large in Pasolinu's career). Friuli is a region that prides itself on being somewhat distanced from Italy. Friuli is known for its peasant culture, which Pasolini revered (tho' it has been disappearing for many decades).

Pier Paolo Pasolini was thus a kid from the sticks, not a city kid at all, not the sophisticated urbanite of Italy's great cities (Milan, Bologna,[10] Venice, Rome, nor the Southern country that he later loved – Napoli, Sicily). Rather, it was a world of small towns and

9 In his essays and articles for magazines over the years Pier Paolo Pasolini discussed Giuseppe Ungaretti, Umberto Saba, and Gianna Manzaini.

10 Tho' he was born in Bologna.

villages and the countryside, bicycle rides, flirting with girls, reading books, writing poetry in dialect ('peace and quiet, girls, mental concentration, fields, idleness, drink', Pasolini noted in a letter of 1940, when he was 18).

But it was also the Friulian dialect (*friulano*) that Pier Paolo Pasolini fell in love with, and Friulian culture. Pasolini was a keen connoisseur of dialects; he composed works in dialect (such as his early poetry), and also employed dialects in his cinema.

Pier Paolo Pasolini was a devotee of language like many modern poets and writers. One thinks of Rainer Maria Rilke, André Gide, Lawrence Durrell, Henry Miller, Alain Robbe-Grillet, Samuel Beckett, etc – writers for whom language and communication itself was a mysterious and utterly compelling force in their lives. Language, as French feminist Hélène Cixous remarked, is the key. For Cixous (who is loved and loathed by feminists nearly as energetically as Andrea Dworkin or Princess Diana), writing is absolutely crucial, and central. Writing is oxygen to Cixous, she must write to live. Cixous asserted in "Difficult Joys" that

> writing, writing poetically, treating language as one of the most important things in the world, today sounds mad. Yet for human beings it is the first most important thing.[11]

Pier Paolo Pasolini was one of those filmmakers who, had he been unable to continue to make movies, would've been quite happy writing (Woody Allen and Ingmar Bergman come to mind).[12] Jean-Luc Godard also took that view: for him, filmmaking and writing were part of the same thing anyway. Writing was 'already a way of making films,' Godard said in 1962 of his time as a film critic, 'for the difference between writing and

11 "Difficult Joys", in H. Wilcox, 1990, 23.
12 There are, of course, some famous film directors who found writing very difficult to do – Steven Spielberg, David Lean, Stanley Kubrick – filmmakers who couldn't write their own scripts, who had to have collaborators and writers. But of course most directors *do not* write their own scripts at all.

directing is quantative not qualitative'.[13] Godard often said he wouldn't stop creating if cinema died: he would move into TV, and if that disappeared, he would move into writing again (ibid., 171).

Other areas which Pasolini might've explored had he lived longer would include opera – several of his contemporaries took up directing live opera performances (Luchino Visconti, Ken Russell, Andrei Tarkovsky, Robert Altman – and even Federico Fellini, who disliked opera, came around to it. Fellini claimed that he only liked Nino Rota's music, and didn't like anything else. In the 1980s, however, Fellini decided he liked opera after all).[14]

Another area was pop promos – maybe too capitalist for Pier Paolo Pasolini, but the right pop act and the right deal might've attracted Pasolini to direct some pop videos. (One of the appeals was that they could be done in a single day, often had a decent budget, and were guaranteed exhibition and an audience).

DVD, Blu-ray and home releases of movies seem an ideal platform for Pier Paolo Pasolini to talk about his works. Some of the most valuable contributions that film directors make are to audio commentaries about their movies (such as Ken Russell, Oliver Stone, Werner Herzog, Mamoru Oshii and Stephen Sommers). Pasolini relating the stories of making *The Gospel According To Matthew* and *The Arabian Nights* would be a treat. (However, some film directors pointedly refuse to talk in audio commentaries about their films, such as Steven Spielberg and Woody Allen. For them, the works speak for themselves).

---

13 *Godard On Godard*, 171.
14 *And the Ship Sails On* (1983) featured an opera star along with other singers, and many other references to opera, and Fellini planned a documentary about opera in 1987 (there were invitations to direct operas, such as at Covent Garden and in Milan).

PASOLINI AND HIS FATHER

The revolt against the Father, against his own father
Carlo Alberto Pasolini, was a violent one for Pier Paolo
Pasolini, and it coloured much of his work. 'The public
aspect of Pasolini's poetry will take the form of a
struggle against all repressive and authoritarian
conventions', remarked Enzo Siciliano (ES, 43), and it
was his father that inaugurated that rebellion. (It was the
loss/ rejection of the father, Siciliano reckoned, that was
fatal for Pasolini, a loss and a pain that never left him).

Pier Paolo Pasolini associated his father and the
father image with 'all the symbols of authority and
order, of fascism, of the bourgeoisie'.[15] Pasolini defined
his father as 'a nationalist and a fascist', and conventional (PP, 14).

According to his biographer, Pier Paolo Pasolini's
father Carlo Alberto was stricken by his son's gay
lifestyle:

he was overwhelmed by the drama of Pier Paolo, by
the "scandal," and accepted it with grief. It brought
him to a kind of insanity. He drank more and more,
and at night cried out that his wife did not love
him. (ES, 40)

As Pier Paolo Pasolini put it, he had placed himself
'in a relationship of rivalry and hatred towards my
father', which made it easier for him to examine that
relationship, compared to that with his mother, which
was more latent (PP, 119). For Pasolini, 'everything
ideological, voluntary, active and practical in my
actions as a writer depends on my struggle with my
father' (ibid., 120). Pasolini was thus conscious of using
his deep-seated feelings as engines for his creative work
(in the way that André Gide said that everything could
be material or fuel for a writer. Famously, Gide remarked
that as he was living his life he was also considering
how it could be exploited in his writing).

According to Sam Rohdie, Pier Paolo Pasolini
15 Quoted in J. Duflot, 22.

THE GOSPEL ACCORDING TO MATTHEW ✝ 22

associated Northern Italia and Bologna with his father, with the bourgeoisie, with fascism, with technology, with capitalism, and with the Law of the Father. That was not the Italy that Pasolini enshrined, but the one he wanted to move away from. Pasolini's Italy was of the South, of Rome and Napoli and Calabria: the South was alive, it was peasants, it was a link to the past, it was non-technological, it was not capitalist (13). However, Bologna has long been a stronghold for the Italian Communist Party (it has held the city since 1945).

That Pier Paolo Pasolini's cinema exhibits a major father complex is clear to all. The ambiguous, anxious attitude towards fathers, father figures, the Sins of the Fathers, and the older generation, is everywhere. In *Pigsty,* the only words spoken in the 15th century tale are when the chief protagonist (Pierre Clementi) announces just as he's about to die: 'I killed my father, I ate the flesh of humans, I shivered with joy' (or something similar). Killing the father – the atmosphere of *Oedipus Rex* and *Theorem* was still in the air, perhaps (these movies – *Pigsty, Theorem, Medea* and *Oedipus Rex* are perhaps Pasolini's most concentrated attacks on the figure of the father).

POETRY AND LITERATURE

Pier Paolo Pasolini was writing poetry and articles from an early age: it's as if, as with poets such as Emily Dickinson or William Shakespeare, he had always written poetry. It was one of the fundamental creative activities in his life. He became disillusioned with politics, with the cultural life in contemporary Italy, with intellectuals, with the passing of the old world (as he saw it – but it had been decaying for 100s of years), yet his poetry remained central to his existence.

Pier Paolo Pasolini's poetry is in free verse – long,

rambling lines and stanzas in the modernist tradition (recalling poets such as Walt Whitman and D.H. Lawrence, who preferred to write in lengthy, loose lines).

Pier Paolo Pasolini's first artistic efforts in the public arena included publishing a literary magazine (in 1941), and his own poems (*Versi a Casarsa*, 1941). He was editor of *Il Setaccio* (*The Sieve*).

By the late 1940s, Pasolini was writing and publishing regularly: *The Diaries*; *Quaderni Rossi*; the play *Il Cappellano*; and *The Cries*, a poetry book. Pasolini's novels (still in print) include *Ragazzi de Vita* (1955)[16] and *Una Vita Violenta* (1959) (both of which have been filmed).

Pier Paolo Pasolini's novel *Ragazzi di Vita* was 'a succès de scandale, drawing positive reviews, heated sales, hostile editorials, and even legal action for obscenity', remarked Shawn Levy in *Dolce Vita Confidential* (190). *Boys of Life* had a run-in in 1956 with the public prosecution office for being 'obscene'. Among the defenders of *Ragazzi di Vita* were Giuseppe Ungaretti, Carlo Bo, Pietro Bianchi and Livio Garzanti.

Reviewing *Una Vita Violenta*, Mario Montanana (a Communist senator), wondered that

> Pasolini does not like poor people, that he despises in general the inhabitants of the Roman shanty-towns, and despises our party even more. The hero, Tommasino, is in reality a juvenile delinquent of the worst kind: thief, robber, pederast.

Enzo Siciliano called Pier Paolo Pasolini a

> frantically manneristic writer – and of a baroque mannerism, a lover of asymmetry, of tormented versifications of topical matter, who made of his style a shining example of the forbidden, who delighted in a "poetics of regression" in order to break the gilded trappings of twentieth-century academicism. (ES, 398)

16 Andrea Di Marco sued Pier Paolo Pasolini for libel in relation to *Ragazzi di Vita* in April, 1962.

An unfinished novel (of 1948), *Amado Mio*, contained autobiographical resonances, coalescing around its central character, Desiderio. In *Amado Mio*, Pasolini secreted 'the meaning of his own obsession,' according to Enzo Sciliano: 'to become father to his boy, so that the latter would mirror, by returning his embrace, all his unsatisfied longings for a son' (114).

The early work, *Amado Mio*, contains a pæan to Rita Hayworth in *Gilda*, as it plays to a cinema of rowdy, young Italians, by moonlight, in the open-air, with the boisterous crowd getting turned on. As the narrator of *Amado Mio* tells it,

> before the image of Gilda something wondrously shared enveloped all the spectators... Rita Hayworth with her huge body, her smile, her breasts of a sister and a prostitute – equivocal and angelic – stupid and mysterious with that nearsighted gaze of hers, cold and tender to the point of languor...

Pasolini was a passionate advocate of Friuli – he was a member of the Friulian Language Academy, the Association for the Autonomy of Friuli, and contributed to the magazine *Stroligùt di cà da l'aga*. Pasolini learnt how to speak Friulian as an adult – it wasn't part of his upbringing: it became part of his poetry – 'I learnt it as a sort of mystic act of love' (PP, 15).

Among Pier Paolo Pasolini's early influences were William Shakespeare (*Macbeth*), whom he discovered at 14,[17] and of course Italy's two giant poets, Francesco Petrarch and Dante Alighieri. Other favourites were André Gide (such as his novel *The Immoralist*[18]), Barbey d'Aurevilly, Niccolò Tommaseo, Johann Wolfgang von

---

17 With *Macbeth* Pasolini entered the world of books, visiting the stalls in the Portici della Morte in Bologna to buy used books.

18 A novel tailor-made for Pasolini, evoking a spiritual journey from Northern Europe to the South, the breakdown of a marriage, the discovery of homosexual encounters in North Africa, and the development of an Existential, outsider persona. Classically, André Gide begins his tale with the anti-hero's father's death, a very Pasolinian device (instantly adding a welter of œdipal associations and an evocation of the Law of the Father). Pasolini didn't need to adapt *The Immoralist* – he lived it (tho' it would have been fascinating to see Pasolini take on Gide).

Goethe, Lautréamont and *Les Chants de Maldoror* (inevitably), Arthur Schopenhauer (his pithy, proto-Existential philosophy is a favourite with many European intellectuals), Villiers de l'Isle-Adam, and Daniell Bartoli (*Uomo al punto*).

As a youth, Pier Paolo Pasolini said he had consumed adventure stories, like many other children, but in his mid-teens discovered Fyodor Dostoievsky, William Shakespeare, Arthur Rimbaud, and authors who were somewhat regarded as rebellious, standing outside of the fascist society of Italy (PP, 17).

There are so many references to the work of Dante Alighieri in Pier Paolo Pasolini's output it's a wonder that he didn't produce a feature film of the *Divina Commedia* (or at least a TV documentary). However, there *are* elements of *The Divine Comedy* in *The Decameron*, in the finale of *The Canterbury Tales,* with its devils, the traveller and his guide (in *The Hawks and the Sparrows* and the 'trilogy of life' films), and of course the *tableaux* from Renaissance art in *La Ricotta* and *The Gospel According To Matthew*.

The significance of Pier Paolo Pasolini's works are often interpreted as a group, and in relation to one another, rather than taken as single pieces to be seen in isolation. Thus, *Accattone* is always related to Pasolini's novels of the rough Roman youth, and the Marxism in *The Gospel According To Matthew* and *Oedipus Rex* is related to Pasolini's political statements. (This interconnectedness was of course encouraged by the maestro himself).

'THE BOURGEOISIE ARE ALWAYS WRONG': MARXISM AND ANTI-BOURGEOIS POLITICS

> I don't think you can make an unpolitical movie.
> Your politics are going to show by permission or
> omission, so that the best you can do is to try and
> focus on them in some way in your movie, organise
> it so that it doesn't happen totally by accident.

Warren Beatty

Only Jean-Luc Godard among comparable filmmakers has a deeper and more visceral loathing of the bourgeoisie than Pier Paolo Pasolini. Oh, how Pasolini *hated* everything bourgeois! – 'I nourish a visceral, deep, irreducible hatred for the bourgeoisie, its self-importance, its vulgarity; it is an ancient hatred, or if you like, a religious one', Pasolini asserted.[19]

As with Jean-Luc Godard, an ingredient of Pier Paolo Pasolini's politics is not so much Marxism as anti-bourgeoisism, anti-capitalism, and anti-consumerism. It is – again like Godard – partly *against things* for the sake of it: *against* the bourgeoisie, *against* consumerism.[20] And it's a politics that is *for* revolution, *for* change, for the sake of it, to turn things upside-down, and to oppose whatever's on offer. (But *how* would Pasolini stem the tide of consumerism and the social decline of his beloved Italy? He doesn't say – because he can't say – because no one can say. Pasolini offers nothing to replace contemporary, capitalist society. His utoptian project is about rewriting or enshrining the past, or the 'Third World').

Pasolini acknowledged that Marxism was a system imposed from the top down by an *élite*, like other political/ philosophical systems. But it gave the illusion that an individual mattered, or had an effect on the system. Andrew Sarris reckoned that 'Italian cinema as a whole – is primarily a Marxist cinema with a deep sense of doubt' (D. Georgakas, 236).

19 Quoted in J. Duflot, 22.
20 However, Pasolini was happy to drive flashy sports cars, one of the loudest symbols of consumer-capitalism.

The aim of shocking the bourgeoisie (that childish goal of too many leftist/ Marxist artists), may derive in part from the attempt at reaching a realm where the bourgeoisie and their ideals do not go. That is, to go beyond the limits of what is accepted by bourgeois society, into the crude, the ultra-violent, the bestial.

It's typical that Pier Paolo Pasolini would side with the policemen in the political unrest of 1968, rather than with the student protesters. Why? Because Pasolini thought the students were bourgeois, and the cops were true working class people.

However, that part of the Pasolini Legend isn't the whole story: Pasolini's famous views about the police (expressed in a poem) were modified by his sceptical views of the police as enforcers of the law in Italy, and his sympathies with the political aspects of the counter-culture (Pasolini, the subject of many run-ins with the Italian authorities, held a sceptical view of the *carabineri*).[21] Subsequently, Pasolini's verses were employed by right-leaning groups and commentators., and twisted around, missing the irony and paradox that Pasolini was exploring.

On his Marxism, Pier Paolo Pasolini reminded Oswald Stack that in Italy everybody is a Marxist, and everybody is a Catholic (PP, 22). 'Pasolini's Marxist critique is sadly too narrow in its view of bourgeois neurosis as a symptom of class decadence under advanced capitalism', according to John Orr in *Contemporary Cinema* (1998, 8).

It's ironic for a left-wing and Marxist radical author like Pier Paolo Pasolini that often for his material he took on very traditional, conservative and right-wing texts and authors: the *Bible*, Ancient Greek mythology, Islamic stories, Geoffrey Chaucer and Giovanni Boccaccio. In fact, historical cinema tends to be conservative at the least, and often right-wing, too (this conservatism doesn't only reflect the markets of commercial cinema).

---

21 See an interesting article by Luca Peretti on Pasolini and Communism: "Remembering Pier Paolo Pasolini" (jacobinmag.com).

The decline of the ideological investment in Communism, socialism and Marxism in the 1970s, following the height of the idealism and activism of the late 1960s, was something that many intellectuals and artists had to face. Hayao Miyazaki, Jean-Luc Godard, Milos Forman, and many Eastern European filmmakers, as well as Pier Paolo Pasolini, confronted the fact that in some societies Communism and Marxism were not only not working, they were becoming as damaging as the mythologies and ideologies they opposed to, or were created in opposition to (such as Western capitalism).

The dream was over. Between the heady days of 1968 (manning the barricades, the student/ youth riots, the anti-Vietnam War protests, the civil rights marches), and the mid-1970s, it was a rapid decline.

'Pasolini's interventions were extreme and unflagging, pleasing to practically nobody across the political spectrum, and, uniquely, were intricately inscribed with the fact of his sexual difference', noted Gary Indiana (14). [22] True – left-wingers and Communists found just as much to get irritated by in Pasolini's pronouncements in the political arena as right-wingers and conservatives. (And Pasolini likely secretly enjoyed the fact that his views wound up leftists as well as rightists).

SOUTHERN ITALY

Pier Paolo Pasolini had a very idealized view of Southern Italy, or rural Italy, or pre-industrial Italy, of peasant Italy, of an Italy before television, cars and two World Wars. It was an Italy that never really existed, but which he wanted to exist. It was an Italy that he loved – the Italy of regions, and regional dialects and languages. It was if Pasolini saw himself as born out of his time –

22 For Indiana, Pier Paolo Pasolini was the wrong sort of gay artist – a Marxist who criticized the political system who wasn't like Franco Zeffirelli, a raging queen (and thus harmless).

he might've been happier in the mediæval era, say, or the Renaissance (I think Pasolini would've got along just fine in the Ancient Roman period – and so would Federico Fellini and Walerian Borowczyk!).

A Northern Italian (he was born in Bologna), Pier Paolo Pasolini revered the South, of Naples, of Calabria. Of course he spent most of his adult life in the Eternal City; yet he always maintained the links to the countryside (keeping a Summer house, for instance).

It was no surprise that Pasolini opted to stage his most well-known movie, *The Gospel According To Matthew*, in Southern Italy, using many non-actors who were chosen by the maestro and his casting team for their interesting faces (as with Federico Fellini).

Accattone had inaugurated numerous approaches to cinema which Pier Paolo Pasolini would pursue throughout his career: a cast of unknowns and non-actors, low budgets, filming on location (and adapting existing settings), and employing recorded music, often classical (rather than specially composed scores).

Choosing unknown performers was about achieving some kind of reality, or a non-fictionalized, non-embellished reality: Pier Paolo Pasolini said in 1973:

> I pick actors whose sheer physical presence suffices to convey this sense of reality. I do not pick them at random but in order to offer examples of reality.[23]

Pasolini wanted the real thing, without making it pretty or cute. I can't think of another filmmaker who so loved extras, or who gave more screen time in terms of close-ups to extras – except perhaps Federico Fellini. And Pier Paolo Pasolini was especially fond of anybody who looked odd – terrible teeth, warts on lips, wall eyes, scars, and faces wrinkled by the Southern Italian sunshine.

The casting directors on Pier Paolo Pasolini's movies deserve all the credit coming their way for gathering such an extraordinary collection of actors and

23 P. Pasolini, *The Guardian*, Aug 13, 1973.

amateurs (such as Alberto di Stefanis, who cast *The Decameron*). Using non-actors is part of the Neo-realist film tradition – such as the Roberto Rossellini film *Francesco* (1950), co-written by Fellini. Movies like *Francesco* showed Pasolini how you could adapt a religious subject for the cinema without stars or professional actors.

Pasolini was happy to direct non-professional actors thru scenes, beat-by-beat, in the Italian cinema manner (by coaxing them from beside the *macchina fotografica*). It worked wonders – Enrique Irazoqui as Jesus in *The Gospel According To Matthew*, for instance. But sometimes it failed: Giuseppe Gentile might possess the sportsman's physique to look like the mythical hero Jason in *Medea*, but he sure can't act.

For Sam Rohdie, the extras in the 'trilogy of life' movies didn't need to act, they just needed to 'be', to appear on camera – their appearance was their characterization and their performance. (It's a version of Pasolini's notion of 'realism' – you simply show reality, and show people as people, and the process of cinema does the rest).

'A SEARCH FOR MAGIC': TRAVELS WITH PASOLINI

Pier Paolo Pasolini's is a cinema of journeys and voyages, eternally restless – films as a continuous search for locations (and as what we could term location scouting movies, Pasolini's are some of the finest). But also a search for the sacred, 'a search for magic', a search for mythology. And it's a quest for a place where those things still hold sway. A search for a time, too, an era of magic and the poetic.

Certainly the exotic is a big draw in Pier Paolo Pasolini's cinema, and for the director too. He did not shoot in North America (tho' he enjoyed visiting it), but took his productions to North Africa, the Middle East, India and Nepal (as well as the wildly alien, end-of-the-line wildernesses of dear, old England!).

Always Pier Paolo Pasolini goes South and East – to Africa, the Middle East, India (and Southern Italy), rather than North, to Germany, Scandinavia, Russia... Some have associated the North in Pasolini's æsthetics to his father, and the Law of the Father (i.e., Northern Italy, Bologna, etc).24 The journey East and South, when taken from Europe, is towards the sun, to heat, to the desert, to the exotic, to the ancient world, to Islam, to old religions, to old mythologies.

As well as India, Pier Paolo Pasolini also visited Africa several times: Kenya in Jan, 1961 and Jan, 1962 (as well as Sudan); Ghana, Guinea and Nigeria in 1963; Africa again in 1970 (for the *Oresteia* film); and Israel and Jordan in 1963 (when he was planning to film *The Gospel According To Matthew* in the Holy Land).

When Pier Paolo Pasolini and his writer chums Alberto Moravia and Elsa Morante visited India in December, 1960, it wasn't for a particular film or book project (tho' a book, *The Scent of India,* duly appeared, as well as a short documentary later, *Notes For a Film In India*, 1969).

PASOLINI THE POET

Was Pier Paolo Pasolini a believer or a non-believer? In what? – in God? Love? Death? Art? Life? Terms like belief, or atheism, or agnosticism, or non-belief, just don't do justice to Pasolini's multi-faceted personality and works. The man and his art were much more complicated than that (also, there are many levels of 'belief', and ways of 'believing').

24 Pasolini's beloved Friuli was in the North, of course, but not grouped with the North for Pasolini – it was beyond-the-North.

Pier Paolo Pasolini was a mass of contradictions only to the extent that many (most?) humans are contradictory. Can a Marxist believe in God? What is the relation between Marxism and materialism to religion and the spirit? These and many other questions have been discussed in relation to Pasolini. As he put it in 1966:

> If you know that I am an unbeliever, then you know me better than I do myself. I may be an unbeliever, but I am an unbeliever who has a nostalgia for a belief.

You only have to look at a couple of movies directed by Pier Paolo Pasolini to see there is a wealth of romance, nostalgia, spirituality, desire and yearning. What was Pasolini's 'religion'? What did he 'believe in'?

Poetry.

If there *are* contradictions, that's because Pier Paolo Pasolini was certainly a contradictory personality. Like Orson Welles, Rainer Fassbinder, Jean-Luc Godard and Andrei Tarkovsky (among filmmakers), Pasolini was a complex person – no single view, no one opinion, no philosophy on its own can sum him up, or condense his views into a coherent whole. (Indeed, every single biographical sketch online, in documentaries, books and newspapers always stresses the seemingly contradictory elements of the Pasolini Legend: religion plus Marxism plus homosexuality plus radical cinema, etc etc etc etc etc).

If there's one single word I would use for Pier Paolo Pasolini, it is poetry. He poeticizes life, poeticizes the world and everything in it. 'To make films is to be a poet', he asserted (PP, 154). 'Pasolini's defence of poetry was a political act of complete committment' (S. Rohdie, 89). Poetry and the poet's life sums up many aspects of Pasolini's personality, and also his approach to art, and to cinema, but it doesn't crystallize everything. With Pasolini, you are always aware of depths and levels below the surface. He may talk a lot in interviews, he may appear forthcoming and affable on camera in interviews (or as the interviewer in his own movies, when he won't shut up or let the interviewee get a word in edgeways), but there are whole oceans of things you don't know about, whole continents where acts, thoughts, ideas and gestures are hidden, or will never be found out, and as everybody who knew Pasolini personally eventually dies as the years pass, we won't know.

With Pier Paolo Pasolini, the legend has become enormous, and of course Pasolini fed it no end in his lifetime, as with filmmakers such as Orson Welles, Alfred Hitchcock, Ken Russell, Jean-Luc Godard and Werner Herzog. Those filmmakers liked nothing better than talking about themselves and their work. There should be a sub-category of film directors who luxuriate in their own eccentricities, in rattling out the same stories and anecdotes. The brief moments of self-deprecation (Ingmar Bergman, Woody Allen, Andrei Tarkovsky, Steven Spielberg) don't fool us for a moment.

In Enzo Siciliano's 1978 biography, Pier Paolo Pasolini comes across as a *very* complex individual: he was a mass of contradictions. Nothing could be simple with Pasolini. There were always a number of levels to consider at the same time.

Pier Paolo Pasolini's relationship with his father Carlo Alberto Pasolini was ambiguous, anxious and filled with conflicting emotions. Pasolini spoke of loving his father until his was three years-old; then came a crisis, and he fell out of love, forever. It was during the time that Susanna was pregnant with Pasolini's brother Guido. What exactly happened isn't clear; certainly it is a classic case of oedipal rebellion, with the father as the erotic rival with the boy for the mother's love (it may have been the Freudian primal scene, Enzo Siciliano wondered, of stumbling upon his parents making love in the kitchen). And it is also a (jealous) rivalry with the younger brother.

There's no need to explore the love-hate relation

with the father and the Law of the Father in P.P. Pasolini's art here, because it's plastered all over his films and his poetry. Pasolini's movies are in part a psychoanalytical investigation into the relationship with the father figure. The movies are their own therapy, their own psychoanalytical cases. The depictions of fathers and the Sins of the Fathers is so obvious it doesn't require any gloss here.

Ditto with his mother – there's no need to explore Pier Paolo Pasolini's relation with his beloved mother, Susanna Colussi Pasolini. That Pasolini adored his mom comes over strongly in his poetry and cinema.

> The mark which has dominated all my work is this longing for life, this sense of exclusion, which doesn't lessen but augments this love of life. (Interview in a documentary, late 1960s)

PASOLINI AND RELIGION

> I suffer from the nostalgia of a peasant-type religion, and that is why I am on the side of the servant. But I do not believe in a metaphysical god. I am religious because I have a natural identific- ation between reality and God. Reality is divine. That is why my films are never naturalistic. The motivation that unites all of my films is to give back to reality its original sacred significance.
>
> Pier Paolo Pasolini (1968)

Whatever he may have said in interviews or written in essays and poetry, Pier Paolo Pasolini was certainly fascinated by many aspects of religion and Catholicism. The imagery and themes of Catholicism, for instance, run throughout his movies – and not because he was Italian, or because he was brought up amongst Catholicism.

You can think of Pier Paolo Pasolini's 'religion' as being poetry; but even here, the crossovers between religion and poetry are numerous, and have been explored by 1,000s of commentators. Enzo Siciliano called Pasolini 'a profoundly religious man, but in his religion the vocative "God" was absent' (ES, 396).

As commentators have noted, Pier Paolo Pasolini's religious faith wasn't in Catholicism, it was in Communism. For him, Communism was natural, inevitable, essential, a way of looking at the world that explained (and fed) his nostalgia for the peasant world, his dissatisfaction with modern life, his hatred of advanced capitalism, his sympathy with the under-class, and his distrust of authority. And there was a social aspect to Communist politics for Pasolini: it brought him together with intellectuals, of course, but he also 'frequented the dance halls on the "red" outskirts of the city' (as Enzo Siciliano explained [162]). Pasolini continued to vote for the Partito Comunista Italiano (Italian Communist Party) and contribute to its publications (though his relationship with the Partito Comunista Italiano was troubled at times).

Of course, being an intellectual and highly educated observer, Pier Paolo Pasolini was inevitably highly critical of the Church, but he was also intrigued by many issues that the Church was linked to. Social control, and State authority, for instance, or issues such as morality and sexual ethics, or the role that Catholicism had in the political and social formation of young people. (And of course, Pasolini was steeped in Catholic art, to the point where it would have probably been absolutely impossible for him to eradicate all traces of that cultural absorption).

In 1971, he said:

> The Church will probably be able to continue for
> centuries to come if it creates an ecclesiastic
> assembly that continually negates and re-creates
> itself. My criticism is against the Church as power
> as it is today. I said that when I was a boy I
> believed, I prayed... but it wasn't anything very

serious. I think there're some facets in my character
that have something of a mystifying quality. I'd
say this is a part of the trauma that dominates my
existence. Nature doesn't seem natural to me, it is a
sort of an act between me and the naturalness of
nature. (1971)

Whether Pier Paolo Pasolini personally 'believed'
or not is not the issue, is not important, and is not even
interesting. It's what Pasolini *did* with those beliefs or
non-beliefs that's valuable, it's how Pasolini engaged
with institutions such as religion, Catholicism, the
State, education, Communism, Marxism, and capitalism
that's interesting. But even those big issues are not
especially compelling on their own, unless, at least for
commercial cinema, they are combined with or put into
drama, fiction, stories and characters.

'Christianity was part of his moral reasoning, the
part that obliged him to interrogate himself (albeit in
the guise of a country priest) on the unrelenting
demands of the body', Enzo Siciliano noted, *pace
Amado Mio* (121).

Pier Paolo Pasolini said he tended to see the world
in too reverential, too childlike terms – if he had any
religion, he remarked, it would be a vague mystical
response to the world (including objects and nature as
well as people [PP, 14]).

PASOLINI THE OUTSIDER

The feeling of not fitting in anywhere in the modern
world can be found throughout Pier Paolo Pasolini's
writings and films (and it makes his work appealing to
modern audiences). You can see how Pasolini would be
right at home in the Middle Ages (as an assistant to
Dante Alighieri or Giotto, say, or in the Ancient Roman
world, as a poet rival to, say, Petronius or Ovid) – yet,

even here, Pasolini would probably still feel that he didn't fit in, would still have that consuming, near-tragic experience of otherness. Pasolini is an exile in his own life, where his poems and films offer a commentary, a layer, a musing on the discontinuities between his life and his art, his life and his heart, his life and his relationships.

We are all exiles, says French philosopher Julia Kristeva. Her experience of displacement (from her homeland of Bulgaria) was an ingredient in her notion of the 'cosmopolitan' individual, the 'intellectual dissident'. As Kristeva knew, strangeness or otherness (being a foreigner) is fundamental to being human: as Kristeva put it, *étrangers à nous-mêmes* (we are strangers to ourselves).[25]

Some of the forerunners of Pier Paolo Pasolini's lifestyle, which combined outsider status, an eccentric and highly individual cultural trajectory, and a homosexual lifestyle, included Oscar Wilde and André Gide. A touchstone for Pasolini, Gide (1869-1951) was cited by Pasolini as an important influence. Easy to see why: early Gide works such as *The Immoralist* and *Fruits of the Earth* are like early Pasolini movies,[26] with their Existentialist, outsider protagonists, their fashionable (French) avant gardism, their depictions of older, white, European guys falling for young, Arab boys (plus the inevitable guilt and post-coital self-loathing), their Catholic/ post-Catholic *milieu*, their high culture and literary allusions, and their enshrinement of the poetry of being alive.

If you enjoy Pier Paolo Pasolini's movies, you will love André Gide's novels (and vice versa). As Pasolini was a 'filmmaker's filmmaker' (like Orson Welles, F.W. Murnau or Sergei Paradjanov), so Gide was very much a 'writer's writer' (as with Rainer Maria Rilke, Francesco

---

25 In *Strangers to Ourselves*, Julia Kristeva describes the foreigner as the 'cold orphan', motherless, a 'devotee of solitude', a 'fanatic of absence', alone even in a crowd, arrogant, rejected, yet oddly happy (4-5). The stranger is always in motion, doesn't belong anywhere, to 'any time, any love' (7).
26 *The Immoralist* is ideal for the Pasolinian treatment. Indeed, *Theorem* has the feel of *The Immoralist*.

Petrarch or Samuel Beckett). C.P. Cavafy, the 20th century Greek poet of lyrical, homoerotic nostalgia, is another reference point for Pier Paolo Pasolini (there are numerous affinities between the two).

PASOLINI THE ICONOCLAST

A controversial figure even today, Pier Paolo Pasolini had run-ins with the Italian authorities many times (he was brought to trial on several occasions). His works were condemned for their blasphemy and obscenity. An early encounter with the authorities occurred when he was accused of pædophilia and homosexuality – with the Ramuscello boys in Casarsa. It was this incident that partly encouraged Pasolini to leave Bologna and to live in Rome (see below).

Altho' critics and admirers found some of Pier Paolo Pasolini's writing and movie-making extreme, it wasn't, compared to some authors: William Burroughs, Marco Vassi, Henry Miller, or even Paul Bowles.

There's no doubt that part of Pier Paolo Pasolini enjoyed shocking people, or simply winding them up – he did it in his newspaper articles, in his poetry, in his movies, and in his documentaries. And he succeeded many times: the number of controversies that Pasolini was involved with is very high – compared to most of his contemporaries (either in literature or cinema).

Things seemed to happen to Pasolini.

> Wholly a man of his time [wrote Enzo Siciliano], he chose to live in the enemy camp, launching polemics and accusations, pushing his intolerable personal situation to the point of paradox, and not troubling himself about anything else. (ES, 399-400)

Pier Paolo Pasolini saw himself as something of an

outsider in Italian culture, a 'disturber of the peace', someone whose contributions were unwanted. Yes – but that didn't stop Pasolini pouring out pronouncements and movies and poems and books! Pasolini wasn't going to hurry home, slam the door and vow never to talk to the press or anyone else again for the rest of his life! He was not someone who could keep quiet. (Instead, Pasolini glorified in attention of all kinds: he was one of those filmmakers who revel in the attention – look at his interviews – you see the same enjoyment of adulation in Orson Welles, in Jean-Luc Godard, in Steve Spielberg, in Francis Coppola, etc).

Pier Paolo Pasolini was involved in a brawl in Rome, at nighttime in a rough part of the city (Via di Panico). The case came to trial on Nov 15, 1961 (around the time that *Accattone* opened in cinemas). Pasolini was charged with 'aiding and abetting', but was fully acquitted.[27] Enzo Siciliano speaks of this period as having 'a climate of persecution', when 'hysteria grew around the public figure of Pasolini' (248).

Yet another brush with the law occurred when Pier Paolo Pasolini was accused of holding up a gas station with a gun (!). The accusations came from Bernardino De Santis, a boy working at the garage, who said that Pasolini had used a black pistol to hold up the garage. The trial took place in Latina on July 3, 1962. (Once again, Pasolini's defence used the concept of research – Pasolini often defended himself by saying that he was researching places and people for future projects). Further scandals are noted below.

Few Italian artists in the same era were attacked and criticized more than Pasolini. 'Pasolini remained un-interruptedly in the hand of judges from 1960 to 1975', as Stefano Rodotà put it in *Pasolini: Judicial Report, Persecution, Death* (1977). Magazines and newspapers such as *Il Borghese, Oggi, Gente* and *Lo Specchio* regularly slandered him. Among Pasolini's loudest critics were Maria Predassi (writing as Gianna Preda) and

27 According to Laura Betti in the *Who Says the Truth Shall Die* documentary, Pasolini was accused some 33 times of different crimes but he was always acquitted. Yet the Italian press kept going after him.

Giose Rimanelli (writing as A.G. Solari).

But why? asked Wu Ming in a 2016 article:

> Why such a persecution? Because he was homo-
> sexual? He was certainly not the only one amongst
> artists and writers. Because he was homosexual and
> communist? Yes, but this isn't enough either.
> Because he was homosexual, communist and
> expressed himself openly against the bourgeoisie,
> government, Christian Democracy, fascists, judges
> and police? Yes, this is enough. It would have been
> enough anywhere, let alone in Italy, and in that
> Italy.

PASOLINI AND HOMOSEXUALITY:
THE PERCEPTION OF PASOLINI'S IDENTITY

It's striking how many commentators on the work of
Pier Paolo Pasolini mention his sexual identity (i.e., his
homosexuality). As if they are now professional,
psychoanalytical experts on sexuality and gender
(almost all critics are not). There is something patronizing about this, as well as something of the tabloid
journalist's pig's nose for snuffling out sensationalism
(yes, and the bastard was gay, too!). As if to be gay is
automatically to be weird, 'other', or perverted.

Every frigging biographical sketch I've read about
Pier Paolo Pasolini mentions his sexuality. Yes, even
those critics who are supposed to be (1) intellectual, (2)
well-read, and (3) critical/ perceptive. And they often
depict Pasolini's sexual preferences as 'dark', or exotic,
or odd. Were they? And how can anybody know?! Why
is his sexual identity seen as such a big deal? Hell,
maybe Pasolini just liked sex! As Spike Milligan said:
'people like to fuck'.

The issue of homosexuality in relation to
Pasolini's media persona is very minor compared to his

public critiques and attacks on institutions such as the Christian Democrat party in Italy, on the bourgeoisie, on con'sumer capitalism, etc.

There are so many assumptions and damaging views in the way that the personality of Pier Paolo Pasolini has been discussed. However, it's true that in some respects the media image of Pier Paolo Pasolini conforms to the stereotype of the ageing homosexual who preys upon boys. Many observers have attested to that, how, according to the Pasolini Legend, he would go out night after night in search of rough trade (often in one of his sports cars). Boys that hung around the Termini railroad station in the centre of Roma, or in the *borgate*, or the bathhouses along the River Tiber (such as the Ciriola below Castel Sant' Angelo).[28] Boys that wouldn't be brought back home, because home meant his beloved Mamma. (His preference was for *ragazzi* with a roguish smile, curly hair on their foreheads, plenty of vitality, and often a reputation as bad boys, as petty criminals).[29]

Famous filmmakers who were homosexual include F.W. Murnau, Jean Cocteau, Andy Warhol, Rainer Werner Fassbinder, Kenneth Anger, George Cukor, James Whale, and more recently, James Ivory, Joel Schumacher, and Pasolini's fellow Italians Luchino Visconti and Franco Zeffirelli (also, Visconti and Zeffirelli didn't, as with Pasolini, hide their sexual identity[30]).

Discussing the idea of the romantic couple in 1970, Pasolini pointed out that societies reject what challenges the norms and the rules – and that includes homosexuality:

Homosexuality is a threat to society. It is incon-

28 Pier Paolo Pasolini was sometimes accompanied by his friend Sandro Penna: they had a joky contest over who could tup the most boys.
29 In Great Britain, in legal history, male homosexuality has been the subject of several laws, including the law on sodomy of 1533 (in Henry VIII's reign), the 1861 and 1885 laws on sodomy and gross indecency; the 1898 Vagrancy Act, the Sexual Offences Act of 1967, and the Criminal Justice Bill of 1991 (however, lesbianism has been largely invisible and unacknowledged).
30 However, Visconti and Zeffirelli didn't loudly criticize the State, the Church and other Italian institutions like Pasolini.

ceivable in any organisms or community, no matter how free. (1970)

Enzo Siciliano in his biography portrays Pier Paolo Pasolini as someone tormented by his passions, his predilections for young, raw boys. 'Pasolini lived in the torment of not being able to give it [his eros] what it demanded of him. And the demand was obscure, indeed dark and nocturnal' (ES, 391).

In 1948, Pier Paolo Pasolini described his homosexuality as something other:

> I was born to be calm, balanced, natural: my homosexuality was something added, it lay outside, it had nothing to do with me. I've always seen it as something beside me like an enemy, I've never felt it to be within me.

Pier Paolo Pasolini revered the rugged, working class *ragazzi* of Rome, Calabria and Friuli, but however much he liked to hang around with them (and have sex with them), he was never one of them. Pasolini was always the intellectual, always the poet, always the guy who wrote newspapers columns and directed movies. He was never a street kid, was never one of the tough, poor *ragazzi* that he liked to cruise at night.

For some observers, Pier Paolo Pasolini was the classic predatory homosexual, the older, gay man who takes to exploring the streets of cities and towns at night looking for willing youths to share the momentary pleasures of sex. It was a habit that Pasolini found hard to break: he enjoyed the danger of it, as well as the ecstasy (he would return from his secretive nighttime jaunts battered and bruised sometimes). According to Enzo Siciliano, most times the erotic encounters consisted of fellatio and masturbation.

Sometimes Pier Paolo Pasolini had to be rescued from his nightly adventures, sore and bleeding (producer Alfredo Bini and production manager Eliseo Boschi would respond to telephone calls to go get Pasolini from some nocturnal spree that'd turned sour

– in Africa and the Middle East as well as in Rome). 'I'm leading not a violent but an extremely violent life', Pasolini wrote in a letter of Oct 5, 1959 (ES, 141).

Pier Paolo Pasolini did have heterosexual experiences. One was with a young mother from Viterbo. Another was with a girl at the beach. Another was with Mariella Bauzano in the early 1950s. And as a kid Pasolini had flirted with girls (and referred to them in his letters). However, Enzo Siciliano wondered if some of these 'girls' were in fact boys (ES, 52).

There were also a number of social and criminal scandals, some of which involved under-age youths and sexuality – which were linked to Pasolini's homosexual practices.

When he was 19, Pier Paolo Pasolini was accused by a neighbourhood child's father of pederasty, when he offered the child some ice cream (this occurred in Bologna in 1941). Pasolini insisted that his intentions were innocent.

One of the biggest scandals in Pier Paolo Pasolini's life, and one which changed the course of his life, occurred in 1949 in Casarsa (his home), when Pasolini (then 27) was overheard talking to some 16 year-old lads in Ramuscello (outside of San Vito al Tagliamento). What happened with the boys at Ramuscello ('probably mutual masturbation', Enzo Siciliano reckoned [135]), which Pasolini had enjoyed (he called it an unforgettable evening), became public when complaints were made to the *carabineri*. In December, 1950, the court acquitted Pasolini of the charges of corrupting minors, but he was convicted of committing lewd acts. In April, 1952, the appeals court absolved Pasolini due to insufficient evidence (ES, 135).

Pier Paolo Pasolini trotted out a defence he used again in later scandals a few times: he was conducting research for a novel, he claimed: 'I was trying an erotic and literary experiment, under the influence of a book I had been reading'. Even if he cited a big cultural name like André Gide, it seems a pretty flimsy excuse.

Pier Paolo Pasolini's erotic encounter with the

Ramuscello boys had other repercussions – such as Pasolini's ousting from the Communist Party, which he found very upsetting (he revered Communism). Pasolini lost his teaching job (as well as the financial security it brought).

The scandal tore into Pier Paolo Pasolini's family – his father went ballistic, raging all night about his son, and his mother locked herself in her room ('Yesterday morning my mother almost went out of her mind, my father is in an unbearable state – I heard him weeping and moaning all night', Pasolini wrote to Ferdinando Mautino). To a friend called over for solace, Giuseppe Zigaina, Pasolini confessed he wanted to kill himself (ES, 137). It was the repercussions of this event that precipitated the move to Roma with his mother, where he remained for the rest of his life.

The pattern of this early scandal of 1949 – Pier Paolo Pasolini preying upon young boys, the social intolerance of homosexuality it evoked, and Pasolini's intellectual defence of his actions – would be repeated a few times in his life.

Another incident involving young boys occurred on July 10, 1960, in Anzio, when Pier Paolo Pasolini was thought to have propositioned some boys in the harbour (the parents of the boys filed a complaint). One of the striking aspects about the career of Pier Paolo Pasolini is that he didn't give up in the face of several scandals.

HOMOSEXUALITY IN PASOLINI'S CINEMA

Critics have noted that although he was a gay filmmaker, homosexuality is not often portrayed in Pier Paolo Pasolini's cinema. Well, there are obvious instances, such as the condemned, male homosexuals in the witchhunting sequence in *The Canterbury Tales*, where one of the victims is publicly burnt to death (while an older one buys himself out), and in *Theorem,* homosexual relationships are explored in more depth (but in *Theorem* the homosexuality is with a visitor who is part-god, part-devil – not an 'average' relationship at all!).

But when you look closer, there are further levels of homosexual elements in Pier Paolo Pasolini's cinema. The preponderance of male brotherhoods, for instance, of men being men together, which you can see in *The Canterbury Tales, The Decameron, Accattone* and, yes, in *The Gospel According To Matthew*. The homosocial relationships are right in the foreground from Pasolini's debut (*Accattone*) onwards. Indeed, *Accattone* is a very gay movie from that perspective (even down to the way that women are treated – their maltreatment further bolsters the homosocial bonds of the guys).

And look at the way that Pier Paolo Pasolini includes so many rough and ready youths in his movies (the *ragazzi* of his 1950s novels), and how the camera lingers over them at length. Pasolini is very fond of close-ups of young *ragazzi* smiling into the camera, as part of the conventional shot-reverse-shot editing pattern of cinema, yes, but the amount of screen time given over to close-ups of attractive, macho young men is very striking.

Brotherhoods and male bonding are fundamental to many other filmmakers' work – it's central to Westerns, to the crime and gangster genres, to the war genre, to action cinema, and is a key element in the cinema of Sam Peckinpah, Howard Hawks, John Woo, Ringo Lam, Martin Scorsese, Francis Coppola, etc etc.

I'm reminded of Michelangelo Merisi da Caravaggio,[31] probably *the* painter (at least in Italy), of beautiful, tough, young men. The homosexuality of Caravaggio is another aspect, of course, but in terms of the art itself, Caravaggio's work is certainly a forerunner

---

31 Other writers have noted the affinities between Pier Paolo Pasolini and Caravaggio: Cesare Garboli drew attention to the similarities, with the art historian Roberto Longhi as the intermediary (Longhi had organized an important exhibition of Caravaggio in Milan in 1951).

of this element in Pier Paolo Pasolini's cinema. And the other artist is of course Michelangelo Buonarroti, the towering genius of the Renaissance, who made the male nude the most sublime, erotic thing you've ever seen (visit the Musée de Louvre to see the *Dying Slave* sculptures, truly orgasmic works of art).

And Pier Paolo Pasolini and his crews did film many men nude. Within the context of heterosexual encounters, that male nudity has a justification. And Pasolini was unusual among many film directors is putting an equal amount of male nudity on screen as female nudity in love scenes (male actors can be more reluctant to disrobe completely – and of course, there are double standards in most cinema, where an actor will stay partially clad, while an actress is fully naked).

As well as nudity,[32] Pier Paolo Pasolini and the camera teams also focussed on the male genitals. In *The Arabian Nights* there are quite a few close-ups of genitals (as well as the usual thrusting butts in sex scenes of heterosexual cinema). *The Arabian Nights* probably contains the most male nudity in Pasolini's cinema, along with *Salò*.

Despite the beauty of Pasolini's imagery, his exaltation of bodies (and men in particular), there isn't much erotic pleasure in some of his works, and sexuality is tied, via his personality, 'to a realm of suffering' which 'inflects his work with melancholy and morbidity', according to Gary Indiana (16).

Pasolini identified with the victim, not the perpetrator, some observed; his masochism was to sympathize with the down-trodden – in Italia, that meant the sub-proletariat (Pasolini invested his social hopes in the sub-proletariat).

Feminists have discussed the male gaze (voyeurism, the look, etc), and wondered if there can be a female gaze in cinema. That there is a homosexual, lesbian, queer and bisexual gaze – or, I would prefer to call it a multi-sexual gaze (why stop at two or three genders?) –

32 Nobody can miss the fact that Pier Paolo Pasolini's last four films are jammed with nudity and sex. (And also in *Theorem* and *Pigsty*).

is clear from the films of Pier Paolo Pasolini, Walerian Borowczyk and Ken Russell.

I'm not talking about the sexual preferences of the filmmakers, but of the gaze, the looks, the desire and the structure of their works. For example, although Ken Russell, Francis Coppola, Martin Scorsese, Bernardo Bertolucci and Michael Powell were heterosexual (at least according to their autobiographies and colleagues and wives and girlfriends), some of their works are supremely gay, queer, lesbian and homosexual.

Pier Paolo Pasolini, though, was not particularly interested in foregrounding that aspect of his personality in his cinema. What does come across, though, and very strongly, is the aspect of *desire*. Sexual desire, desire for life. Which's often intensely romantic and poetic, sometimes nostalgic, sometimes ironic, sometimes masochistic, and sometimes vitriolic.

The most unbridled expression of desire in Pier Paolo Pasolini's work is in the three 'life' movies, 1971, 1972 and 1974. But the desire on display is nearly all heterosexual (*Salò* explores desire within an eccentric, S/M environment).

PASOLINI CRITICISM

A huge amount of articles, essays and books have appeared about the works of Pier Paolo Pasolini, focussing on his poetry, his novels, his essays/ statements and his movies. In short, Pasolini has been taken *very* seriously, with critics and journos assuming that he is an important figure with significant things to say. I would imagine that Pasolini himself would be stunned, delighted, and perhaps embarrassed by the number of pieces written about his work, and how he has been placed in the same company as many of his cultural heroes.

I would recommend, as the first point of call, the amazing biography by Enzo Siciliano (sadly out of print). Among the studies of Pier Paolo Pasolini's films, Sam Rohdie, B. Babington, Pamela Grace, Philip Kolker, John Orr, A. Pavelin, and Gary Indiana are useful.

There are far fewer biographies of Pier Paolo Pasolini in print than one might think. In fact, for years no biographies have been in print in English. The biography by Enzo Siciliano, *Pasolini,* published in 1978 by Rizzoli (in Italian), is among the finest (it was translated in 1982, and published in 1987). Retrospectives of Pasolini's work were mounted at the Museum of Modern Art in 2012 and the British Film Institute in 2013.

Enzo Siciliano concentrates very much on Pier Paolo Pasolini the public figure in Italian cultural life, and on Pasolini's poetry: there is far less in his biography on Pasolini's cinema, for instance, than on Pasolini's poems (Siciliano quotes from the poetry at length). Siciliano also employs the poems in a problematic manner: to illustrate Pasolini's thoughts and even some of his experiences. Assessing and explaining someone's life through their poetry is full of difficulties, filled with assumptions about what poetry is, how it works, how poets write poems, and how poetry relates to the poet's life.

In short, poetry is not autobiography, or documentary, or history. Very often it has no relation to the poet's life whatsoever. Robert Graves called poetry a 'spiritual autobiography', but even that is not always the case.

With Pier Paolo Pasolini, however, some of his poems definitely do reflect upon his experiences, and many poems do express his own views. But it's still a very stylized, literary kind of mirror, reflecting back only what the poet chooses.

Pier Paolo Pasolini has been discussed widely in cinema circles, but when you look into it, there are far fewer really good books about Pasolini's cinema than one might expect (certainly compared to contemporaries such as Jean-Luc Godard or Orson Welles). And many of the best studies are now out of print (including Enzo Siciliano's essential biography).

In studies of the cinema of Pier Paolo Pasolini's cinema, the context and the references tend to be Neo-realism, and to that select band of Italian filmmakers who have been exported and critically revered: Fellini, Rossellini, Visconti, Antonioni, de Sica, Bertolucci, etc.

Sure – those are the great artists of Italian cinema of the 1950s to 1970s. But they are not really representative of Italian cinema of that era. Rather, cinema in Italy of the 50s through 70s was a thriving industry of remakes, sequels, rip-offs, exploitation movies, *mondo* movies, populist comedies (hugely popular), *James Bond* cash-ins, and endless genre movies (Spaghetti Westerns, *gialli* (horror/ thriller), crime, erotica, and of course the *peplum/* sword & sandal movies), plus the many visiting productions from North America (resulting in the 'Hollywood On the Tiber' cycle). If a movie – from anywhere – was successful, Italian cinema dived in and had a cash-in movie filmed and released within weeks (same with the Hong Kong film business).

We don't think of Pasolini as a director of sequels and franchises, but he *did* sequelize his own movies: *Mamma Roma* follows up *Accattone*, *The Hawks and the Sparrows* led to further collaborations with Totò (in the short films for anthologies, and a feature-length sequel to *The Hawks and the Sparrows* was planned), *Medea* is a follow-up to *Oedipus Rex,* and the 'trilogy of life' pictures can be regarded as a film series.

Pier Paolo Pasolini distanced himself from Neo-realist cinema; while Neo-realism was dead in Italy, it had migrated to England and France, Pasolini noted (PP, 137). He didn't like the British version of the New Wave at all (very few Europeans did!), tho' of course he greatly admired Jean-Luc Godard.

Inevitably, Pasolini would be critical of Neo-realist cinema and distance himself from it (as Federico Fellini and Bernardo Bertolucci did), partly because we know that Pasolini (and Fellini and Bertolucci) didn't like being part of a group, or being pigeon-holed and labelled.

However, Pasolini, like Fellini, certainly employed some of the formal approaches of Neo-realism (even if he denied using them): in her 2005 essay on *Rome: Open City*, Marcia Landy listed some of the styles and subjects of Neo-realist cinema:

> a predominant use of location shooting, deep-focus and long-take photography, non-professional actors, a loose form of narration, and a documentary look, plus in the intermingling of fiction and nonfiction, the privileging of marginal and subaltern groups, and a focus on contemporary situations. (J. Geiger, 404)

The decline of the Neo-realist form of cinema coincided with the changes in Italian society after WWII. As David Cook explained in *A History of Narrative Film*:

> In practice, it was a cinema of poverty and pessimism firmly rooted in the immediate postwar period. When times changed and economic conditions began to improve, neorealism lost first its ideological basis, then its subject matter. (453)

Another factor was the Andreotti Law, instituted in response to the glut of North American movies in Italy in 1949. The Andreotti Law taxed imported films and promoted home-grown products. (Several European nations have attempted to control American cultural imports and promote their national arts).

For David A. Cook (in *A History of Narrative Film*), at his best Pier Paolo Pasolini 'succeeded in creating an intellectual cinema in which metaphor, myth, and narrative form all subserved materialist ideology' (1990, 633).

Gary Indiana described Pasolini as:

> Indefatigably productive, ingenious, exasperating, narcisstically didactic, slyly self-promoting, abject, generous, exploitative, devoted to the wretched of the earth with honest fervor and deluded romanticism...

Pierre Leprohon, in one of the standard books on Italian cinema (1972), was suspicious of the merits of Pier Paolo Pasolini's work: 'originality, violence, controversiality and a taste for (often confused) symbols', Leprohon asserted, with anachronistic music, and it's deliberately, irritatingly mystifying (207).

For David Thomson (an idiosyncratic and not always reliable film critic), Pier Paolo Pasolini's films weren't up to the level of his theories and poetry: there was too much portentousness in Pasolini's imagery, Thomson reckoned, adding:

> His strident compositions were clumsy and monotonous, and his appetite for faces often overrode the ability to edit shots together fluently. The style was top-heavy, just as the meanings of his films were too literary, too immediate, and too inconsistent. (1995, 575-6)

Of course I don't agree with any of that. 'Monotonous'?! Hardly. And why is being 'too immediate' a problem? But you could agree that some of the imagery and the *mise-en-scène* didn't match up with the grand themes and issues, that sometimes the imagery is too grandiose for the stories and the characters (or vice versa).

How would I define myself? It's like asking the definition of infinity. There's an interior infinity and an exterior infinity. When I think of myself, I think of something infinite. It's impossible to define myself. For you I'm definable but for me I'm infinite. I'm the mirror of exterior infinity, it's impossible for me to define myself. I could create... some slogans, a few funny things in conversations, in salons, perhaps... I could quote something Elsa Morante said about me: "I'm a narcissistic individual who has a happy love of myself." I must add that I have an unhappy love for the world. Or maybe, I could say I'm a true devil, not a false devil like Sanguineti or the *avant garde* writers.

Pier Paolo Pasolini (1966)

The death of Pier Paolo Pasolini at age 53 has loomed large in his legend (as with the deaths of figures such as Marilyn Monroe, Jim Morrison, Jimi Hendrix and Bruce Lee). The details are still shrouded in mystery and controversy. No one knows precisely what happened, or will confess the truth. (It does seem as if some people *do* know who was responsible, but refuse to say). Anyway, nobody can agree exactly what went on that fateful night of November 1-2, 1975.

Some of the events of the night of Nov 1 and Nov 2, 1975 are agreed upon: that Pier Paolo Pasolini picked up the 17 year-old hustler Giuseppe Pelosi in Rome; that they ate in a restaurant; and that they drove in Pasolini's sports car to Ostia (a typical evening for Pasolini, thus far).

After that, there are many versions of what happened. That Pasolini was beaten and run over by his own car seems certain.

Other details of the murder have come to light:

• the green sweater that didn't belong to Pasolini in the car;

• the bloody handprint on the roof of the car;

• that witnesses claimed they saw at least one

motorbike and possibly a car following Pasolini's vehicle;

• that a skinny kid could not have killed the bigger, athletic Pasolini;

• that Pelosi didn't have any blood on him;

• that the damage sustained by Pasolini was far beyond what Pelosi could have inflicted;

• that, if other people were involved, the murder seems inept;

• that the motives are obscure – for Giuseppe Pelosi, but also for other groups (such as a local gang).

Giuseppe Pelosi confessed to Pier Paolo Pasolini's murder (and was duly imprisoned). Pelosi claimed that Pasolini had proposed things that he didn't want to do (including, preposterously, sodomy with a wooden stake). Pelosi's motives for the murder have never been explained satisfactorily.

In 2005, Giuseppe Pelosi retracted his confession, which he claimed had been made due to threats to his family. Pelosi gave more names in 2008.

Several high profile members of Italian society have asked that the case be re-opened, including former mayors and lawyers, as well as journalists.

When the case was re-opened in 2005, Sergio Citti, Pier Paolo Pasolini's long-time lover and colleague, said that Pasolini had been going to meet someone who had stolen reels of the film *Salò* (with a view to extorting money). Others have also reckoned that film canisters stolen on Aug 27, 1975 from the Technicolor lab in Rome might've been involved (as well as *Salò*, some of the negatives of *Casanova* were taken – 74 cans of film. Some have suggested that the thieves mistook the negatives of *Salò* for those from *Casanova*. Producer Alberto Grimaldi (he was producing both films) refused to pay the thieves the half a billion Lire they demanded).

ı The extortion scenario doesn't make total sense – not least because it's the producers, the production companies and the studios who control the money in the film industry, not directors. Also, killing someone means you won't get the money you're extorting. That

Pasolini would go to meet some small-time crooks intent on extracting some Lire out of him at night in a lonely spot like Ostia seems unconvincing.

Several theories have been proposed for the death of Pier Paolo Pasolini. That he irritated some groups (and institutions) is well-known – that his views were not welcome in some quarters of Italian society; that he was known as a Marxist and Communist who criticized the social and political status quo; that he wrote articles published in Aug, 1975 which criticized Christian Democrats and other right-wing organizations for the decline of Italian society, etc. But then, many writers and artists have stirred up controversy (and some were louder and more outspoken than even Pasolini). And being a Communist in Italy is common (Pasolini remarked that everyone in Italy was a Catholic, and a Communist).

Anyway, one or more neo-fascist groups have been put forward as possible culprits, plus a local criminal gang (partly because witnesses said several people (perhaps five) murdered Pier Paolo Pasolini, not Giuseppe Pelosi on his own. Laura Betti and others have claimed that a car containing four people followed Pasolini's vehicle). Links have also been suggested between neo-fascist groups and the Italian secret services. (The neo-fascist connection makes sense – it was neo-fascist groups that caused trouble at screenings of Pasolini's films in the early 1960s).

For Bernardo Bertolucci and others, it was a kind of public execution, an over-the-top act of punishment, probably backed by conservative groups in Italy who wanted Pasolini silenced, or to make an example of him. Bertolucci wondered if the perpetrators even knew what they were doing, or if they knew of the real motives behind the murder they were hired to carry out. Certainly, whoever killed Pasolini knew that they could get away with it, that they wouldn't be caught, that they had a scapegoat lined up, and that the Pasolini's supporters would not have the means to bring them to justice.

The death of Pier Paolo Pasolini has provided plenty of speculation and gossip-mongering. Inevitably commentators refer to his homosexuality, to his habit of cruising or seeking out rough trade, to his apparent sadomasochism (even with suggestions of a kind of suicide), to the brutality of his last film, *Salò,* and so on. But the sex/ masochism angle, though sensational, isn't the whole story by any means.

With its combination of spectacle, sex and mystery, Pasolini's murder is a 500-word newspaper piece that writes itself. When you add in aspects such as conspiracy, or extortionists, or neo-fascist groups, or political organizations such as Christian Democrats, you have an explosive cocktail that damns segments of Italian society. Pretty much every piece on Pasolini mentions his sensational demise.

Even philosophers such as Julia Kristeva have had their say (in *Tales of Love*):

> Masochism, which, we are told, is essentially and originally feminine, is a submissiveness to the Phallus that the soulosexual knows well and can assume until death in order to become the "true" woman – passive, castrated, nonphallic – that his/ her mother was not. Mishima, mistaking himself for Saint Sebastian, and even Pasolini, allowing himself to be executed by a hoodlum on an Italian beach, carry to the limit the slavish moment of male eroticism appended to a deathful veneration of the Phallus. (78)

Pasolini on set:
with opera superstar Maria Callas during Medea (above).
And with Enrique Irazoqui during The Gospel (below).

Pasolini and Welles during Curd Cheese (1963).

3

THE WORKS OF
PIER PAOLO PASOLINI

I love life fiercely, desperately... Love of life for me
has become a more tenacious vice than cocaine. I
devour my existence with an insatiable appetite.

Pier Paolo Pasolini[1]

Pier Paolo Pasolini directed thirteen feature films (one is
a documentary), and also many shorter pieces, including
contributions to anthology movies. His feature movies
are:

Beggar (*Accattone,* 1961)
Mother Rome (*Mamma Rome,* 1962)
Love Meetings (a.k.a. *Lessons In Love = Comizi
d'Amore,* 1964)
The Gospel According To Matthew (*Il Vangelo
Secondo Matteo,* 1964)
The Hawks and the Sparrows (*Uccellacci e
Uccellini,* 1966)
Oedipus Rex (*Edipo Re,* 1967)
Theorem (*Teorma,* 1968)
Pigsty (*Porcile,* 1969)

1 In L. Valentin, "Tête-à-Tête avec Pier Paolo Pasolini", *Lui*, April, 1970.
Andrea Dworkin used that Pasolini quote – 'I love life so fiercely, so
desperately' – in her novels.

Medea (*Medea*, 1969)

The Decameron (*Il Decamerone*, 1971)

The Canterbury Tales (*I Racconti di Canterbury*, 1972)

The Arabian Nights (*Il Fiore Delle Mille e Una Notte*, 1974)

Salò, or The 120 Days of Sodom (*Salò, o le Centoventi Giornate di Sodoma*, 1975)

Pier Paolo Pasolini's contributions to episode or anthology[2] movies are:

The Anger (*La Rabbia*, 1963)

Curd Cheese (*La Ricotta*, episode in *RoGoPaG*, 1963)

The Earth Seen From the Moon (*La Terra Vista Dalla Luna*, episode in *The Witches* = *Le Streghe*, 1967)

What Are the Clouds? (*Che Cosa Sono le Nuvole?*, episode in *Caprice Italian Style* = *Capriccio all'Italiana*, 1968)

The Sequence of the Flower Field (*La Sequenza del Fiore di Carta*, episode in *Love and Anger* = *Vangelo '70/ Amore e Rabbia*, 1969)

Pier Paolo Pasolini's shorter works include:

Location Hunting In Palestine (*Sopralluoghi in Palestina Per Il Vangelo Secondo Matteo*, 1965)

Notes For a Film In India (*Appunti Per un Film Sull'India*, 1969)

Notes For a Garbage Novel (*Appunti Per un romanzo dell'immondizia*, 1970)

Notes Towards an African Oresteia (*Appunti Per un'Orestiade Africana*, 1970)

The Walls of Sana'a (*Le Mura di Sana'a*, 1971)

12 December 1972 (*12 Dicembre 1972*, 1972)

---

2 Advantages for filmmakers with anthology movies included: they didn't have to originate them or raise the cash – the producer did all of that; they could be filmed in one or two weeks; they could dig out unmade ideas; they could write their own scripts or come up with their own ideas; and they often had more freedom than with a feature film.

Pasolini and the Shape of the City (Pasolini e la forma della città, 1975)

✻

Pier Paolo Pasolini's 1955 novel *Ragazzi di vita* was adapted into a movie by Jacques-Laurent Bost and Pasolini: *La Notte Brava* (a.k.a. *Bad Girls Don't Cry,* a.k.a. *The Big Night,* Mauro Bolognini, 1959). It was produced by Antonio Cervi and Oreste Jacovini for Ajace Film and Franco-London Film. In the cast were: Rosanna Schiaffino, Laurent Terzieff, Jean-Claude Brialy, Franco Interlenghi, Antonella Lauldi, Mylène Demengeot and Elsa Martinelli.

A chapter from *Ragazzi di vita* was adapted in *La Canta dell Marane* (1960, dir. Cecilia Mangini). It was produced by Giorgio Patara.

Una Vita Violenta (A Violent Life, dirs. Paolo Heusch and Brunello Rondi) was adapted by Ennio De Concini, Franco Brusati, Paolo Heusch, Brunello Rondi and Franco Solinas in 1962. *A Violent Life* was produced by Aera Films/ Zebra Film.

✻

Pier Paolo Pasolini worked on about 15 scripts b4 directing his first feature, *Accattone,* in 1961. As a screenwriter, Pasolini contributed to movies (working with many other writers) such as:

• *La Donna del Fiume* (1954, with 5 other writers: Bassani, Franchina, Vancini, Altovitti and Soldati),

• *Il Prigioniero della Montagna* (1955, with Trenker and Bassani),

• *Nights of Cabiria* (1956, alongside 3 other writers: Fellini, Flaiano and Pinnelli),

• *Marisa la Civetta* (1957, with 2 writers: Demby and Bolognini),

• *A Farewell To Arms* (1957, with Ben Hecht and John Huston),

• *Giovani Mariti* (1958, with 5 other writers: Currelli, Martino, Bolognini, Franciosa and Camanile),

• *La Notte Brava* (1959, with Jacques-Laurent Bost),

• *Marte di un Amico* (1960, with 5 other writers: Berto, Biancoli, Rossi, Guerra and Riganti),

• *I Bell'Antonio* (1960, with Brancati, Bolognini and Visentini),

• *La Lunga Notte del '43* (1960, with Bassani, Vancini and Concini),

• *La Giornata Balorda* (1960, with Moravia and Visconti),

• *Il Carro Armato dell'8 Settembre* (1960, with Baratti, Bertolini and Questi),

• *La Ragazza In Vetrina* (1961, with Cassuto, Emmer, Sonego, Martino and Marinucci),

• *The Grim Reaper* (1962, a.k.a. *La Commare Secca*,[3] with Citti and Bertolucci),

He also co-wrote with Sergio Citti the films *Ostia* (1970) and *Storie Scellerate* (1973), both of which Citti directed.

✲

Pier Paolo Pasolini's books of poetry include:
Poesie e Casarsa (1942)
Diarii (1945)
Tal cour di un frut (1953/ 1974)
La Meglio gioventù (1954)
Le Ceneri di Gramsci (1957)
L'Usignolo della chiesa cattolica (1958)
La Religione del mio tempo (1961)
Poesia in forma di rosa (1964)
Trasumanar e organizzar (1971)
La Nuova gioventù (1975)
and *Roman Poems* (1986)

Pier Paolo Pasolini's fiction and narratives include:
Amado Mio - Atti Impuri (1948/ 1982)
Ragazzi di vita (*The Ragazzi*, 1955)
Una Vita Violenta (*A Violent Life*, 1959)
A Dream of Something (1962)
Roman Nights and Other Stories (1965)
Reality (*The Poets' Encyclopedia*, 1979)

3 Pier Paolo Pasolini had conceived *The Grim Reaper* (writing a five-page treatment), but decided to make *Mamma Roma* instead. Producer Antonio Cervi had bought the project from Pasolini, and decided to let Bernardo Bertolucci have a go at directing it, after seeing the script he had commissioned from Bertolucci and Sergio Citti. Bertolucci admitted that his first film as director (he was only 21), *The Grim Reaper*, was made very much in the Pasolinian mold.

Petrolio (1992)

Pier Paolo Pasolini's volumes of essays and writings include: *Passione e ideologia* (1960), *Canzoniere italiano, poesia popolare italiana* (1960), *Empirismo eretico* (1972), *Scritti corsari* (1975), *Lettere luterane* (1976), *Le belle bandiere* (1977), *Descrizioni di descrizioni* (1979), *Il caos* (1979), *La pornografia è noiosa* (1979) and *Lettere (1940–1954) (Letters, 1940-54*, 1986).

Pier Paolo Pasolini directed plays. In Turin he directed a version of *Orgia* in November, 1968. The cast included Laura Betti, Luigi Mezzanotte and Nelide Giammarco.

Pier Paolo Pasolini's theatre work includes: *Orgia* (1968), *Porcile* (1968), *Calderón* (1973), *Affabulazione* (1977), *Pilade* (1977), and *Bestia da stile* (1977).

Films/ TV shows/ documentaries have been made after Pier Paolo Pasolini's death from his works (some have quoted from his poems and plays), including:

Laboratorio teatrale di Luca Ronconi (1977)
Mulheres... Mulheres (1981)
Calderon (1981)
Die Leiche murde nie gefunden (1985)
L'altro enigma (1988)
Who Killed Pasolini? (1995)
Complicity (1995)
Il pratone del casilino (1996)
Le bassin de J.W. (1997)
Una disperata vitalità (1999)
Orgia (2002)
Salò: Yesterday and Today (2002)
Pasolini prossimo nostro (2006)
'Na specie de cadavere lunghissimo (2006)
La rabbia di Pasolini (2008)
Pilades (2016)

Of the thirteen features directed by Pier Paolo Pasolini, only one is an acknowledged masterpiece: *The Gospel According to St Matthew* (taking its place alongside meisterwerks such as *8 1/2*, *The Searchers,*

Sunrise, Ran, Rashomon, Ordet, Persona, Vertigo, The Magnificent Ambersons, Citizen Kane and *The Godfather*). Some Pasolini pictures are highly regarded (*Theorem, Salò, Accattone*), some are minor (*Mamma Roma*), some deserve to be much better known (*The Arabian Nights, Medea, Oedipus Rex*), some are almost wilfully obscure (*The Canterbury Tales, Theorem*), some are very patchy (*The Hawks and the Sparrows,* parts of the 'trilogy of life' films), only parts of *Pigsty* are any good,[4] and one is a disaster (*Love Meetings*). But only *The Gospel According To Matthew* has become an out-and-out classic, that can take its place in the top ten lists of the critical academy. *The Gospel According To Matthew* is no. 30 in *Sight & Sound*'s 2012 poll of top movies among directors, and is included in the Vatican's list of important films (which the Pontifical Council For Social Communications produced in 1995, for the 100th anniversary of cinema). Other Italian films on the Vatican's list are *Rome: Open City, Bicycle Thieves, The Road, 8 1/2, The Leopard* and a forerunner of *The Gospel, Francesco.*

And of Pier Paolo Pasolini's short fiction films (for anthology movies), most are disappointing (*The Witches, Capriccio all'Italiana, Love and Anger*), with only two attaining greatness (*Curd Cheese* and *The Anger*).

However, some critics and filmmakers have put *Salò* into their top ten lists, and Bernardo Bertolucci places *Accattone* in there (as have some other critics). Occasionally a film like *The Arabian Nights* or *Oedipus the King* makes it into a critic's top ten. (The Italian movies that regularly crop up in top ten movie lists include *The Leopard, The Road, Bicycle Thieves, La Dolce Vita, The Conformist, Voyage To Italy* and *Rome, Open City*. The single most beloved Italian movie around the world for film critics and film directors is definitely *8 1/2*, the astonishing and enormously

---

4 Yes, we know that *Pig Fry* is a poetical-political-polemical fable, a savage satire about survival and being human and capitalist consumerism and why aren't there any cafés on Mount Etna where you get a cheeseburger and a decent cup of coffee?

entertaining exploration of a modern film director in crisis helmed by Federico Fellini – closely followed by *La Dolce Vita*).

One should note, too, that directing 13 pictures over 15 years (from 1961-1975) is very productive (plus the anthology pieces and the documentaries). I wish that Pier Paolo Pasolini had started directing earlier (he was 40 when *Accattone* was released), and also that we might have seen the incredible work that Pasolini would no doubt have created from 1975 onwards (his *St Paul*, his *Socrates* – even, maybe, his *Terms of Endearment 3*, his *Rocky 12*, his *Star Trek 17*).

PASOLINI AS EUROPEAN *AUTEUR*

Although Pier Paolo Pasolini is classed with other European *auteurs* as a maker of small-scale art films (as if only North American or internationally-financed pictures could be 'epic' or large scale), in fact many of Pasolini's films as director have an enormous scope (and they were also part-financed by American companies). Sure, some of Pasolini's pictures are intimate and small-scale, but many of them happily contend with hundreds of extras, props, animals, costumes and a huge number of different locations and sets. In many movies directed by Pasolini the frame is teeming with human life – in the mediæval trilogy and in *The Gospel According To Matthew*. Pasolini, in some ways, is the European equivalent of Cecil B. DeMille or D.W. Griffith as a creator of historical epics.

Of course, there have been plenty of European, costume epic films over the years, but Pier Paolo Pasolini's films are very different from those international movies which are usually co-productions between, say, French, Italian, German, Spanish, Swedish or British film companies. Pasolini's films do not have the style, flavour or feel of the typical 'Euro-pudding' with their starry casts, glamour, and self-conscious apeing of Hollywood cinema.[5] Instead, Pasolini goes completely his own way, doesn't pander to creating star parts or scene-stealing cameos, doesn't cast U.S. actors, doesn't have easy-to-follow plots, doesn't shoot in English (or mid-Atlantic), and his cinematic approach is instantly recognizable (and has proved inimitable – very few film directors have the vision, the guts, the energy, the sheer stubbornness or, crucially, the *patience* to pursue that kind of grand, vast filmmaking).

Some of Pier Paolo Pasolini's Italian contemporaries produced large-scale historical films: Federico Fellini, Bernardo Bertolucci and Luchino Visconti, for instance. But Bertolucci's historical epics, from *1900* to *The Last Emperor* and *The Sheltering Sky*, were always commercial, European-American productions (in style and casting, if not in financing). Incredible as many of Bertolucci's later movies were, they were always slickly and glossily turned out, more than half in love with the creation of finely-crafted visuals (what Jean-Luc Godard called the cinema of Max Factor, his comments *pace Schindler's List*. Pasolini thought that Bertolucci had sold out to commercialism with *Last Tango In Paris*). Luchino Visconti's later films also have that eager eye on the international market. (Notice too that Pasolini doesn't do the usual thing of recreating the past accurately of historical movies: no, he preferred to produce characters and settings by analogy. Thus, the *Bible* wouldn't be filmed in Israel or Palestine, but in Calabria and Sicily).

Comparing the cinema of Pier Paolo Pasolini with that of Bernardo Bertolucci,[6] Bruce Kawin and Gerald Mast (in *A Short History of the Movies*) assert that Pasolini's movies are

> more abstract, more elliptical, more complexly

5 However, Pasolini's later films were part-financed by American companies.
6 Pier Paolo Pasolini remarked that Bertolucci's 'real master is Godard' (*Pasolini On Pasolini*, 138).

structured, and more ferociously aggressive moral-political investigations, enlivened and propelled by dazzling bursts of unforgettable imagery... (338)

In his history of Italian cinema, Gian Brunetta remarked that

> Of the entire generation of 1960s filmmakers, none stood out like Pier Paolo Pasolini. He was a postwar one-man band, capable ot transforming everything he touched into gold, from painting, poetry, and narartive to cinematography. Even his life and death were works of art. (238)

Somehow, Pier Paolo Pasolini's films remained stubbornly his own, far more idiosyncratic and eccentric than most of his contemporaries, except filmmakers such as Federico Fellini (Fellini's films were always highly self-conscious and comical in their evocations of history – *Fellini Satyricon*, for example, or *Roma*). Sometimes reaching for camp eccentricity appears laboured and clunky in cinema; for Pasolini, as for Fellini, Walerian Borowczyk and Ken Russell, it seems almost effortless (indeed, it is their natural habitat; when people drew attention to the vulgarity, the eccentricity, the eroticism and the silliness of their movies, they would reply, eh? I don't know what you mean. Because for them, it was natural to make movies like that!).

No doubt Pier Paolo Pasolini was a powerful talent in cinema, but let's not forget that he was aided by some of the greatest artists in Italian cinema, some of whom have been called geniuses: Danilo Donati (costumes), Dante Ferretti (production designer), Nino Baragli (editor), Sergio Citti (writer/ director), Giuseppe Rotunno and Tonino Delli Colli (photographers) and Ennio Morricone (composer).

There must have been times when Pier Paolo Pasolini's producers pleaded with the *auteur* to at least include some big names in some cameos, or to cast one or two star actors. But no, Pasolini simply didn't. However, he and his casting directors did put some well-known faces into his movies, include Silvana Mangano, Anna Magnani, Terence Stamp, Orson Welles, Totò, Hugh Griffith, Jean-Pierre Léaud, and Maria Callas. (And of course Pasolini helped to make Franco Citti a star, at least in Italy).

But I'm sure some of Pier Paolo Pasolini's producers wished he'd used plenty more stars, or used them in the conventional way (that would be the instinct of Italian producers such as Dino de Laurentiis and Carlo Ponti). There would be all sorts of factors involved here, not least money – the budgets of some of Pasolini's movies were small, compared to big, international co-productions, and to Hollywood A-pictures. Also, I would guess that some film stars wouldn't want to appear in the kind of movies that Pasolini was making (and also, they wouldn't do some of the things that the movies required, such as nudity. Sure, Marlon Brando might bugger Maria Schneider in *Last Tango In Paris*, but he did it fully clothed!).

It's intriguing to note that Pier Paolo Pasolini made three ancient world movies: *The Gospel According To Matthew*, *Medea* and *Oedipus Rex*, and three Middle Ages movies: *The Arabian Nights*, *The Decameron* and *The Canterbury Tales*. He was very happy in distant history (most filmmakers, if they film historical periods, go back to the mid or early 20th century (often their early years, or that of their parents), or to the 19th century[7] at most). Indeed, the last significant work that Pasolini produced that was set in the contemporary period in feature movies was one half of *Porcile* (the other half was set in the 15th century). His next four films after 1969 were historical pieces.

You can easily discern the influence of the cinema of Pier Paolo Pasolini on filmmakers such as Sergei Paradjanov (a huge admirer of Pasolini), Federico

7 Pier Paolo Pasolini's works are steeped in Victoriana – the hysterical melodrama, the Gothicism and Romanticism, the early Industrial Revolution, the emerging metropolises, the industrialization of desire in mass prostitution, early capitalism, etc.

Fellini, Francis Coppola, Oliver Stone, Terry Gilliam (and the Monty Python team),[8] Derek Jarman, Peter Greenaway, Bernardo Bertolucci, Martin Scorsese, Jeunet and Caro, Guillermo del Toro and Abel Ferrara. In 2003 Gian Brunetta noted Pasolini's continuing impact on Italian filmmakers such as Mario Martone, Luigi Faccini, Nico d'Alessandria, Aurelio Grimaldi, Pappi Corsicato, Daniele Ciprí and Franco Maresco (239).

> Pasolini's life's work and his cinema continue to speak to us thanks to his cultural nomadism, his ability to mix and hybridize all codes, his asystematic working method, and his ability to tap into the pulse and capture the soul of minorities and regional identity. (239)

FIRST WORKS IN CINEMA

In Bologna, Pier Paolo Pasolini saw some of the classics for the first time: Charlie Chaplin, Jean Renoir, René Clair, etc. 'That's where my great love for the cinema started' (PP, 30). Films like *Rome, Open City* and *Bicycle Thieves*[9] made a big impact on the young Pasolini (ibid.).

Pier Paolo Pasolini had written his first film script in 1945 (aged 23), called *I calzon* or *Lied*. When he arrived in Roma (in 1950), he began writing movie scripts. Some of the early screenplays were co-written (such as *La Donna del Fiume*, with Giorgio Bassani).

In the mid-1950s, Pier Paolo Pasolini was working for movies as a scriptwriter. He published his key works

8 One can see the influence of Pier Pasolini Pasolini in the Ancient Greek sequence in *Time Bandits* (Terry Gilliam, 1981), or in Monty Python's *Life of Brian* (the desert sequences in both films also allowed the two Terrys (Jones and Gilliam) to recreate Pasolini, whom they loved, as well as a bit of the Biblical epics – *Ben-Hur* and *The Ten Commandments*).

9 He went to Udine (from Casarsa) specially to see *Bicycle Thieves*. He wasn't so young, tho' – *Bicycle Thieves* was released in 1948, when Pasolini was 26.

in this period – such as *Ragazzi di vita* and his poetry book *La Meglio gioventù*.

When Pier Paolo Pasolini was dating Sergio Citti in the mid-1950s, he became friendly with many of the *ragazzi* of the *borgate*, the real-life street kids who would become non-professional actors in his first movies, from *Accattone* onwards.

Pier Paolo Pasolini was most productive in the years prior to his entry into film production, according to his biographer Enzo Siciliano: from 1953 to 1961. This was the period when he published novels (*Ragazzi di Vita, Una Vita Violenta*), poetry (*La Ceneri di Gramsci, La Religione del mio tempo*), 13 film scripts, translations (*Oresteia*), and magazine articles (such as for *Officina*).

SCRIPTS

All of the movies that Pier Paolo Pasolini wrote before taking up directing with *Accattone* were *co*-written: Pasolini was *not* the sole screenwriter on *La Donna del Fiume, Il Prigioniero della Montagna, Le Notti di Cabiria, Marisa La Civetta*, etc. Instead, he was part of writing teams which included Basilio Franchina, Florestano Vancini, Antonio Altovitti and Mario Soldati (*La Donna del Fiume*), Luis Trenker, and Giorgio Bassani (*Il Prigioniero della Montagna*), Federico Fellini, Ennio Flaiano and Tullio Pinelli (*Nights of Cabiria*), etc. Other films Pasolini contributed to were: *The Big Night, La Giornata balorda, Giovani mariti, Morte di un amico, Il Carro armato dell '8 settembre, La Ragazza in vetrina* and *La Cantata delle marane.* Pasolini worked with Bassani (1916-2000) on several films, including *Una Notte del' 43.* Bassani dubbed Orson Welles in *Curd Cheese,* and he wrote the novel *Il Giardino dei Finzi-Contini* (later filmed by Vittorio de

Sica).

It's also worth noting that before he started to direct with *Accattone*, Pier Paolo Pasolini had already had some of his works made into movies – though he didn't direct them. A chapter of the important Pasolini novel *Ragazzi di Vita* was adapted in *La Canta dell Marane* (1960, dir. Cecilia Mangini), and *Ragazzi di Vita* was made into a movie in 1959, as *La Notte Brava* (= *The Big Night,* dir. Mauro Bolognini), and *Una Vita Violenta* (= *A Violent Life*) was filmed by Ennio De Concini, Franco Brusati, Paolo Heusch, Brunello Rondi and Franco Solinas in 1962 (*Una Vita Violenta,* dir. Paolo Heusch and Brunello Rondi).

✻

Only a very few filmmakers write and direct their movies. I don't mean co-write, I mean who are the sole writers of their films. And even fewer filmmakers write and direct *from their own ideas* (i.e., they come up with the fundamental concept). Because most movies are adapted from existing material, whether it's comic-books, plays, books, computer games, TV shows, musicals, newspaper articles, or even theme park rides (plus remakes, sequels, reboots, etc).

And Pier Paolo Pasolini is no different: although we think of him as an *auteur*, writing and directing his movies (each one with the possessive credit: '*un film scritto e diretto da'*), in fact maybe half of his movies are based on existing material. They do not come from ideas and stories that Pasolini has conceived himself. Instead, they are adaptations – usually of classic literature: mediæval literature in three movies (the 'trilogy of life' series), three ancient world sources (*The Gospel According To Matthew*, *Medea* and *Oedipus Rex*), and the Marquis de Sade (*Salò*). So Pasolini didn't invent the concepts, the characters, the stories, the situations, the themes, the settings, the interactions, the relationships or many other elements of those adaptations.

The movies that are based on Pier Paolo Pasolini's own ideas and stories include: *The Hawks and the*

Sparrows, Accattone, Mamma Roma, Theorem, Curd Cheese, The Earth Seen From the Moon and *Pigsty*. Also, Pasolini did *not* write everything himself: he co-authored his scripts with writers such as Dacia Maraini, Pupi Avati, Giorgio Bassani, and Sergio Citti.

Pier Paolo Pasolini didn't take up pot-boilers, sleazy novels, airport fiction, computer games, theme park rides, TV comedies, sit-coms, radio shows, comicbooks or the backs of cereal packets to adapt into movies: he took up the very greatest literature, heavyweight authors like Sophocles, Euripides, Aeschylus, the *Bible*, Giovanni Boccaccio, Geoffrey Chaucer, the Marquis de Sade and *The Thousand and One Nights*. Well, that's a *very* impressive list! Nobody can doubt the high ambition or the seriousness of the master's approach!

For Jean-Luc Godard, all of the work in making a film is *already done* before the cameras started rolling. The real work of making the film was the scriptwriting and the preparation. 'Most people think they work only when the camera is rolling, but that's not it. When the camera rolls, everything is done already'.[10] That certainly applies to Pasolini – it's all about the conception and the writing.

FLAWS IN PASOLINI'S CINEMA

I am writing about the movies directed by Pier Paolo Pasolini primarily as movies, as movie experiences, in a deliberately simple and direct manner. But of course there are *thematic* and *narrative* and *political* and *psychological* and *theoretical* perspectives to these films which are rich and inspiring.

However, there are times in watching a Pasolini movie when you think:

10 *Interviews*, 1998, 174.

This is twaddle.[11]

I don't care if he's a major poet and political rebel and cultural iconoclast! It's as if Dante Alighieri directed *Deep Throat*!

Observers of the Legend and Cult of Pasolini in the early 1970s might've looked at the 'trilogy of life' movies with exasperation and dismay: when is Pasolini, they might've thought, going to stop bothering with these silly saucy frolics and get back to something worthy of his immense talents, like *Medea* or *Oedipus Rex*? (Well, Pasolini *did* come back to something very serious after the three Middle Ages romps, but it was *Salò, or The 120 Days of Sodom*! – a film that was so far in the other direction, it wasn't what audiences were expecting, and probably not what the Pasolini admirers wanted).

Unfortunately, with the less-than-successful movies in the Pier Paolo Pasolini canon – such as *Love Meetings, The Hawks and the Sparrows, Pigsty* and *The Canterbury Tales* – it becomes more difficult to sustain the hi-falutin' theoretical approach. I mean, if you didn't know that Pasolini directed *The Canterbury Tales,* would we even be discussing it today? Wouldn't it have been relegated to the marginal critical discourses of cult movies or *mondo* cinema? An entertaining, weird, over-the-top slice of 1970s kitsch, but ultimately small potatoes?

Not *everything* by a great filmmaker has to be 'great' (or can be 'great'), does it?[12] Orson Welles completed twelve features (a comparable number with Pier Paolo Pasolini's thirteen features): seven are masterpieces, by my reckoning – *Kane, Ambersons, Othello, Touch, Macbeth, F For Fake* and *Shanghai* – but his 1955 movie *Mr Arkadin* (a.k.a. *Confidential*

11 This thought – am I watching piffle? – occurs with many directors who are highly critically acclaimed – Steven Spielberg, Sergio Leone, Billy Wilder, Martin Scorsese, John Woo, Vincente Minnelli, even Alfred Hitchcock, John Ford and D.W. Griffith.
12 Like many filmmakers (such as Woody Allen, Tim Burton and Hayao Miyazaki), Pier Paolo Pasolini said he never went to see his own films (PP, 108). Sometimes he saw them at film festivals, but he'd never dared to go see one of his movies in a public theatre.

Report) was, by his own admission, a failure (whichever you look at, in whichever botched, public domain version you get to see it, *Mr Arkadin* is incredibly disappointing). *Mr Arkadin* was an important personal project for Welles, but the post-production had been unhappy (a recurring motif in Welles' film career), and the film had been re-cut by the producer (Louis Dolivet).

Or take Francis Coppola: an all-round filmmaker with few peers and a truly colossal talent, Coppola has directed at least three masterpieces (*The Godfathers 1* and *2* and *Apocalypse Now*, though some would include *The Conversation*, and I would include more), but many critics found *Jack* (1996) perplexingly lightweight, and Coppola's two early movies – *Finian's Rainbow* (1968) and *You're a Big Boy Now* (1966) – are uneven (some would say mis-conceived and very dissatisfying – certainly *Finian's Rainbow*, as a Fred Astaire musical, is under-whelming).

To a degree, Pier Paolo Pasolini suffered like Orson Welles and Francis Coppola from a similar problem, seen in conventional critical terms: they were very successful early in their careers. Everything Welles did after *Citizen Kane* was compared with *Citizen Kane*, and his films never escaped that blinkered view from critics.[13] And Coppola is routinely satirized by critics as the man who directed *The Godfather* but went into artistic 'decline' in the 1980s with *The Cotton Club* and *One From the Heart.*

Rubbish, of course, but persistent rubbish.

Pier Paolo Pasolini, meanwhile, launched a filmmaking career with a minor masterwork, *Accattone*, and produced the staggering, 100% classic *The Gospel According To Matthew* three years later. As with Orson Welles and Francis Coppola and other filmmakers, early successes mean other movies can get made, but the stigma of early triumphs can colour the critical reception of later works. And in the case of Welles and Coppola, critics' emphasis on the early triumphs

13 Which is also applied all the time to Woody Allen, where audiences prefer his early, funny films.

becomes obsessive (both Coppola and Welles became completely exasperated by everybody harking on about those early works, even while they appreciated that at least people were talking about them!).

I'm sure that the later films of Pier Paolo Pasolini tried the patience and devotion of even his most ardent admirers (as with the later work of Jean-Luc Godard, Walerian Borowczyk, Ken Russell and Terry Gilliam). You can imagine Pasolini-worshippers turning up to theatres to see *Pigsty* in 1969 or *The Canterbury Tales* in 1972, and wondering if their Freudo-Marxo-Poetico God was losing his marbles. Jean-Pierre Léaud getting freaky with pigs in a film about cannibalism? Eh?! Hugh Griffith humping on top of Charlie Chaplin's daughter in a movie stuffed with spotty, greasy, British non-actors?

*

When you watch the films of Pier Paolo Pasolini again and again, some of the technical aspects and the flaws do rankle: the shaky, handheld camera,[14] the patchy sound, the endless shots of people walking, and too much Ninetto Davoli.

There is a *lot* of filler in Pier Paolo Pasolini's later films. Filler meaning, for example, shots of people walking in landscapes and towns. Now, the Pasolini sympathizers can point out the atmospherics, the mood, the Existential loneliness, the exquisitely-poised, onto-logical *ennui*, etc, of a shot of a guy walking across a volcano (*Pigsty*) or thru an anonymous, Middle Eastern town (*The Arabian Nights*). But Pasolini detractors can rightly criticize such images as pointless, redundant, or dramatically, poetically empty – the characters have already been established, the story is already in progress, the chief locales have been explored, so four shots of a guy getting from A to B are not necessary, and even harm the narrative flow.

Take a movie everybody has seen – *Jaws* (1975): do

14 Pier Paolo Pasolini operated the *macchina* himself sometimes. Unfortunately, he's no Stanley Kubrick, Ridley Scott or Ken Russell. He can't hold a camera. (One of the reasons for his terrible camerawork might be that he's yelling instructions at his actors at the same time!)

we need to watch Police Chief Brody driving for 15 minutes down to the dock where he joins the crew of the *Orca* boat? No – we cut straight to it. Do we need to see all fifteen hours of the connecting flights from the U.S.A. to the island off the coast of Costa Rica in *Jurassic Park* (1993) – plus four hours waiting in the terminal at Panama? No – we cut straight to the island. (An Ancient Greek text might say, 'And then he went to Thebes'. But that doesn't mean we need to see five lengthy shots of a guy walking to Thebes!).

Endless shots of people walking are a sure sign that a filmmaker is out of ideas. Yes, even a hyper-super-mega-genius like Pasolini. There's no juice in such shots (even isolated, Existential, metaphysical, onto-logical, outsider-ish juice). The filmmaker has admitted to the audience: *I have no idea how to dramatize the script or the story.* (This occurs even in *The Gospel According To Matthew*).

ANTI-CINEMA

When you consider all of the films of Pier Paolo Pasolini, sometimes it seems as if these movies *don't* want to be liked, or enjoyed (at least in the usual manner). As if, as with Carl-Theodor Dreyer, Robert Bresson and Andrei Tarkovsky, Pasolini wasn't going to make it easy for the viewer. And sometimes it can appear as if Pasolini's movies are being deliberately off-putting. Not 'offensive' or 'obscene', just plain difficult or obscure. A kind of anti-cinema, where expectations are wilfully, stubbornly scuppered. (Yes, there is definitely in Pasolini a delight in being difficult for the sake of it, as with Jean-Luc Godard).

For example, how would a Pier Paolo Pasolini movie play in a big cinema multiplex today? Reactions might run from laughter, scorn and ridicule to dismay and walk-outs. These are not movies that're going to preview well! They would die a death in the preview process, where unreleased movies are shown to invited audiences from the general public, getting a near-zero rating from the score cards. (Pasolini's personality, his financial contracts – and his reputation – would mean his films would be exempted from the preview process. Is a Pasolini movie going to be screened before an audience culled from shopping malls in San Diego who're then going to 'judge' his movie? I don't think so!).

They are not funny when they're meant to be funny, they are not scary when they're meant to be scary, they are not thrilling when they're meant to be thrilling, they are not dramatic when you expect/ hope them to be dramatic, they are not romantic when you think they might be romantic. They don't do what audiences would expect them to do. The technical aspects let Pier Paolo Pasolini's movies down, from the sound (the crude voice dubbing, the lack of sound effects (or 'immersion'), and the poor sound mixes),[15] to the picture (the too-shaky camerawork, and the sometimes indifferent staging).

There's an impossible-to-miss self-analysis in Pier Paolo Pasolini's cinema, a love-hate relationship with the material: as with the movies of Jean-Luc Godard, you can feel Pasolini's films arguing with themselves, simultaneously loving as well as distrusting the material, the themes, even individual shots. Like all artists, Pasolini wants to have it all ways: to evoke a scene of, say, extras in exotic costumes in a dusty, Mediterranean setting, but also to critique the subject and the very idea of making a movie in the first place.

This restlessness and dissatisfaction permeates not only Pier Paolo Pasolini's cinema but also his poetry,

15 Oh, how I wish that Alfredo Bini or Franco Rossellini or Alberto Grimaldi, the principal producers of Pier Paolo Pasolini's movies, had said, OK, we will use some of the budget to buy some decent sound equipment. This time it's live sound for us! Direct sound! Sound recorded on the set! *Si, si,* no more crappy dubbing at Cinecittà for us! (But the maestro of course preferred to deal with the sound in post-production).

and his whole work. And his personality, too, as those who knew him attest. Pasolini, everybody agrees, was a very complicated person.

✳

The cinema of Pier Paolo Pasolini does not do other things that audiences expect from movies. They do not employ conventional dramaturgy, for example. They avoid the conventions of rising action and cause and effect. So the flow of the drama and the narrative from scene-to-scene of your average movie is negated. Pasolini's movies do not build and build with suspense or tension or drama. Many scenes are self-enclosed, with little relation to scenes before or after.

And when you couple that avoidance of conventional dramaturgy with the intense stylizations of Pier Paolo Pasolini's cinematic approach – the flattened, static, *tableau* approach, for instance, or the paucity of dialogue or exposition – it creates a cinema that can be tough-going for some viewers. You can't slide thru a Pasolini movie easily, quickly and cheaply (with no investment): you have to *work*. It's not easy-to-digest television, like *C.S.I.* or *Friends*.

Pier Paolo Pasolini wasn't interested in action, either, or staging impressive spectacles (the 1st A.D.s would organize a vast array of extras, animals and props, which would then be filmed with a single, wobbly, handheld shot from a single viewpoint).[16] Like Jean-Luc Godard, Pasolini was indifferent to action (Godard famously filmed action as quickly as possible; he just couldn't be bothered with it). Pasolini wasn't interested in the glamour of cinema, or in making people look gorgeous, like the Hollywood Dream Factory (tho' he would insist on very extravagant costumes and hats. Which would then be filmed somewhat casually – unlike Walerian Borowczyk, who has probably the most acute and sensual feeling for clothes in all cinema).

---

16 No multiple cameras, either, or additional takes for safety, to make sure that a scene had been captured.

Sam Rohdie noted that 'Pasolini's documentaries were feigned. His past was not real, but a fragment framed, cut out. Reality was mutilated to make it all the more beautiful' (1995, 109). Pasolini realized that his essay/documentary pieces were for a minority, intellectual audience (PP, 140).

Pier Paolo Pasolini's documentaries are niche, certainly, and they are let down by misguided concepts, some dubious ideology, and poor technical aspects. But with the right producer, or maybe the right commissions from television companies, I reckon that Pasolini might've been amongst the finest documentary film-makers in cinema. He possessed all of the skills required to deliver some great material, except for the discipline and rigour to really make the material fly. Plus, with a major TV company behind him, he could have drawn on the resources necessary to complete the ambitious projects he wanted to make. (But he would also need a very strong TV producer who could say 'no' to his face).

Take the documentary made in Africa and Italy about staging an African version of Aeschylus' *Oresteia* – *Notes Towards an African Oresteia* (1970). The concept is full of ideological holes, and the execution is scrappy at best, and downright dreadful at worst.

So dump all of that material, and start again with a decent team of filmmakers and decent resources, and put the director himself in the picture (it's silly to squander a striking and well-known personality on camera like Pasolini, and have him hide behind a microphone back in Roma. Put Pasolini front and centre. And let's also see Pasolini directing his cast of amateurs in Africa).

Compare Pier Paolo Pasolini's documentaries with two geniuses of the medium in the same Euro-art arena: Werner Herzog and Jean-Luc Godard. Herzog has produced a striking and lively set of documentaries and film essays, often about exotic subjects in far-flung places (the Amazon, Africa, caves, etc). Like Pasolini, Herzog often appears in his documentaries, exploring places and interviewing people. He is a far more sympathetic interviewer than Pasolini, who tended to dominate his interviewees, and to ask them rhetorical questions (as if he'd already decided what he wanted his documentary to say). Herzog's documentaries are quirky and very distinctive (Herzog's German-accented voice-overs identified them as thoroughly Herzogian).

Jean-Luc Godard, meanwhile, is a master of the film essay form – half of his fiction movies, for example, might be characterized as film essays. Godard produced several fascinating film essays about his feature films, which he called notes for films (and Godard can talk about cinema as few people can, including Pasolini. Godard is a formidable intellectual talent). And with *Histoire(s) du Cinéma,* Godard created an epic history of cinema (between 1989 and 1998). *Histories of Cinema* was a major work, and has generated a good deal of critical comment. As well as being a history of cinema, it was also a history of the age – and a history of Godard himself.

DOCUMENTARIES ABOUT PASOLINI

Pier Paolo Pasolini has fascinated TV documentary producers – there was a documentary of 1970 (filmed with Pasolini's co-operation), and *Who Says the Truth Shall Die* (Phil Bregstein, 1981). Several documentaries have appeared on *Salò – Fade To Black* (2001), *Salò: Yesterday and Today* (2002), *Enfants de Salò* (2006, French), *Pasolini Prossimo Nostro* (2006, Italian) and *The End of Salò* (2008). Pasolini's murder was explored in *Who Killed Pasolini?* (1995). A ficionalized account of Pasolini was released in 2014 (with Willem Dafoe as the great man).

PASOLINI.

Pasolini (Abel Ferrara, 2014) was a biographical portrait of the last days of Pier Paolo Pasolini. Starring Willem Dafoe, Maria de Medeiros, Ninetto Davoli, Adrianna Asti and Riccardo Scamarcio, produced by Thierry Lounas and Fabio Massimo Cacciatori for the production companies Urania Pictures/ Dublin Films/ Belgacom/ Canal Plus, and scripted by Maurizio Braucci, *Pasolini* was a curiously flat and unengaging take on an incendiary filmmaker and poet. For Pasolinians, there was not only nothing new here, and the opportunities for depicting a complex and compelling artist were squandered. *Pasolini* took a de-dramatized approach, flattening the aspects of this passionate artist into a series of boring images and boring dialogues.

We see: Pasolini working on the post-production of *Salò;* a snippet of Pasolini's home life (with his mother Susanna prominent (played by Pasolini regular Adriana Asti – she was Amore in *Accattone*)); an interview with a journalist; a visit from an effervescent actress;[17] and extracts from a novel that Pasolini was working on.

Pasolini was one of those works in which nothing much happens – either visually, narratively, dramatic-ally, psychologically or philosophically. More like notes for a possible movie about Pier Paolo Pasolini (in the Godardian manner). It's scrappy. Bitty.

Time passes... *Pasolini* ends... a pointless group of images and sounds. Cinema at its worst.

Pasolini came alive a tad when Ninetto Davoli entered the frame – sort of playing himself (and shadowed by his former self, played by Riccardo Scamarcio), in an illustration of an unmade film idea from Pasolini about a spiritual journey/ religious skits, which included a visit to a gay and lesbian Sodom and Gomorrah (a festival where couples tup and the audience around them jeers and cheers. Presumably this is meant to be the 1973 unmade film project *Porno-Teo-Kolossal*). Not a patch on what Pasolini himself

17 Is that meant to be Laura Betti? (Played by Maria de Medeiros).

would've done with a modern-day Sodom and Gomorrah scenario, of course.

Pasolini recreated the night in November, 1975, when the director was murdered after picking up a youth. This played out as expected, but without the political/ ideological/ blackmailing motives (instead, the three youths who round on Pasolini attack him partly for homophobic reasons, yelling insults as they kick him. That fudged the issue, avoiding an opportunity to explore the more controversial issues surrounding Pasolini's demise).

4

ASPECTS OF
PASOLINI'S CINEMA

PIER PAOLO PASOLINI AND ITALIAN CINEMA

Pier Paolo Pasolini made his thirteen feature movies as a
film director between 1961 and 1975, the years of a
boom in the Italian film business, and of the European
New Wave (but he had been working on co-written
scripts thru the Fifties). This period of Italian cinema
was marked by the regeneration of production after
WW2, with movements such as the development of Neo-
realism (embodied in productions such as *Rome: Open
City,* Roberto Rossellini, 1945 and *Bicycle Thieves,*
Vittorio de Sica, 1948). However, Neo-realist cinema was
not popular in Italy itself, but overseas (especially
North America). The significant filmmakers of this
period were, with Rossellini and de Sica, Luchino
Visconti and Alberto Lattuada. North American
companies increasingly used Italian studios (such as
Cinecittà): they followed the money, which couldn't be
repatriated. When M.G.M. made *Quo Vadis* in Italy in
1950, other U.S. studios followed (and the Yanks visited
Italy throughout the 1960s).

Actually, how 'Italian' is Italian cinema? Pasolini's
and Fellini's later films, for example, were backed by
North American companies (such as United Artists). It

was the same with Visconti and Antonioni, as director Glauber Rocha of Brazil's New Cinema pointed out in the mid-1960s: 'Italy does not really have a national film industry, a truly Italian cinema, anymore' (in D. Georgakas, 17).

In the 1960s, Federico Fellini, Michelangelo Antonioni, Bernardo Bertolucci, Marco Bellocchio, Sergei Leone and the Tavianis were among the key film directors in Italy, as well as Pier Paolo Pasolini. The film stars included Marcello Mastroianni, Monica Vitti, Anna Magnani, Gina Lollobrigida, Sophia Loren, Vittorio Gassman, Totò and Silvana Mangano (Pasolini used Totò and Mangano the most). Among film producers of the period, such as Alberto Grimaldi and Alfredo Bini (who produced Pasolillni's films), two stand out in the Italian industry: Carlo Ponti[18] (married to Loren) and Dino de Laurentiis (married to Mangano); Pasolini worked with all of them).

The 1960s, according to Gian Brunetta,

> would prove to be the years of the greatest experimentation, freedom, and expressive riches. Not everything in the cauldron was made of gold, but the average qualitative level was the highest of all time. (171)

The Italian film industry reacted swiftly to any big hit movie, hurrying copies and sequels into production. Thus, successful movies such as *Spartacus* (1960), *Cleopatra* (1963), *Ben-Hur* (1959), and *Hercules* (1958) led to instant cash-ins. As Howard Hughes noted in *Cinema Italiano*:

> The story of Italian cinema is essentially a series of creative explosions, interspersed with fallow periods of audience exhaustion. If a film was popular, literally dozens of imitations would be made to cash-in at the domestic and international

18 Carlo Ponti (1912-2007) is one of the legends of the Italian film industry. Ponti produced some 140 movies, including many film classics, such as *La Strada, Boccaccio '70, Doctor Zhivago, War and Peace, Closely Watched Trains, Cléo From 5 To 7,* and three Michelangelo Antonioni flicks, *The Passenger, Blow-Up* and *Zabriskie Point.*

box office. This intense technique often resulted in each fad enjoying rather limited longevity, as the glut quickly satisfied audience interest. (ix-xi)

Thus, there was a craze of muscleman movies with mythological or ancient world settings, inaugurated by *Hercules*[19] (1958),[20] which lasted from 1958 to 1964. The Spaghetti Western fad, sparked by the *Dollars* films starring Clint Eastwood, ran from 1965 to 1970 (but continued into the 1970s). The *James Bond*-inspired spy cycle ran from 1963 to 1967. Gothic horror flicks were popular from 1960 to 1965 (and again in the 1970s with the *gialli*). 1960 was a triumphant year for Italian cinema, with *Rocco and His Brothers* and *La Dolce Vita* becoming big critical and commercial successes. Pasolini's cinema had its own cash-ins (the 'trilogy of life' movies were obvious candidates for rip-offs, which were released rapidly following the success of *The Decameron*. Producers saw that they could deliver sex romps much cheaper, by leaving out the elaborate set-pieces with extras and animals).

Along with Germany, Spain, Holland and of course France, Italy has been one of the most significant film production territories in Europe. The number of productions made each year and the number of tickets sold (i.e., punters going to the cinema) is among the highest in Europe.

Pier Paolo Pasolini benefited from the boom years of Italian film production, when it was making more movies per year than Hollywood: 242 films were produced in 1962, for example, compared to 174 in North America. 245 films in Italy in 1966, compared to

19 The Italian 1958 *Hercules* (the first one), starring Steve Reeves (Mr Universe) and helmed by Pietro Francisci, was so successful it inaugurated a series of Italian 'muscle-men', sword-and-sandal epics – some 180 films. *Hercules* cost $120,000 and made $20 million, and was released in 1959 thru Warners (producer Joe Levine had paid $120,000 for the rights). Its budget was less than 1% of that of Hollywood's *Ben-Hur* or *The Ten Commandments*, yet it made somewhere between 1/8th and 1/3rd as much (a producer's dream!). Levine launched *Hercules* with $1.1 million of advertizing, including on television ('the most aggressive campaign any film ever had', as William Goldman put it). 20 The couple in *A Violent Life* go to see a *Hercules* movie at the cinema.

168 in the U.S.A. 237 productions in 1974, compared to 156 in America (the recession hit Hollywood badly in the early 1970s).

In the 1960s and the 1970s, the period when Pier Paolo Pasolini was active as a film director, Italy made more movies than any other European country, including France (which since then has become the premier country for production *and* consumption), and more people went to the cinema in Italy than in any other nation (this's if you exclude Russia from Europe — which most people did in the Cold War era).

So film culture is immensely significant in Italy (even though de-regulated, hyper-capitalist television in the Silvio Berlusconi era has over-shadowed it). And the star filmmakers, like Federico Fellini, Luchino Visconti, Bernardo Bertolucci, Michelangelo Antonioni and Pier Paolo Pasolini, have become well-known outside film circles. And Dino de Laurentiis is a legendary mogul whose movies (and those produced by his daughter Raffaella) have generated billions.[21]

Dino de Laurentiis (1919-2010) was probably the most well-known Italian producer of recent times, a formidable mogul who moved from Italian movies (*Il Bandito, Bitter Rice, Anna, Europa '51, La Lupa, La Strada*), to North American co-productions (*War and Peace, Ulysses*), to international movies (*Barabbas, Bandits In Rome, Serpico, Barbarella, Three Days of the Condor* and *The Valachi Papers*), and epics (*The Bible, Waterloo, The Bounty* and *Dune*). De Laurentiis produced all-out commercial ventures (such as *King Kong, Death Wish, Hurricane, Orca the Killer Whale, Flash Gordon, Conan the Barbarian, Year of the Dragon, Body of Evidence,* and *Hannibal*), but also movies by art maestros like Ingmar Bergman, Federico Fellini, Luchino Visconti, Michael Cimino, Milos Forman, David Lynch, Vittorio de Sica and Robert

21 Jean-Luc Godard sent up Italian producers such as Carlo Ponti and Dino de Laurentiis (whom he's worked with), in his film *Passion* (1982), who always turn up with a beautiful woman on their arm. The producer in *Passion* yells: 'where's my money?', 'what have you done with my money?' It's one of the recurring phrases in the film business (usually yelled out, as of course it should be).

Altman (such as *Buffalo Bill, Face To Face, Desperate Hours, Lo Straniero,* and *Blue Velvet*). In North America in the 1980s, de Laurentiis founded D.E.G. (De Laurentiis Entertainment Group) in North Carolina, which flourished until it ended in 1988 (with, some said, debts of $200 million).

Dino de Laurentiis' career is truly remarkable – and long-running (he began producing during the German Occupation of Italy). He formed Real Cine in 1941 (when he was 23), produced *Il Bandito* (Alberto Lattuada, 1946), when he was 28, and married actress Silvana Mangano (who appeared in Pier Paolo Pasolini's *Theorem, The Decameron, The Witches* and *Oedipus Rex,* among others). With Carlo Ponti, de Laurentiis formed Ponti-De Laurentiis in 1950 (they owned the Farnesina Studios in Rome). De Laurentiis created Dinocittà outside Rome, where *The Bible, The Great War* and *Barabbas* were based. (Dinocittà has since become a movie theme park).

PASOLINI AND FELLINI

In the late 1950s, Pier Paolo Pasolini became part of Federico Fellini's court.[22] They had met at the Canova (Franco Rossi had brought them together). They took to wandering around Roma at night, with Pasolini introducing Fellini to some of the locations he drew inspiration from: Idroscalo, Tiburtino Terzo, Pietralata and Guidonia. The maestro had brought in Pasolini (and his partner, Sergio Citti) to help with some of his scripts (such as advising on the dialect in *Nights of Cabiria*[23] – dialect being one of Pasolini's passions). Pasolini wrote

---

22 Totò parodied *La Dolce Vita* in *Totò, Peppino and La Dolce Vita* (1960).
23 The settings of *Nights of Cabiria* – the outskirts of Roma, the scrubland and the caves – were employed several times in Pasolini's early films.

about 40 pages of the screenplay, according to Moraldo Rossi, but Fellini hardly used any of it.[24]

Federico Fellini later invited P.P. Pasolini to sit in on auditions at Cinecittà for projects such as *La Dolce Vita* (1960). Although some in the Fellini camp resented the maestro becoming so close to Pasolini, it was not a long-lasting friendship.[25] Fellini's wife Giulietta took 'an immediate dislike to the homosexual Pier Paolo as a corruptor of innocent young souls'),[26] and Fellini's regular screenwriter, Ennio Flaiano, refused to work with Pasolini on *La Dolce Vita*. Flaiano (known as a cynical, spiky writer) wrote a skit about it – "*La Dolce Vita* According To Pasolini" (which Fellini begged him not to publish).

Pier Paolo Pasolini had hoped that Federico Fellini (and his new company, Federiz, formed with the publisher Angelo Rizzoli), would back his first movie as director, *Accattone*[27] (Fellini and Rizzoli were also planning movies by Vittorio De Seta, Ermanno Olmi, Marco Ferreri and of course Fellini. But in the end, Fellini wasn't bothered about becoming a movie mogul – he only wanted to make his own films).

Tests for *Accattone* were shot (in September, 1960),[28] including two scenes: at via Fanfulla da Lodi, in the pine woods, and outside Castel Sant'Angelo. Pasolini later recalled meeting with Fellini to discuss them (after hearing nothing from the maestro): but it

24 Quoted in *Fellini On Fellini* 1995, 50.
25 It was a lively friendship, tho', according to Enzo Siciliano, 'a deep human attachment' (ES, 223).
26 Quoted in T. Kezich, 178.
27 *Accattone* announces its quirkiness from the outset: after those Renaissance-elegant opening titles, and the breezy, rarefied tones of J.S. Bach, what is the first shot of the movie? A pretty aerial view of the Eternal City? Oh no, this is not going to be a film featuring dignified professional actors spouting Shakespeare or Petrarch! Instead, it's a close-up of the ugly mug of Fulvio, joshing with the lads in their customary position: sitting outside the café in the side street. The final shot of *Accattone* is of Balilla, crossing himself as he looks down at the dying Accattone.
28 This was Pier Paolo Pasolini's first experience of being a film director, at least with his own material. His model was the 'absolutely simplicity of expression' in *The Passion of Joan of Arc*, directed by Carl-Theodor Dreyer. Another influential film for Pasolini was the 1950 *Francesco*, the portrait of St Francis and his followers directed by Roberto Rossellini using all non-professional actors (except for Aldo Fabrizi).

became apparent that Fellini and Rizzoli were not going to get behind *Accattone* (which in the event was produced by Alfredo Bini[29] – it was Bini who persuaded Pasolini to make *Accattone*).[30] According to Moraldo Rossi, Pasolini 'had staked everything on Fellini, but Fellini had dropped him'.[31] And from that point, Fellini and Pasolini fell out, sniping at each other's projects in the press.

PIER PAOLO PASOLINI'S COLLEAGUES

Critics typically talk about Pier Paolo Pasolini's movies in awed, auteurist terms, as if the director did *everything* in his movies. He didn't, though: he directed them, sometimes appeared in them in cameos, and wrote or co-wrote most of them (Pasolini did, however, believe in the *auteur* theory, unlike almost every filmmaker).[32] Thus, his films usually have the credit:

scritto e diretto da
or: *un film scritto e diretto da*

But one must always remember that Pier Paolo Pasolini was surrounded by some legends in Italian cinema – such as designers Dante Ferretti and Danilo Donati, DPs Giuseppe Rotunno and Tonino Delli Colli, producers Alfredo Bini and Alberto Grimaldi, and composer Ennio Morricone. And numerous others: by the 1960s, when Pasolini started to direct features, the Italian film industry boasted some of the finest, most

29 Mauro Bolognini saw photographs of the tests, and suggested the project to Bini.
30 E. Siciliano, 227.
31 Quoted in C. Constantin, 1995, 50.
32 Pasolini insisted that he 'always thought of a film as the work of an author, not only the script and the direction, but the choice of sets and locations, the characters, even the clothes. I choose everything – not to mention the music' (PP,32).

imaginative and skilled technicians and talents in the world. (Italian cinema was on a high, an up, a boom in this period).

The *auteur* credit, the 'un film de' credit, is dishonest and dumb. Who drew up all of the contracts (sometimes thousands for big movies)? Who oversaw the insurance, taxes, and liabilities? Who bought the cloth for the costumes? Who built the sets? Who booked the hotels? Who carried the lights up ten flights of stairs?[33] Who drove the actors to the locations? Who created the opticals for the titles? Who logged all of the rushes and takes? Who rented the vehicles? Who processed the exposed celluloid?[34] And who does 100s of other jobs in movie production?

Not the director.

This is a simplistic argument of who does what in movies, but *auteur* theory has also been disparaged on ideological, political, social, philosophical and cultural grounds.

The producers of Pier Paolo Pasolini's movies included Alfredo Bini, Alberto Grimaldi, Franco Rossellini (brother of Roberto Rossellini), Carlo Lizzani, Dino de Laurentiis, and Gian Vittorio Baldi. Bini produced the early works, Rossellini the middle period pictures (late 1960s), and Grimaldi the later ones.[35]

ALFREDO BINI (Dec 12, 1926-Oct 16, 2010)[36] is a hugely important figure[37] in the cinema of Pier Paolo Pasolini.[38] That he not only produced Pasolini's movies (and took a chance on him with his first film as director), but also supported the movies and stood behind them (when they attracted controversy), is also not to be under-estimated. Producing Pasolini's films wasn't the

---

33 No elevators in some of those old buildings.

34 I could go on!

35 The only problems he had with producers, Pasolini said, were *Pigsty* and *Medea*, which were flops.

36 Pasolini was four years older than Bini.

37 Occasionally you see snipes at Bini – but that goes with the territory of being a film producer. It doesn't detract from Bini's significance in Pasolini's film career.

38 'My contemporary from Gorizia | red-haired, hands in his pockets, | heavy as a paratrooper after mess-hall', as Pasolini characterized Bini in a poem in *Il padre salvaggio*.

easiest gig in town, I would imagine, adding all sorts of unforeseen challenges that went beyond your run-of-the-mill producing duties. I bet you had to be on top of your game to keep up with Pasolini.

> Bini had confidence in me at a time when that was extremely hard: I knew nothing about the cinema, and he gave me *carte blanche* and let me work in peace. (PP, 138)

Alfredo Bini formed Arco Film in 1960, and the companies Finarco and Gerico Sound. Bini produced most of Pier Paolo Pasolini's earlier movies (such as *RoGoPaG, The Gospel According to St Matthew, Mamma Roma* and *Accattone* and, later, *Oedipus Rex*). Bini's other producer credits included films helmed by Mauro Bolognini (*The Mandrake*, 1965), *El Greco* (1966), a rival version of *Satyricon* to the Federico Fellini film (1969), *Simon Bolivar* (1969), *Gli Eroi* (*The Horse*, 1973), *Lancelot du Lac* (Robert Bresson, 1974), and adaptations of theatrical plays aimed at the video market. He was married to actress Rosanna Schiaffino.

ALBERTO GRIMALDI (Mch 28, 1925-Jan 23, 2021, born in Naples) produced Pasolini's last four films, from *Il Decamerone* to *Salò*. Grimaldi was a lawyer from Naples; he had formed Produzioni Europee Associate S.p.A. in Roma in 1961. He had made plenty of $$$$ by producing the *Fistful of Dollars* Spaghetti Westerns starring Clint Eastwood. Grimaldi went on to become a big cheese in the Italian film industry – producing several Federico Fellini films, for instance, plus *Last Tango In Paris, 1900, Burn!, Trastevere, Man of La Mancha* and *Bawdy Tales*. One of Grimaldi's last producing jobs was *Gangs of New York* (2002). Grimaldi had a distribution deal with United Artists (hence, the films were released thru U.A. in North America, including the Pasolini productions).

United Artists was investing, like other North American studios in the 1960s, in European productions (brokering deals with Dino de Laurentiis as well as

Alberto Grimaldi and other Italian producers). United Artists wanted prestige pictures – 'more complex, larger-scale pictures' than Spaghetti Westerns (see below).

The films produced by Alberto Grimaldi often had erotic content – in the 1970s alone, there was *Last Tango In Paris*, the 'trilogy of life' films, *Salò, Novecento* and *Casanova* (dir. Federico Fellini, 1976). But that also reflects the era, when eroticism meant box office.

Many of Pasolini's later films were backed by Les Productions Artistes Associées along with Alberto Grimaldi's Produzioni Europee Associate (so they were Italian and French co-productions). Les Productions Artistes Associées had been founded in 1963 in Paris. Their movies included *Last Tango In Paris, Le Cage aux Folles, The Night Porter, 1900, Man of the East, The Story of Adele H., Roma, The Train, Burn!,* and *Moonraker* (the *James Bond* film).

UNITED ARTISTS. In the early Seventies, United Artists was known as one of the more adventurous of the Hollywood studios, and backed some of the more eccentric or left-of-centre productions. (U.A. was instrumental in forging the 'New Hollywood' cinema, for instance). From its early days, United Artists was known as a filmmaker-friendly studio, on the side of the filmmaker-as-artist. It was set up by Mary Pickford, Charlie Chaplin, Douglas Fairbanks and D.W. Griffith in 1919, where it was known as a company that would control marketing and distribution of the artists' products, rather than a conventional film studio (it didn't have sound stages and production facilities, didn't own cinemas, and didn't have a roster of stars).

By the 1960s, among United Artists' successes were the *Pink Panther* franchise (led by Blake Edwards and Peter Sellers), the Beatles films (*A Hard Day's Night* and *Help!*), and the ever-reliable *James Bond* franchise. (There were flops in the 1960s, however, such as the very costly picture *The Greatest Story Ever Told* (1965) – $20 million, and disappointments such as *Chitty Chitty Bang Bang* (1968, cost: $10m), *Battle of Britain* (1969, cost: $12m) and *The Private Life of Sherlock Holmes* (1970, cost: $10m). These productions were part of the over-spending cycle of the late Sixties.)

In the 1970s, *Rocky* was an important franchise for U.A. – the Chartoff-Winkler movies were sequelized several times. Chartoff and Winkler made a *ton* of money from United Artists' *Rocky* series (the first *Rocky* movie cost $1.5 million and took $55.9 million in North American rentals alone – equivalent to $487m in 2005 dollars). Among Chartoff and Winkler's productions was the controversial movie *The Last Temptation of Christ* (1988), which they had set up with Paramount in the early 1980s.

And let's not forget editor NINO BARAGLI (1925-2013), who cut nearly all of Pier Paolo Pasolini's features. Thus, Baragli (three years younger than the maestro), is one of the most important figures in Pasolini's cinema, and in Italian cinema of recent times (yet some film critics don't even mention him). Baragli worked with all of the major Italian filmmakers, including Federico Fellini, Luchino Visconti, Sergio Leone, Bernardo Bertolucci, Damiano Damiani, Mauro Bolognini, Massimo Troisi, Alberto Lattuada, Tinto Brass and Roberto Benigni, and directors such as Gabriele Salvatores and Margarethe von Trotta (for many of those directors, Baragli worked on many of their projects).

Editing is always underrated by film critics, even critics you'd think would know better (partly because critics don't really know what editing is. I think film critics should spend a day or so with a film editor, to learn exactly what the job entails). Among Baragli's credits were important collaborations with Sergio Leone (the *Fistful* Spaghetti Westerns and *Once Upon a Time In America*), *Ginger and Fred* and *The Voice of the Moon* (Federico Fellini), and *Mediterraneo*.

Editing a Pier Paolo Pasolini production, though, meant working with intuitive, spontaneously-shot material, where eyelines didn't match, where inserts and close-ups were often not filmed (plus all of the other 'coverage' of a scene of a typical movie), where non-naturalistic and discontinuous images had to be welded together. Pasolini didn't arrive on set with a regular shot list, and didn't approach scenes in a conventional manner. Editing a Pasolini film would be a challenge, with different requirements from your average film or TV show. Luckily, Nino Baragli was a master editor – some critics have called him a genius.

As for costumes, in DANILO DONATI (1926-2001), Pier Paolo Pasolini had one of the great costume designers (and set designers) of recent times: Donati's feeling for costume is simply astonishing.[39] Solely in the realm of *hats* and *headgear*, Donati has few peers. If you want to study the history of costume in cinema, you have to include lengthy research into Danilo Donati, or the cinema of Federico Fellini and Luchino Visconti. (In many ways, in Pasolini's cinema, as with Vincente Minnelli, Walerian Borowczyk and Ken Russell, it's all about the clothes).

For Pier Paolo Pasolini, Danilo Donati designed *RoGoPaG, The Gospel According To Matthew, The Hawks and the Sparrows, Oedipus Rex, Pigsty, Salò* and the 'trilogy of life' movies. For Federico Fellini, Donati designed *Satyricon* (1969), *The Clowns* (1971), *Roma* (1972), *Armarcord* (1973), *Casanova* (1976), *Ginger and Fred* (1986) and *Intervista* (1987). As well as working for Visconti, Fellini and Pasolini, Donati also provided costumes for films such as *The Taming of the Shrew* (1967), *Romeo and Juiliet* (1968), *Bawdy Tales* (1973), *Caligula* (1979), *Flash Gordon* (1980), *Red Sonja* (1985), *Nostromo* (1996), *Life Is Beautiful* (1997) and *Pinocchio* (2002).

On a Pier Paolo Pasolini production, costume designers were often encouraged to go all-out, and not hold back from outrageous designs. A huge challenge were the ancient world and mediæval movies – especially the ones set in archaic societies. Not least among the challenges would be getting all of the

---

39 Pier Paolo Pasolini praised Donati's genius with costume – 'he does all that, extremely well, with excellent taste and zest' (PP, 32).

costumes to those remote locations in Africa or Turkey (or even Southern Italia). No doubt quite a few costumes were manufactured near the set, using local workers (which would require a whole new way of working). For some of the historical productions, the wardrobe dept also had to clothe huge numbers of extras – and on budgets that were a fraction of their Hollywood equivalents. Yet each Pasolini movie has a look in costume design that's unique: a single frame, or a single still photograph from a Pasolini movie is instantly recognizable as coming from Danilo Donati. If there was a touring exhibition of costumes from Pasolini's movies, I would be first in line. (You can see some of Donati's costumes today at Cinecittà).

DANTE FERRETTI (b. 1943) is one of the superstars of production design in recent cinema. His list of credits is extraordinary by any standards. Ferretti worked with Pier Paolo Pasolini as production designer on *Medea, The Arabian Nights, The Decameron, The Canterbury Tales* and *Salò* (and as an assistant on earlier pictures, such as *The Gospel According To Matthew*). Ferretti also designed for Federico Fellini – *City of Women, And the Ship Sails On, The Voice of the Moon* and *Ginger and Fred,* and films such as *The Night Porter, Tales of Ordinary Madness, The Name of the Rose, Hamlet, Titus, The Adventures of Baron von Munchausen, Bram Stoker's Dracula, Sweeney Todd* and *Interview With a Vampire*; Ferretti worked with Martin Scorsese on *The Age of Innocence, Kundun, The Aviator, Bringing Out the Dead* and *Casino,* and with directors such as Tim Burton, Francis Coppola, Terry Gilliam, Jean-Jacques Annaud and Marco Ferreri.

Pier Paolo Pasolini would research the designs for his films from paintings, Ferretti said. Ferretti recalled that he was

> always a little intimidated by Pasolini. He was like a poet or a priest, and his approach to filmmaking was architectural: his shots were always like geometrical *tableaux*, with the camera dead centre.

TONINO DELLI COLLI (1923-2005) began, with *Accattone,* a long-running collaboration with Pier Paolo Pasolini that must rank as one of the finest in recent cinema – alongside Federico Fellini and Giuseppe Rotunno, Bernardo Bertolucci and Vittorio Storaro or Jean-Luc Godard and Raoul Coutard. Delli Colli (a year younger than Pasolini) was the cinematographer on eleven out of the maestro's thirteen feature films[40] (plus the episodes for anthology films). He was also DP for Federico Fellini, Roman Polanski, Jean-Jacques Annaud, Claude Chabrol and Sergio Leone (you can see Delli Colli at work with Fellini in *Interview*, 1987).[41] Delli Colli was known for subsuming his style into the material, and what the director wanted. He didn't impose his style on the movie, he served the movie. (He was described by Enzo Siciliano as short, Roman, nervous and given to uncontrollable rages, but was gentle with Pasolini.[42] From Delli Colli Pasolini learnt much of the art and practice of cinema).

> Come on, Tonino, come on,
> set it at fifty, don't be afraid
> of the light sinking – let's take
> this unnatural shot![43]

Tonino Delli Colli recalled: 'Our relations were perfect. [Pasolini] was an incredibly sweet and kind person, and he had respect for everyone on the set.' In terms of camera movement and style, Pier Paolo Pasolini preferred a simple visual approach: Pasolini was not interested in tricks, gimmicks or the 'magic' of cinema (even the greatest of filmmakers are full of tricks and gimmicks: Orson Welles, D.W. Griffith, F.W. Murnau, Jean Cocteau, Akira Kurosawa, Ingmar Bergman and

---

40 And Tonino Delli Colli would've shot the other movies if it weren't for scheduling conflicts.

41 He filmed the famous Spaghetti Westerns, for instance.

42 Delli Colli was described by Gideon Bachmann as a 'small, wiry man'.

43 Pasolini, *La Poesie*, 337.

Jean-Luc Godard. And Federico Fellini, of course, used every trick available).[44] Pasolini liked the 50 mil lens, Delli Colli said,[45] which gave a slightly compressed, squashed image, but approximated to the field of vision of the naked human eye.

GIUSEPPE ROTUNNO (1923-2021) is one of the great cinematographers of Italian cinema: he was DP on many classics, including the incredible *The Leopard* (1963), and worked for Federico Fellini (as his chief cameraman, from the late 1960s to the end of Fellini's life), Luchino Visconti,[46] Terry Gilliam (*Baron Munchausen*), Bob Fosse (*All That Jazz*) and John Huston (*The Bible*). Rotunno also lit films such as *Candy, The Secret of Santa Vittoria, Carnal Knowledge, Popeye, Red Sonja* and *Five Days One Summer.* Solely for his work for three Italian maestros – Fellini, Pasolini and Visconti – Rotunno should be regarded as one of the greats among photographers.

SERGIO CITTI (1933-2005) was a very important collaborator in the cinema of Pier Paolo Pasolini – he worked on the scripts, on the dialogue, and was an assistant director (as well as having a relationship with the maestro). Born in Rome, Citti was one of the longest-serving members of the Pasolini Movie Circus, following the master everywhere.

In 1970, Sergio Citti stepped up to become a film director: Pier Paolo Pasolini co-wrote Citti's first two films as director: *Ostia* (1970) and *Bawdy Tales* (1973). If anyone could step in to direct in Pasolini's absence, it would be Citti.

Sergio Citti's subsequent films included: *Beach House* (1977), *Happy Hobos* (1979), *Il Minestrone* (1981), *Mortacci* (1989, *We Free Kings* (1996), *Cartoni Animati* (1997), *Vipera* (2001) and *Fratella e Sorello* (2005). *Sogni e Bisogni* (1985) was a TV mini-series.

---

44 Sergio Citti, in the 1970 documentary on Pier Paolo Pasolini, insists that *he* didn't use zooms or dollies or other trickery on his movies, as Pasolini did.

45 Delli Colli said that Pasolini liked to use either long lenses or wide angle lenses.

46 Rotunno started out on Visconti productions such as *Senso* and *White Nights.*

SILVANA MANGANO. One of Pier Paolo Pasolini's favourite actresses was Dino de Laurentiis' wife Silvana Mangano (1930-89): she appeared in *Theorem, The Decameron, The Earth Seen From the Moon* (the episode in *The Witches*), and *Oedipus Rex*. As well as films helmed by Pasolini, she was in *Ulysses, Barabbas, Black Magic, Mambo, Tempest, Il Processo di Verona, Gold of Naples, Five Branded Women, Conversation Piece, Dune* and *Death In Venice* (many of those movies were produced by de Laurentiis). Like Sophia Loren, Gina Lollobrigida, Anna Magnani and Alida Valli, Mangano was an icon of Italian cinema; her face, which could melt the camera, was instantly recognizable (she was a hit aged nineteen in *Bitter Rice* (1949), walking in rice fields with her skirt up around her thighs).

LAURA BETTI (1927-2004) was another of Pier Paolo Pasolini's special actresses, appearing in many of his films (and providing the voice in others). Betti was one of his most important friends. The bond between Betti and Pasolini could be fiery, however – she would yell at him, hurling insults, and Elsa Morante, listening, would interject: 'If you two want to make love, stop doing it in words' (ES, 261). Betti was possessive over her friendship with Pasolini, pushing away anyone who threatened it (such as Maria Callas).

ALBERTO MORAVIA (1907-1990, born in Rome) was a favourite author with Italian filmmakers – most of his fiction was adapted into movies (including *The Conformist, La Romana, Agostino, Gli Indifferenti*, etc). Moravia also wrote films.

Novelist ELSA MORANTE (1912-85) was an valued advisor and encourager for Pier Paolo Pasolini, and influenced several of his film projects (such as advising on the music for *The Gospel According To Matthew* and others). Morante's husband, author Alberto Moravia, was a fellow colleague and traveller (he appeared in *Love Meetings* and went on trips with Morante and Pasolini, such as to India in 1960).

FRANCO CITTI

Apart from six Pier Paolo Pasolini movies, Franco Citti (1938-2016) has also appeared in mainly Italian movies – by Bernardo Bertolucci (*La Luna*), Sergio Citti, Sergio Pastore, Elio Petri, Franco Rossi, Antonio Bido, Antonio Avati, and two *Godfather* movies.

While Nino Davoli represented the lighter side of Pasolini's art, the Charlie Chaplin aspects which mocked existence, Franco Citti, from *Accattone* onwards, embodied the murky, egotistic, and degenerate sides of the Pasolini persona, with its tendency towards self-loathing, violence and depression. Citti played Pasolini's grandiose but doomed hero Oedipus (his finest role for the maestro, along with Accattone), a ruthless crook (in *The Decameron*), a fellow cannibal (in *Pigsty*), the Devil in *The Canterbury Tales,* an enigmatic demon (in *The Arabian Nights*), and an arrogant pimp (in *Mamma Roma*).

Franco Citti's characters operate on the wrong side of the law, are introspective and difficult, and see themselves as Existential rebels (who feel that the whole world is against them). They want an easy life (they think they deserve it), and they can't understand why everybody isn't falling over themselves to do their bidding. They are charismatic and independent (which makes them initially attractive), but they implode under pressure (and arrogance).

NINETTO DAVOLI

While actors such as Franco Citti might be associated with Pier Paolo Pasolini's cinema in its arty, handsome, dramatic mode, just as significant were actors such as Ninetto Davoli (b. 1948, Calabria).[47] With his toothy

47 Davoli's parents were Calabrian peasants.

grin and frizzy hair, Davoli is terrific as hapless, lusty, rather dim youths on the make. Energetic, naïve, indefatigable, cowardly, Davoli is an unlikely leading man: he can never be the romantic lead, he is always the ordinary guy looking for the easiest way out.

Enzo Siciliano portrays Davoli as having a

> slight and skinny build, pimples on his face, kinky hair, and incredibly "merry" eyes... His voice was raucous, his physicality pliant and emaciated. His histrionics had a melancholy tinge and conveyed from the depths an inexpressible emotional anxiety. (284-5)

Ninetto Davoli was also Pier Paolo Pasolini's lover (from 1963, when Davoli was 15) – and they lived together for years after they'd ceased being lovers. So Davoli plays a special role in Pasolini's cinema on many levels[48] (he is also, like Franco Citti, a manifestation of the street kid from the Roman shanty towns, the kind of youth that Pasolini liked to hang out with).

Enzo Siciliano characterized the relationship of Pier Paolo Pasolini and Ninetto Davoli after the eroticism had gone as a male friendship of near-equals (tho' Pasolini was 26 years older). Pasolini wasn't a father figure to Davoli, Siciliano reckoned, and they were not dependent on each other. But Pasolini was in despair when Davoli wed (in January, 1973).

In the midst of filming *The Canterbury Tales* Ninetto Davoli told Pier Paolo Pasolini that he was getting married (during shooting in Bath in the West Country). According to Enzo Siciliano, Pasolini was distraught: 'Pier Paolo's despair was uncontainable. He wanted to die' (ES, 338). The high emotion behind the camera may have coloured the movie (Pasolini composed many poems about his relationship with Davoli).

In a 1965 poem, Pier Paolo Pasolini wrote:

---

48 'Pasolini deserves credit for foregrounding his relationship... with Davoli, who was not from the class in which the director's chic friends thought he should look for a boyfriend, and for his public frankness about this infatuation', commented Gary Indiana (91).

Ninetto is a herald
and overcoming (with a sweet laugh
that blazes from his whole being
as in a Muslim or a Hindu)

And that's exactly how Pasolini cast him in some films: in *Theorem*, he's the angelic messenger who visits the morose Milanese family; in *Oedipus the King*, he's the herald who guides Oedipus to the Sphinx.

However, altho' Pier Paolo Pasolini became infatuated with Ninetto Davoli and put him in quite a few films following *The Hawks and the Sparrows*,[49] he is a somewhat limited actor in terms of range (Davoli on screen tries the patience of even the most committed Pasolinian devotees). But Pasolini was quite enamoured of Davoli – especially when Davoli was teamed up with Totò (after *The Hawks and the Sparrows*, Pasolini cast Davoli in a series of films alongside Totò, including the episodes in *The Witches* and *Love and Anger*).

MAKING A FILM WITH PASOLINI

I imagine that Pier Paolo Pasolini, though a perfectionist in some areas of filmmaking, would not push his actors to numerous takes.[50] It seems as if Pasolini and the team are searching for the spontaneity of performances that *haven't* been rehearsed and blocked at length. There must be times when Pasolini would ask for many takes, but I bet in general he would shoot one or two takes then move on.

'I always shoot very short takes' (PP, 132). Pier Paolo Pasolini's cinema is constructed from short pieces of film – not for him lengthy takes where the camera and the actors're hitting many marks, and seven minute

---

49 And a brief cameo in *The Gospel*.
50 Sometimes Pasolini would ask for retakes with the camera still running – asking his actors to do the scene repeatedly without cutting.

takes run thru numerous beats. 'I never use the long take (or virtually never). I hate naturalness. I reconstruct everything' (ibid.). And he didn't shoot a single master shot to cover a scene – 'I never do a whole all in one take' (ibid.). However, there *are* many examples of lengthy takes in Pasolini's films (or lengthy by the standards of today's cinema).

Sometimes Pasolini would shoot a scene with both actors in shot, and ask them not to get too close, so that he wouldn't have to film a reverse angle. That way, a scene could be covered with a single shot (Pasolini like to move fast, and get shots done quickly).

Like George Lucas in the age of digital filmmaking (and the *Star Wars* prequels), Pier Paolo Pasolini spoke of shooting as 'collecting material': he was gathering content that he would shape later into a movie (in the editing room). Thus, there were opportunities for spontaneity and improvization from the non-professional actors, and later in post-production the best bits from the takes would be selected and put together.

'While crews complain about being cold and wet on locations, I wonder if Pier Paolo Pasolini's crews moaned about the heat (Pasolini and co. filmed in hot, dry climes far more than in rainy, chilly regions). I bet a Pasolini shoot moved fast, too – I bet the crew didn't sit around on the grass, drinking and chatting and dancing to Euro-pop as depicted in *La Ricotta*, either. Instead, I bet it was one or two takes for each set up, then swiftly on to the next set up.

Filming a Pier Paolo Pasolini movie would provide many opportunities for cinematographic challenges for DPs – candlelight, firelight, magic hour, sunrise, sunset, plus lighting all sorts of existing locations, some of which would probably be miles from the nearest town, and with no power nearby (thus, many of the African and distant European locations in Pasolini's movies were filmed during daytime, using available light augmented by lamps. Because filming at night in remote locations is tough – and expensive).

Camera operators on a Pier Paolo Pasolini movie

would need to be physically fit, too – there would be much clambering over rocks in hot sun to reach that perfect spot under an over-hanging cliff, or climbing Mount Etna[51] yet again in gales or heat. And Pasolini often preferred to have the cameras handheld, so the operators would be shouldering heavy cameras all day.[52] (On the plus side, most scenes would be filmed in one or two takes – no going to 12,457 takes like Jackie Chan, Michael Cimino or Stanley Kubrick for Pasolini!).

Pasolini was fond of staging scenes as *tableaux*. Carl-Theodor Dreyer often used the frontal, *tableau* style – in *Ordet* (1955), for instance.[53] Theo Angelopoulos took it up in films like *Ulysses' Gaze* (1995). Sergei Paradjanov was a master of the form (in *The Color of Pomegranates*, 1969). Walerian Borowczyk used it in all of his films. Werner Herzog exploited the *tableau* approach in movies such as *Aguirre, Wrath of God* (1972)[54] and *Heart of Glass* (1976 – in which he also hypnotized the cast!).

For the first features, Pier Paolo Pasolini and his DP Tonino Delli Colli filmed in black-and-white (Delli Colli, like many cinematographers, spoke nostalgically of b/w, and preferred it in many respects to colour film). By the Sixties, tho', colour film stock was cheaper, and distributors and television wanted colour (everybody wants colour except for filmmakers). Pasolini stuck with monochrome longer than necessary, perhaps (as did filmmakers like Federico Fellini and Ingmar Bergman), tho' the pressure of the marketplace prevailed, and from around 1966 onwards, his movies were in colour.

Colour was more complicated for Pier Paolo

---

51 A favourite Pasolini location.

52 Thus, tripod shots were dispensed with – no need to carry a tripod if the shot's going to be handheld anyway.

53 Many of the compositions in *Ordet* are flattened, with the performers arranged in a tight, flat space at right angles to the camera. It's a frontal, *tableau* approach to composition that Carl-Theodor Dreyer favoured in other movies. You might say that action is staged this way in *Ordet* because it derives from a theatrical play, and the film set is a replica of a stage. No. That has nothing to do with it: this is how some filmmakers like to block their actors (Walerian Borowczyk was the same, and so was Sergei Paradjanov).

54 *Aguirre* employed stylized *tableaux,* scenes which were consciously staged as paintings or portraits.

Pasolini, and it took more planning. Pasolini's approach to colour films was to take out all of the colours he didn't want: there are too many colours in real life, Pasolini remarked. He said he chose to shoot *Oedipus Rex* in Morocco[55] 'because there are only a few main colours there – ochre, rose, brown, green, the blue of the sky' (PP, 63). That's one reason why some filmmakers preferred to film in the studio, where the settings could be controlled entirely.

The running times of Pier Paolo Pasolini's films as director tend to be in the 80-110 minute range (with *Accattone* and *The Gospel According To Matthew* and others going over slightly). One wonders what sort of movies Pasolini might've made in the era of the 1990s, 2000s and after, when movies (and not only prestige productions), ran to 140 and 150 minutes. We might've seen longer, perhaps more rambling pictures (Pasolini was headed that way, though, with the 'trilogy of life' movies).

Compared with his contemporaries, it's striking how much of Pier Paolo Pasolini's output is comical: his first three fiction features were dead serious, but for his fourth feature, *The Hawks and the Sparrows,* Pasolini and the team attempted a comedy (with mixed results). Short films of the period, such as in the anthologies *RoGoPaG* and *The Witches*, were also comedies. And large parts of the 'trilogy of life' pictures were humorous (or they tried to be). A good reason for making the 'trilogy of life' series was to tackle something upbeat and positive after the gloom and seriousness of *Pigsty, Medea* and *Theorem.*

However, contemporaries of Pasolini's such as Federico Fellini and Jacques Tati were far more skilled with comedy, and Pasolini's attempts at humour are often badly conceived and badly executed (excellent editing is absolutely foundational for screen comedy, and Pasolini's films really do lack that, even with cutting by the great editor Nino Baragli). Pasolini is

---

55 *Edipo Re* was shot in Italy and Morocco (including San Petronio, Bologna).

also *way* too indulgent with his performers (with Totò and Ninetto Davoli in particular. Totò is a great screen clown, but you can see even him struggling with the material and the situations. Davoli, meanwhile, relies too much on charm, energy and enthusiasm. Pasolini's comedies hope to get by on Marx Brothers-type clowning around, but it doesn't work. Mel Brooks and the Zucker-Abrahams-Zucker team insisted that the performers or the director shouldn't try to be funny – it was the script, the situations and the characters that were funny. And that was what Pasolini's comedies lacked – amusing characters and situations).

Indeed, it's curious that Pier Paolo Pasolini persisted in attempting to direct (and write or co-write) movies in a comical mode, when they clearly were not working. Surely people in Pasolini's entourage pointed out to him that his so-called comedies were not funny – and worse, they might damage Pasolini's reputation as a world-class director? (Or did no one dare to voice their opinion to the director? Would *you* have the guts to tell Pasolini to his face that his comedies stank?[56]).

Well, anyway, the maestro kept going, from *The Hawks and the Sparrows* and the anthology movies of the mid-Sixties onwards, to the mediæval trilogy. (It's possible that nobody dared to suggest to the maestro that the comedies weren't amusing. And anyway, *The Decameron* had been a big hit in Italia in 1971, encouraging the production of further historical comedies).

One of the chief reasons why the comedy of the 'trilogy of life' films and others can seem laboured, or haphazard, or incomprehensible is due to that issue that irks so many TV broadcasters and film distributors: cultural translation. Humour is often difficult to translate not only into different languages but different cultures and societies. Thus, comedy stars can be huge in Asia (Stephen Chow Sing-chi, for example), but almost unknown in the Western world (Stephen Chow is *very* funny – *Royal Tramp, Fight Back To School,*

56 Not if you wanted to keep all of your fingers! Just kidding.

Shaolin Soccer, The Mad Monk, etc – but nobody knows who Chow is in the West, and he's rarely celebrated).

Some of the producers of
the films directed by
Pier Paolo Pasolini.
Alberto Grimaldi (left).
Franco Rossellini (below),
and Alfredo Bini (bottom).

Pasolini with Totò during The Hawks and the Sparrows (top).
And with Anna Magnani during Mamma Roma (above).

ACTORS AND ACTING

Like Tim Burton, Woody Allen and Ken Russell, Pier Paolo Pasolini preferred actors who just 'got it' straight away, without needing lots of discussion, coddling, encouragement, and analysis. No lengthy sessions of questions and answers between actors, producers and directors, and no arguments about the characterizations. 'I choose people for what they are and not for what they pretend to be', Pasolini remarked (PP, 49).

> In general, I choose actors because of what they are as human beings, not because of what they can do. Terence Stamp was offended by this because I never asked him to demonstrate his acting ability. It was like stealing from him, using his reality. I had a similar experience with Anna Magnani on 'Mamma Roma.' She also felt I was stealing from her. (1968)

Actors were given the screenplay, but Pasolini preferred to talk them through their roles. As with many directors (such as Ken Russell), it was in the chats before filming that Pasolini really did much of his directing. The scripts might be adjusted slightly during shooting, usually in response to what an actor was doing.

The trouble with the non-acting, Robert Bressonian approach to film performance is that it can too easily come over as wooden, uninspired or just plain *boring*. There are instances in the cinema of Pier Paolo Pasolini, as well as Robert Bresson, Michelangelo Antonioni and Carl-Theodor Dreyer (four of the key exponents of the non-performance performance style), where any heat/ juice/ drama/ tension/ suspense in a scene is deflated or negated. Yes, that may be one of the goals of Bresson, Antonioni, Dreyer and Pasolini, but there are trade-offs with every performance style. (More recent proponents of po-faced non-acting include Mamoru Oshii and Theo Angelopoulos).

✳

You have to admit that Pier Paolo Pasolini's appearances in his own movies were, like those of many

other film directors, not especially special (quite a few
film directors are convinced they can act). He was no
Orson Welles or John Huston. But at least he didn't
deliberately send his movies up, like Jean-Luc Godard
did in his cameos in his own films.[1] And Pasolini is a
significant presence in his documentaries, too – he had
no problem appearing before the camera, interviewing
people (or simply talk-talk-talking), or providing
voiceovers (which sometimes sound like he is making it
up on the spot).

SAINTS, SINNERS AND STRANGERS (OUTSIDERS)

Filmed like mediæval saints[2] (or martyrs) in the modern
world, Pier Paolo Pasolini's characters – Accattone,
Stracci, Zumurrud, Ninetto – were ancient souls, who
didn't fit into contemporary society, as Sam Rohdie
explained in his book on the *maître*: they were
outsiders, eternally at odds with their society; they are
useless in terms of economy and capitalist production;
they are innocents in a corrupt land; they are
otherworldly, and as such were revolutionary: 'their
otherworldliness, essentially their uselessness, made of
them revolutionary in *this* world' (123), but not because
they existed within this world, but because they refused
it, they didn't compromise with it.

And yet the Pasolinian sanctification of these
subproletarian characters was æsthetic and artistic, not
practical or even social: that is, it was a sacralization of
the subproletariat that could only take place in cinema

---

1 Jean-Luc Godard's best cameo is in *First Name: Carmen*, where he
plays a director who commits himself to hospital because he can't – or
won't – make movies anymore. And Godard's worst cameo is in *King
Lear*, in which he sports a wig of electrical cables and plugs, chomps on
a cigar permanently, and speaks out the side of his mouth like a would-
be wise guy. It's *so* bad!
2 In *Accattone*, they refer to themselves as saints. What they really mean
is martyrs.

and poetry and similar arts. As Sam Rohdie commented, Pier Paolo Pasolini gave his characters

> a sacred halo, as if they were sanctified angels. He made them into Masaccio saints, Caravaggio apostles, a Mantegna Christ, a Piero della Francesca Madonna, the Christs of Pontormo and Rosso Fiorentino. (123-4)

THE POETRY OF CINEMA

> The cinema should always be the discovery of something. I believe that the cinema should be essentially poetic.
>
> Orson Welles[3]

Pier Paolo Pasolini was a poet: his aim was to be 'purely poetical and natural'.[4] Pasolini remarked that he was 'the least Catholic of all the Italians I know' and that his religion was 'probably only a form of psychological aberration with a tendency towards mysticism'. Pasolini said he saw the world in childlike, reverential ways (PP, 14).

Poetry was an early love of Pier Paolo Pasolini's – he started to write poems in the Friulan dialect, poems of the hermetic, Symbolist kind (he cited Stéphane Mallarmé, Giuseppe Ungaretti, Eugenio Montale and Rainer Maria Rilke as influences [1969, 15]). He began publishing his books of poetry in the mid-1940s (with *Poesie e Casarsa* in 1942 and *Poesie* in 1945).

Instead of one recognizable style, as with Robert Bresson or Orson Welles, underneath Pasolini's cinema was his own recognizable tone. 'You can always feel underneath my love for Dreyer, Mizoguchi and Chaplin – and some of Tati, etc, etc' (PP, 28). Of Dreyer,

3 O. Welles, interview, in A. Sarris,1969.
4 In A. Pavelin, 33.

Mizoguchi and Chaplin,[5] Pasolini said: 'all three see things from a point of view which is absolute, essential and in a certain way holy, reverential' (PP, 43). (Notice that Pasolini cites big, serious names in cinema, not commercial, exploitation directors such as Roger Corman or William Castle.) You can't cheat in style, Pasolini maintained, but you could cheat with the content (PP, 83).

'One sees, often, an *idea* of sensuality instead of sensuality, a *concept* of comedy', Gary Indiana commented (20). Pier Paolo Pasolini's films come across as essays or notes for movies that might be made. They are films of ideas, of possibilities for future projects. The comedies aren't funny, but they contain seeds that might be explored in further works.

Pier Paolo Pasolini defends himself in this respect by insisting that his films are not finished works: rather, they are questions. 'My films are not supposed to have a finished sense, they always end with a question. I always intend them to remain suspended' (PP, 56-57).

> I've never wanted to make a conclusive statement.
> I've always posed various problems and left them
> open to consideration. (1971)

'I don't want to be paternalistic, or pedagogical, or engage in propaganda, or be an apostle', Pasolini insisted in 1970 (yet part of his personality couldn't help being a teacher).

Jean-Luc Godard was greatly admired by Pier Paolo Pasolini – to the point where some of Pasolini's films are infused with the spirit of Godard (such as *Pigsty, Theorem* and *Salò, or The 120 Days of Sodom*). Most committed filmmakers in the 1960s in Europa were inspired by Godard's films: Godard's 1960s movies remain one of the most extraordinary groups of works in cinema history.

---

5 Charlie Chaplin and silent movie comedy was a touchstone for Pasolini, according to Sam Rohdie; Chaplin is *hommaged* in many Pasolini movies. But what did Chaplin himself think of the often very strange tributes to him in Pasolini's films?

And so many filmmakers have tried to put some Jean-Luc Godard on the screen as well as Pier Paolo Pasolini: Francis Coppola, George Lucas, Oliver Stone, Martin Scorsese, Luc Besson, Jean-Jacques Beineix, Bernardo Bertolucci, Terence Malick, Donald Cammell, Abel Ferrara, Rainer Werner Fassbinder, Wim Wenders, Peter Greenaway, and Robert Altman. But not even cinema giants like Coppola or Pasolini have managed it as successfully as the maestro himself. As they say, Godard is still the Man.

Pier Paolo Pasolini said he wasn't much fond of North American cinema (PP, 136), and the American films he did like were directed by Europeans who had moved to the U.S.A. (such as Fritz Lang and Ernest Lubitsch). Among American directors Pasolini has cited John Ford and Orson Welles.

Though he regarded himself as 'born from the Resistance' and a Marxist, Pier Paolo Pasolini was inevitably drawn to what he called 'irrational' and 'decadent' literature.

Pier Paolo Pasolini's form of cinema was (like that of Andrei Tarkovsky or Walerian Borowczyk) the 'cinema of the image', one of André Bazin's two definitions of cinema (the other was the 'cinema of reality').[6] Pasolini had more in common with Soviet silent cinema than with Italian Neo-realism, with Dziga Vertov and Sergei Eisenstein rather than Roberto Rossellini.[7]

Pier Paolo Pasolini used the formal aspects of cinema (quotation, pastiche, parody, analogy, repetition, rhyme) to foreground its construction, its writing, to make the viewer aware of the process of fictionality. Terence Stamp (*Theorem*) said Pasolini made films in a particular way which could be called 'using the camera to write poetry'.[8]

To watch Pasolini's films [commented Sam Rohdie] is to watch a parable, a type of non-fictional fiction,

---

6 A. Bazin, 1960, 9f, 23f.
7 S. Rohdie, 1995, 3.
8 M. Cousins, *Scene By Scene*, Laurence King, 2002, 83.

evidently made up and false, yet whose falsity is there to express a truth. (1995, 3)

Orson Welles made the same distinction: like Pier Paolo Pasolini, Welles advocated a theatrical, abstract, expressive kind of cinema. Welles' take on the realism vs. artificiality debate was simple: his films might be 'unreal', might be 'theatrical' and 'baroque', but they were 'truthful'.[9] Welles' goal was to make something that wasn't necessarily 'real', but was 'true'. It could be unreal, stylized and theatrical, but it had to be true to life.

'Cinema represents reality with reality; it is metonymic and not metaphoric' (PP, 38). Yes but exactly what 'reality' is, and what 'reality' is in cinema, is difficult to define, Pier Paolo Pasolini admitted. The first question to ask when people use terms like 'reality' or 'realism' is: *whose reality? Whose realism?*

Alain Robbe-Grillet's comments (made at the time of 1962's *Last Year At Marienbad*) summarize the position of Pier Paolo Pasolini neatly:

> I don't think either the cinema or the novel is for explaining the world. Some people believe there's a certain definite reality and all that a work of art has to do is pursue it and try to describe it... I don't think believe a work of art has reference to anything outside itself. In a film there's no reality except that of the film, no time except that of the film... The only reality is the film's, and as for the criterion of that reality, for the author it's his vision, what he feels. For the spectator, the only test is whether he accepts.[10]

For Pier Paolo Pasolini, cinema was not an image but 'an audio-visual technique in which the word and the sound have the same importance as the image' (PP, 146). Pasolini said that it was easy to see, by looking at a page, if a text was in poetry or prose, but in cinema it was more difficult. A cinema of poetry could be

9 'In my case, everything has to be real', Pier Paolo Pasolini insisted, 'even if only by analogy' (PP, 90).
10 A. Robbe-Grillet, *The Observer*, Nov 18, 1962.

produced by particular techniques. For Pasolini, certain sounds could get closer quicker to the mystery of reality than written poetry.

> Even a sound image, say thunder booming in a clouded sky, is somehow infinitely more mysterious than even the most poetic description a writer could give of it. A writer has to find oniricity through a highly refined linguistic operation, while the cinema is much nearer to sounds physically, it doesn't need any elaboration. All it needs is to produce a clouded sky with thunder and straight away you are close to the mystery and ambiguity of reality. (PP, 150)

For Pier Paolo Pasolini, cinema was 'substantially and naturally poetic', because it was dream-like,[11] and because things in themselves were 'profoundly poetic':

> a tree photographed is poetic, a human face photographed is poetic because physicity is poetic in itself, because it is an apparition, because it is full of mystery, because it is full of ambiguity, because it is full of polyvalent meaning, because even a tree is a sign of a linguistic system. But who talks through a tree? God, or reality itself. Therefore the tree as a sign puts us in communication with a mysterious speaker. (PP, 153)

Even the most banal films could contain the poetry of cinema, Pier Paolo Pasolini said, but the cinema of poetry proper was a cinema 'which adopts a particular technique just as a poet adopts a particular technique when he writes verse' (PP, 153). In short: 'to make a film is to be a poet'.

Pier Paolo Pasolini believed in the notion of the author of a film. He said he was the author not only of the script[12] and the direction, but of everything else (such as the choice of sets, locations, characters and

---

11 'Cinema is already a dream' (PP, 150)

12 Many of Pasolini's scripts didn't alter much during production. And the filmmakers shot pretty much what was in the script. For *The Hawks and the Sparrows*, a sequence was filmed but cut (for running time). For *Accattone*, a scene was cut because the film was too long.

costumes [PP, 32]). True, Pasolini's stamp is all over his movies, but he could not have made them without a large group of collaborators, such as regular actors like Ninetto Davoli, Silvana Mangano, Laura Betti, and Franco Citti, and production crew such as Nino Baragli (editor), Tonio Delli Colli (DP), Umberto Angelucci (assistant director), Ennio Morricone (music), Dante Ferretti (production designer), Alfredo Bini, Franco Rossellini, and Alberto Grimaldi (producers).

Once again, let's not forget the actors: no matter how well a script is written, or the concept of the film is conceived, it is actors on set who have to express it all. So Pasolini *did not* do everything himself! (But his reputation persists even today in overshadowing everybody else).

In Pier Paolo Pasolini's poetics of cinema, reality and cinema commingle, as a system of signs.

> The cinema is a language which expresses reality with reality. So the question is: what is the difference between the cinema and reality? Practically none.

(Though in postmodern theory, the difference is practically everything). To express people, Pier Paolo Pasolini used people; to express trees, Pasolini used real trees, as he found them in reality. In a interview in the *New York Times* (1968), Pasolini stated:

> the cinema forced me to remain always at the level of reality, right inside reality: When I make a film I'm always in reality, among the trees and among the people; there's no symbolic or conventional filter between me and reality as there is in literature. The cinema is an explosion of my love for reality. I have never conceived of making a film that would be a work of a group, I've always thought of a film as a work of an author, not only the script and the direction but the choices of sets and locations, the characters, even the clothes. I choose everything, not to mention the music. (PP, 29)

No veils or no distantiation between the filmmaker and reality – and no metaphors either.

> Reality doesn't need metaphors to express itself...
> In the cinema it is as though reality expressed itself
> with itself, without metaphors, and without any-
> thing insipid and conventional and symbolic. (ib.,
> 38)

However, despite Pier Paolo Pasolini's penchant for realistic, non-metaphorical or non-symbolic cinema, he did not like naturalism. He aimed for realism, not naturalism. 'I believe deeply in reality, in realism, but I can't stand naturalism', he asserted (PP, 39).

Pier Paolo Pasolini repositioned himself *vis-à-vis* the Neo-realism tradition (in Italian cinema) and the films of Roberto Rossellini, saying that the naturalistic, credulous and crepuscular everyday reality of Neo-realist cinema was not his style. The detachment, warmth and irony of Neo-realism were 'characteristics which I do not have', commented Pasolini (PP, 109). Maybe – but Pasolini's cinema, and not only his early works, exhibit many of the elements of Neo-realist cinema. In the late 1960s, Pasolini said he did not go to the cinema anymore for entertainment, unless he could be sure the film was going to be worth seeing (PP, 136).

PASOLINI AND PAINTING

Pier Paolo Pasolini is known as a Mannerist (the same accusations have been made of Bernardo Bertolucci, Walerian Borowczyk and Peter Greenaway). Sometimes critics also use the term 'Baroque' (yes, even film critics, God bless them!, don't know their art history as well as they should). Yet altho' the Mannerist artists – Pontormo, Michelangelo, Rosso, Mantegna – were cited often by the maestro, he also revered the Early Renaissance artists (Giotto, Duccio, Piero, Masaccio, Angelico, etc).

Pier Paolo Pasolini was something of a 'Renaissance' man, in the sense of being happy to work in a number of disciplines: poetry, painting, criticism/ essays, short stories, novels, films, reportage and theatre. He was 'Renaissance' in another sense, taking much of his inspiration from (mainly Italian) Renaissance art (in the deployment of religious imagery in *The Gospel According To Matthew*, for example).

The two favoured periods of painting in Pier Paolo Pasolini's cinema were the Early Renaissance (Giotto di Bondone, Duccio Buoninsegna, Masaccio and Piero della Francesca), and the High Renaissance, Mannerism and Baroque (Michelangelo Buonarroti, Jacopo Pontormo, Sebastiano del Piombo, Giovanni Battista Rosso and Andrea del Sarto). Pasolini spoke of being deeply influenced by the Early Renaissance masters like Giotto and Masaccio – to the point where, in cinema, he automatically composed shots using their visual techniques (where 'man stands at the center of every perspective', as Pasolini put it). Even moving shots were like the lens was moving over a painting. 'I always conceive the background of a painting, like a stage set, and for this reason I always attack it frontally' (and even tho' he sometimes fought against the Renaissance pictorial approach, he could never lose it completely, because it was so deeply embedded in his psyche). Books of art were used on the set to help with setting up shots.

STYLE

One can cheat in everything except style.

Pier Paolo Pasolini

Pier Paolo Pasolini said he didn't have a cinematic style of his own, like Charlie Chaplin or Jean-Luc Godard: his style was made up of many influences and inspirations; he was a *pasticheur*, he said (among the filmmakers that Pasolini cited were Jacques Tati, Carl Theodor Dreyer, Kenji Mizoguchi, Chaplin and Godard). The dream in *Wild Strawberries* (1957) was admired by Pasolini – 'remarkable, it comes very close to what dreams are really like' (PP, 150). Anyway, what counts, Pasolini insisted, wasn't the form or even the content, but the violence and intensity of the work, 'the passion I put into things' (PP, 28). Tsui Hark, a dragon emperor among film directors, said a similar thing: sometimes, it's not the characters, or the stories, or the themes that interest a filmmaker, but the *attitude* of the piece. In 2011, Tsui said (in *Twitch*):

> The best thing actually to do is write according to what you feel. If you feel your heart would take you to the point where you would want to express something to do with the story or the film. Sometimes it's not the story; sometimes it's the way you tell the story. Sometimes it's the attitude you have with the story. The attitude is something you build and you accumulate for a long time for no reason and no logic, it's there. When you write that way, you might want to make it that way.

Pier Paolo Pasolini's cinema is full of conventional and clichéd elements. Some are so obvious that they're seldom remarked upon, as if Pasolini is somehow exempt from being treated like any other filmmaker, as if he soars above narrative conventions (in the legend that is Pasolini the Poet, Pasolini the Saint). He doesn't: the motif of the death of the hero is a good example: films like *Accattone, Mamma Roma, Pigsty, Theorem* as well as the tragedies close with the demise of the main characters.

✻

Not known as a technically brilliant filmmaker, or rather, a filmmaker for whom technique was an end in itself, or something that had to be got absolutely right, as with F.W. Murnau, Andrei Tarkovsky or Alfred Hitchcock, Pier Paolo Pasolini could nevertheless orchestrate the technical arsenal of cinema to do anything he wanted. But Pasolini is the opposite of a technical film director, the polar opposite of someone like Jackie Chan or Stanley Kubrick, who would shoot take after take until they got what they were looking for.[13] But for directors like Pasolini and Jean-Luc Godard, that approach to filmmaking would be ridiculous, wasteful, and pointless (Godard, like Werner Herzog, preferred to shoot one or two takes. No more were necessary).

Pier Paolo Pasolini did share one thing with perfectionists like Jackie Chan, Michael Cimino, Fritz Lang and George Lucas of course: total control. I bet there was no question as to who was the top guy on set in a Pasolini movie. Pasolini regarded cinema as the work of one man, an author. Terry Gilliam commented that in Italy the director is treated like a maestro (à la Luchino Visconti and Federico Fellini). Consequently, when Gilliam was shooting *The Adventures of Baron Munchausen* in Roma in 1988, one of the things he couldn't get used to was that production crew were reluctant to offer suggestions, and Gilliam preferred to work as a team.

---

13 The final shot of *The Shining*, the slow tracking shot towards the hotel wall and the 1920s photograph, took ages to film. Stanley Kubrick wanted it to be as fluid as possible. The camera crew tried changing the dolly cart; they put it on a track; they took it off the track; they loaded it with more weight; they put more people on it (in V. LoBrutto, 1997, 444).

The idea of re-shooting that tracking shot again and again, until it was as smooth and perfect as possible, just wouldn't occur on a Pier Paolo Pasolini set! (Or a Jean-Luc Godard set!). Forget it!

Consider the works of Pier Paolo Pasolini in print, theatre, TV or cinema (and in numerous interviews), and a host of concerns and themes will pop out time after time:

- Politics is part of pretty much everything that Pasolini did or said in the public arena.
- Communism – Pasolini was in constant dialogue with Communism, and with the Partito Comunista Italiano (which he voted for and was once a member[14]).
- Pasolini celebrated peasants, the under-class, and never lost his reverence for them.
- Southern Italy and its peasants were very important for Pasolini (he linked the area and its inhabitants to the Third World).
- The love of the Friulian dialect is part of Pasolini's exaltation of all things sub-proletarian and working class.
- The progress of Italy towards being a modern, capitalist nation was a recurring concern for Pasolini (in particular how modern technology would affect his beloved peasant class).
- For Pasolini, consumerism[15] was nothing less than 'a real anthropological cataclysm', and 'pure degradation'.
- Pasolini venerated his mother, and had a very ambiguous relationship with his father.
- Pasolini had a vision/ theory of cinema as poetry, as a means of mythicizing life.
- Pasolini was searching for the epic and the mythological in everyday life (and said he saw it everywhere).
- Sexuality – altho' many commentators always draw attention to Pasolini's homosexuality, it actually plays a much smaller role in his works than the Pasolini Legend would suggest.

✳

14 He had been thrown out of the Communist Party following the sex scandal in 1949.
15 Pasolini said he detested consumerism 'in a complete physical sense'.

Nothing is resolved to a point of bliss or unity in the cinema of Pier Paolo Pasolini: his art is one of eternal strife and dissatisfaction. There is a conflict between opposites, and the oppositions are instantly familiar:

Male	Female
Men	Women
Masculine	Feminine
Father	Mother
Present	Past
Youth	Age
Realism	Fantasy
Reality	Poetry
Heterosexuality	Homosexuality
North (Europe/ Italy)	South (Europe/ Italy)
Bologna	Rome
Italy	Third World
Europe	Asia/ Africa
Christianity	Communism
Capitalism	Marxism
Wealth	Poverty
Bourgeoisie	Proletariat

PRE-MODERN, PRE-INDUSTRIAL, PRE-CAPITALIST

Pier Paolo Pasolini enshrined pre-industrial Italy, the Italy of his youth, which he reckoned was being eroded in the modern era, with its advanced (North American/ Western) capitalism, its technology, its science. By the 1960s, much of the world that Pasolini yearned for was rapidly disappearing underneath concrete and tenements (it was a similar story of suburbanization all over the developed world).[16] Pasolini neglects to recognize that young people in the Western world embraced all things

16 Yet if you visit Italy today it can still feel archaic.

American with incredible fervour. They *wanted* America, even more than America or the Americans did! (As director Elio Petri remarked, America had already been colonizing Italy culturally from the 1930s – via Hollywood cinema).

In short: after the war, *teenagers in Europe* <u>*wanted*</u> *all things American.*

They *yearned* for the U.S.A. following World War Two. The choice was: America or Europe? Dreary, war-torn, impoverished Europe or glitzy, out-size America? Pop acts in Britain such as the Beatles and the Rolling Stones opted for the Great American Dream. The coolest youth culture was American. The clothes. The music. The movies. The cars. The places. The language...

As Paul McCartney put it, Route 66 and the American South in the blues music that he and John Lennon loved sounded so much more glamourous than dear, old England:

> We know about the Cast-Iron Shore and the East Lancs Motorway but they never sounded as good to us, because we were in awe of the Americans. Even their Birmingham, Alabama, sounded better than our Birmingham.[17]

Let's remember that after WWII much of Italy was in pieces and it received around $1.2 billion in aid (from the Marshall Plan and other initiatives) from the U.S.A. (only France and Britain received more U.S. assistance). Like it or not, Italy and America were intimately linked politically and ideologically as well as economically and socially in the postwar era.

Anyway, these yearnings of Pier Paolo Pasolini's for earlier times which were thought to be better (even if they actually weren't), occur in many artists. Fifty years before Pier Paolo Pasolini, for instance, D.H. Lawrence (1885-1930) had spoken with incredible fury of the ugly, industrial Midlands, and how his England ('England, My England') was being destroyed by modern social and industrial forces (the Midlands is far

17 B. Miles. *Paul McCartney*, Secker & Warburg, London, 1997, 201.

worse today than in Lorenzo's time). And before Lawrence, Thomas Hardy had decried the advances of the modern era and the Industrial Revolution.

And so it goes, back and back, so that artists and writers can never reach that Eden, that Paradise, when all was better, richer, deeper, purer, juicier. No it wasn't. This is age talking, this is growing up to become an adult talking. Because if you are an eighteen year-old today, in the 21st century, I bet you could be having a *fantastic time*! But in thirty years, you'd look back and think, darn, things were cooler thirty years ago!

You can't win, because you can't turn back time. You can't be 17 again. What? Did Pier Paolo Pasolini want to return to the 1920s, the decade of his birth? Or – why hold back? – why not go back to the 1810s (pre-industrialization)? Or the 1580s, the height of Pasolini's beloved Renaissance era? Or, hell, why not go back to the Roman Empire?!

Truth is, Pier Paolo Pasolini's comparisons of then and now, of the 1930s with the 1960s, are simply more of his dualistic worldview, his penchant for oppositions, for automatically and violently slamming two eras, two political views, two artforms, two whatevers together. That's how Pasolini made art, by setting something up he could kick against (whether it was capitalism, or consumerism, or technology, or fascism, or old age, or poverty, or concrete jungles). With Pasolini, it's always 'us and them', 'me and that', 'I and those'.

Pier Paolo Pasolini knew that his mythical, ancient past didn't exist, and probably had never existed. But, as with God, or belief, or religion, an Eden was necessary for his existence.[18] He needed to believe that primitive cultures were more in touch with nature, or more 'authentic', or more substantial as communities, even if they weren't, even if nothing like his idealized, utopian communities ever existed.

The *idea* of the ancient world – and the Third World

18 One of the recurring motifs in the 'trilogy of life' movies (and in other Pasolini movies) is the notion of miracles. Many times characters are speaking in awed tones of a *miracolo*. And in Fellini's cinema.

– is thus vital to Pier Paolo Pasolini's project: it might never have had any 'reality', outside of essays, and discussions, and films, and poems (the past as cultural imaginary), but that didn't matter. Because it was useful for Pasolini to have an invented, mythical past with which to accuse the present day (for falling short of his ideals, his utopia). The utopian, idealized past was also a realm, as Sam Rohdie pointed out (1995, 110), in which Pasolini could play and explore, and in which he was in control.

Pier Paolo Pasolini's utopias were not to be found in the real, contemporary world, which was too capitalist, too bourgeois, too consumerist and too superficial for him. Instead, he looked to exotic climes (to Southern Italia), to the Third World (particularly to Africa, the Middle East and India), and to the distant past (of the ancient world). The notion of *ancestors*, then, is crucial – Pasolini explored the idea of people living today who had ancestors going back to the ancient world.

The exaltation of peasant, primitive societies in Pier Paolo Pasolini's philosophy has a right-wing, regressive and racist component, as Sam Rohdie noted: this nostalgia for archaic, pre-modern societies (communities which Pasolini claimed to have found in Africa and the Middle East), chimes with the writings of Claude Lévi-Strauss, with D.H. Lawrence and Gustave Flaubert, with Marguerite Duras' novels of the Orient, and, most problematically with racist and Nazi theorists such as Ernest Renan and Arthur de Gobineau.

Pier Paolo Pasolini might've known what was wrong with contemporary society in the West, but he didn't know how to put it right, or how to make his utopian visions come to fruition. Of course. It's much easier to attack, to identify targets and hit them, than it is to build a whole new world. (No artist of recent times has come up with a complete, complex, and convincing vision of how a utopia/ paradise/ new world would work).

Artists complain about modern society, and in TV

and films super-villains are always destroying the world (or trying to). But *no one* has any idea at all what to put in its place. (We could get into a really fascinating topic here – the formation of alternative communities or societies in the modern era. For example, communities that have been developed along women-only, or feminist and lesbian lines (several female communes/ communities have been founded in the U.S.A.). Many would-be utopias tend to be very small, and often last only as long as the lifetimes of the original founders. When the creators die, or leave, alternative communities often go into decline and break up).

PASOLINI AND AMERICA

Pier Paolo Pasolini remained a European film director, and didn't leave for North America like some of his contemporaries. Nor did he venture into co-productions with North American companies. And he tended to cast from European (mainly Italian) actors, and didn't use North American actors, like many of his contemporaries. He also didn't take up North American subjects: his movies stay in Italy, or they venture into the Middle East, Africa, Britain or India (whereas a filmmaker such as Jean-Luc Godard has explored probably the most passionate love-hate relationship with the U.S.A. in all of cinema). Pasolini's films are Italian, made by and for Italians, even when their subjects are Ancient Greek or Arabian. However, thru producer Alberto Grimaldi and his distribution deals with United Artists, Pasolini was linked to the North American movie business (and some of his movies were financed with U.$. dollars; this occurred throughout the Italian film industry).

Pier Paolo Pasolini visited Gotham in October, 1966, for a retrospective of his cinema organized by

Richard Roud, an important showcase for Pasolini's work in the New World. Pasolini loved N.Y.C. (it was his first trip to the U.S.A.).

> I'm in love with New York. I have a passion beyond words for it. Like Romeo and Juliet – love at first sight. It is the most beautiful city in the world. I love the huge mingling of enormous amounts of people, races. The mixture of cruelty and innocence. New York is a piece of mythical reality, as beautiful as the Sahara Desert.

ON EROTICISM AND VOYEURISM

A significant ingredient in the cinema of Pier Paolo Pasolini is the emphasis on voyeurism: every movie contains sequences of people looking and being looked at. And, like the cinema of Tsui Hark, Alfred Hitchcock or Orson Welles, Pasolini is a master at orchestrating the network of looks and camera angles: consider the angles and the viewpoints that Pasolini and the DPs select, for instance, or how editor Nino Baragli cuts those shots together.

It's not only the erotic aspect of voyeurism and scopophilia that Pier Paolo Pasolini's cinema activates – power and the relationship of power between the observer and the object are more to the point than sex. 'Desire' is a better term than sex or eroticism – 'desire' with all its philosophical associations with the Lacanian lack, with loss, with distance, with Kristevan abjection, with Foucauldian power. Yes – *distance* – the looking and looked-at-ness in Pasolini's cinema emphasizes the sadness and loss evoked by the distance between people. Looking is not pleasurable in Pasolini's work – the observers are not getting off on looking: rather, looking reminds them of their own loneliness, their separateness from everything. Pasolini made a remark about sex in cinema that resonates here, how seeing sex emphasizes sadness and distance.

As for sex, titillation, nudity – well, Pier Paolo Pasolini didn't use *those* particular ingredients the same way anyone else did, either. Sex and nudity are some of the tried and tested and above all *cheap* means of getting an audience's attention (maintaining it is something else). Hence so much of exploitation cinema, *mondo* cinema, cult cinema, and European (art) cinema, has used the genres of horror, fantasy and thriller (all cheap genres to produce), and included plenty of naked bodies. Or any scenario where characters can disrobe and get freaky. Sex and nudity are simply easier to market than, say, abstract concepts like Ludwig Wittgenstein's philosophy of language or the notion of pessimism in the philosophy of Arthur Schopenhauer.

So if Pier Paolo Pasolini wasn't going (to be persuaded) to use stars in his movies, a producer might think, at least we'll have some T. and A. to be able to market the picture – something for the film poster and the trailers (in the way that producers Joe Levine and Carlo Ponti asked Jean-Luc Godard to shoot some nude scenes featuring Brigitte Bardot in *Contempt*.[19] As Levine told Godard, the 1963 movie 'didn't have enough ass in it'. So Godard, Raoul Coutard and co. duly filmed B.B. naked[20]).

But Pier Paolo Pasolini wouldn't do that! Yes, there *would* be naked bodies and people Doing The Deed in his movies, but the sex would be either desperate or off-the-wall, or the bodies wouldn't be slinky, European vixens and handsome, buff men.

---

19 Joe Levine and Carlo Ponti, wanted Brigitte Bardot to be seen nude in *Le Mépris*. Levine demanded reshoots of Bardot nude, and Godard drew up a budget which he thought Levine might not pay, being twice what it should be. But Levine OK-ed it and the scenes were filmed: Bardot nude with Michel Piccoli, Bardot nude on different coloured rugs, Bardot running by a lake, and Bardot with Jack Palance (dressing after sex, tho' this wasn't used).

20 That must've been a tough day of filming: 'OK, Brigitte, now you take your clothes off, *bien*?'

Sometimes, the over-use of handheld camera can be irritating in the films of Pier Paolo Pasolini. So much effort has clearly gone into the production design, the costume design, the props, the art direction, the casting, the hair and make-up, the lighting and the visuals of Pasolini's films, it seems wasteful or irresponsible (at first) that all that hard work should be captured with a shaky camera (a *very* shaky camera at times – there are many ways of doing a handheld shot!). But the viewer soon gets used to it, and the handheld camera becomes a cinematic device that Pasolini and the camera operators employed repeatedly to achieve a sense of poetic immediacy and urgency to their narratives.[21] The handheld camera becomes a tool of someone totally confident about capturing the action in front of the lens. (One can't imagine studio executives in a Hollywood studio being satisfied with that kind of loose, improvized camerawork if they had been financing Pasolini's films. Of course, self-consciously shaky camerawork has become fashionable in TV and movies since the 1990s, but it's fake, simulating *cinéma verité*, and is never as haphazard as the handheld camerawork in Pasolini's movies).[22] (You can see Pasolini at work filming *Salò*, where it seems that he operated the *macchina* himself sometimes, and you can see that he is wobbling the camera at times).

Other *auteurs* employed handheld camerawork far more than usual – Walerian Borowczyk comes to mind, and also Ken Russell (which Russell often operated himself – his camerawork is instantly recognizable). In their movies, the handheld camera isn't used to evoke a 'documentary' approach, or to emulate an actor's

---

21 Enzo Siciliano has rationalized the shaky camerawork by saying that it expresses 'the sign of his hand, the visual possibility of his retina. Style tries to be life, life in its entirety' (240).

22 The actors are always in focus and framed nicely and well-lit, for a start. The framing is traditional, even if the camerawork seems shaky. And the self-conscious, wobbly camerawork is always integrated into familiar editing patterns and dramatic structures. Not so with Pasolini's cinema.

movement or viewpoint, it is a whole stylistic manner bound entirely to the material and the drama.[23]

SOUND

One reason given for the tradition of dubbing in Italian cinema is the lack of decent equipment following WWII (and the absence of it during the war). Yes, true, you could use that excuse at the start of the 1960s, but not by the end of the 1960s, when so many hit movies had been filmed in Italy. And movies that shot in Cinecittà, such as 1963's *Cleopatra,* used direct sound (when Italy was the biggest film production centre in Europa). Besides, the cost of a Nagra tape recorder, a couple of mics, a boom and some electrical cables isn't really *that* much (even provincial film schools have them).

There are other reasons, however: one is that Italian sound stages could be noisy (and were not constructed to the same sound-proofed standards of state-of-the-art studios. Cinecittà, for instance, might possess the largest stage in Europe, but it had only had one indoor restroom). Another reason is that the casts of Italian movies often comprised actors who spoke different languages. A key reason is probably the cinema distributors and exhibitors, who wouldn't want to pay the extra costs for sound editing and mixing (with looping, actors can sit in a studio and dub their lines in a few hours). Also, apparently, Benito Mussolini (a big influence on Italian cinema) didn't want to hear foreign languages in movies, so they were dubbed in Italian.

For overseas versions of his films, Pier Paolo Pasolini said he preferred subtitles rather than dubbing (PP, 40). Jean-Luc Godard preferred dubbing to subtitling for foreign prints – he thought it was more

---

23 And also for speed – Borowczyk liked to use the handheld camera to start shooting quickly once everything was ready.

honest. As Godard noted in *Histoire(s) du Cinéma*,[24] postwar Italian cinema was filmed without sound – instead, the great Italian poetry (Ovid, Dante) replaced the sound.

And not only is the sound added afterwards in all Italian cinema after WWII, it's often a completely new cast. As in any industry which relies on voices, like radio, or TV commercials, or feature animation, producers and directors will have their favourite voice actors (often they're also the actors who dub Hollywood movies for Italian distributors). Pasolini would have likely certain voice actors in mind when he was casting their screen counterparts, for example.

Pier Paolo Pasolini followed the example of Federico Fellini in the use of sound. For Fellini, direct sound wasn't a big deal, and he didn't think highly of the fetishization of it in North American movies. In short, Fellini much preferred to add the sound on after shooting. It was also because Fellini liked to talk to his actors during takes (or, as U.S. director Elia Kazan observed on a visit to a Fellini set: he 'yelled at the actors'). So a take on a Fellini film often had the maestro telling his actors what to do. Famously, Fellini had his performers simply recite numbers if they didn't know the text.

The point is, when you are replacing the entire soundtrack to a movie, and not using any live sound recorded on set at all, there is an enormous *potential* for exploring some really interesting things in sound and music and dialogue. Unfortunately, the films directed by Pier Paolo Pasolini don't often take advantage of that (compared to the king of post-synchronized sound-tracks, Orson Welles. And even when some of Welles' experiments were spoilt by technical faults, as in *Othello* or *Macbeth*, and interference from studios or producers, the results are still fascinating). The truth is, Pasolini as a film director is far less compelling in the realms of sound compared to some other filmmakers

24 Pier Paolo Pasolini appears in *Histoire(s) du Cinéma*, with Jean-Luc Godard intercutting a photograph of the maestro with a painting by Piero della Francesca (from *The Legend of the True Cross*).

(even tho' he thought of cinema not as simply an image, but as an audio-visual experience). Part of this is attributable to the poor technical facilities in sound in Italian cinema.

Pier Paolo Pasolini preferred to dub voices on later: he reckoned that dubbing 'while altering a character, also makes it more mysterious; it enlarges and enriches it. I'm against filming in sync' (PP, 39). It was part of Pasolini's penchant for pastiche and anti-naturalism: 'I believe deeply in reality, in realism, but I can't stand naturalism' (ibid.).

It was also because many of the actors in Pier Paolo Pasolini's films were non-professionals, and weren't used to the rigours of acting, such as remembering cues and dialogue (so their voices were replaced by professional actors back in Roma). And Pasolini also liked to direct actors during takes (like Federico Fellini), from behind the camera (again, this is also partly due to using non-professionals, who needed more guidance than professional actors).

Often even the professional actors in a Pier Paolo Pasolini movie didn't dub their own voices.[25] Pasolini liked this – and he liked to have two non-professional actors create a character: one to perform it on set, and one in the dubbing theatre.[26] In fact, Pasolini would travel to parts of Italy to hire actors who weren't Roman or part of the film business, because he was after unaffected, untrained, working class voices, or a particular regional accent. (Thus, the performances in Italian cinema are actually a double act: the actor *and* the voice actor).

25 The voice dubbing actors in *The Gospel* include Enrico Maria Salerno, Cesare Barnetti, Gianni Bonagura, Pino Locchi and Emanuela Rossi.
26 Pier Paolo Pasolini also said that he wasn't interested in actors who depended on their voices (PP, 40).

Too many film critics had (and still have) little idea about the music that Pier Paolo Pasolini included in his movies – particularly what is now known as 'world music'. After several decades of 'world music' circulating in the media and popular culture, we can spot particular sounds and musics, we are used to hearing those sounds – but critical accounts of the 1960s tended to flounder (but musical appreciation is often way down the list for film critics, and they also don't have the intellectual capabilities to assess it. Also music can be fiendishly challenging to *really* describe (try describing the physical sound of a piano). Hence, critics talk about everything else – the musicians, the singers, the lyrics, the celebrities, the fashions, the concerts; anything but the actual music).

Notice that the classical music composers that Pasolini liked to use in his films tended to be German/ Austrian – Bach, Mozart, Webern, Orff, etc – rather than Italian. Pasolini did employ Antonio Vivaldi, but often neglected the big names of Italy, such as Verdi, Rossini, Puccini, Monteverdi, etc.

Sometimes the music in a Pier Paolo Pasolini-directed movie is allowed to burble along, without editing, punctuation or dramatic significance: altho' Pasolini is often described as a genius with putting music in movies, occasionally the underscore meanders thru scenes at a low volume for too long (this usually occurs with existing recordings). And his films do that with genius composers such as Vivaldi, Bach and Mozart (for musos, this is sacrilege, demeaning, a crime against music, turning music into muzak).

Also, the music is often mixed far too low – this may be due to the unsatisfying sound mixes on the home entertainment releases of movies. (Sometimes movies are remixed for DVD and video releases, but often they're not: the sound mixes of the films directed by Pier Paolo Pasolini, stemming from 1961-1975, will probably all be the original mono mixes).

There are times in Pasolini's movies when you wish that some effort had been undertaken during pre-production (1) to select the *final* pieces of music for a film, and (2) to clear the rights to use the music. Adding the music later often doesn't work in sections featuring singing and dancing. There are wonderful scenes captured in the historical movies (*Medea, Oedipus Rex, The Arabian Nights*, etc) of players playing and singers singing which have completely different music dubbed over them.

PASOLINI, BOROWCZYK AND JARMAN

The cinema of Walerian Borowczyk (1923-2006) has many affinities with that of Pier Paolo Pasolini: both come from the same highly intellectual, highly educated, European backgrounds which valorize *avant garde* art, philosophy (Existentialism), Surrealism, de Sade, etc. Both were mavericks, who worked on the fringes of commercial cinema. Both produced contro-versial, Euro-art movies which included plenty of eroticism and nudity as well as politically provocative subject matter. Borowczyk's debut feature, *Goto: Island of Love*, was seen as an allegory about a Communist state, echoing Borowczyk's own experience of growing up in Poland. It amused Borowczyk, for example, that *Goto: Island of Love* was banned in fascist Spain as well as Eastern Bloc nations. In the truly remarkable *Immoral Tales* (1974), Borowczyk attacked European fascism in the 20th century, with his take on the 'Countess Dracula' myth – in which Countess Báthory collects and slays a group of virgins in order to bathe in their blood (*Erzsébet Báthory* was set in Eastern Europe in 1610, and starred Pablo Picasso's daughter Paloma in her only film role). With its scenes of mass degradation and nudity, of naked victims being herded and controlled like concentration camp inmates, *Immoral Tales* chimes closely with *Salò*.

Derek Jarman (1942-1994) was one of a number of filmmakers who cited Pier Paolo Pasolini as an inspiration. Jarman worked with Ken Russell in the early 1970s (on *The Devils* and *Savage Messiah*). Jarman came to critics' attention with the gay film *Sebastiane* (1976), a totally Pasolinian piece. Jarman wanted the film to be like Pasolini, but it turned out (or was sold or consumed) as gay soft porn (though it wasn't). Jarman spoke of a 'romance in the camera' that he saw 'all over the Pasolini films – something vulnerable, an archaic smile. I see it in our films, nowhere else. This is all I really want to film' (1991, 143).

Attempting a film in the manner of Pier Paolo Pasolini on one's first feature was very ambitious (Derek Jarman had already made many short Super-8 films by 1976). But Pasolini is by far the greater artist than Jarman in every respect. None of Jarman's films come close to even Pasolini's middling efforts. There is simply a welter more life, more humour, more emotion, more imagination and more invention in Pasolini's cinema than in Jarman's cinema. Take the use of non-actors, which both directors liked to do a lot: Pasolini could compose a poetry of unusual faces and characters from the simplest means, while in Jarman's pictures the non-actors drift about aimlessly. Pasolini had a genius for choosing fascinating people and orchestrating them within sequences, and putting them in amongst his professional actors which's pretty much unique in cinema. Absolutely no other filmmaker employs extras like Pasolini. By contrast, too often the non-professional actors in Jarman's movies are dull people doing dull things.

Pasolini making documentaries in Africa (top) and India (above).

Filming The Arabian Nights
in Isafahan (left).
Filming Salò (below).

Pasolini's books and films on display in Rome's biggest bookstore

PART TWO
✦
THE GOSPEL ACCORDING TO MATTHEW

Philosophically, nothing that I have ever done has
been more fitted to me than *The Gospel According
To Matthew* because of my tendency always to see
something sacred, mythical and epic quality in
everything, even in the most simple and banal
objects and events.

Pier Paolo Pasolini (1971)

1

IL VANGELO SECONDO MATTEO

THE GOSPEL ACCORDING TO MATTHEW

INTRODUCTION.

Among the most successful and satisfying of the portrayals of Christ's story is *The Gospel According To Matthew* (*Il Vangelo Secondo Matteo*, 1964, Italy/ France),[1] directed by Pier Paolo Pasolini (Pasolini did not want the prefix 'St' to be inserted in his title for *The Gospel According To Matthew*, which was added by the British distributors). I first saw *The Gospel According To Matthew* on television, on April 20, 1984. In the *Sight and Sound* list for top 100 films in 2012, *The Gospel According To Matthew* is 30th in the directors' list.

Alfredo Bini, Pier Paolo Pasolini's regular producer of the era, and an enormously important member of the Pasolini operation, produced *The Gospel According To Matthew*. It was Bini who saw the possibilities of the movie straight away, and who worked very hard to get *The Gospel According To Matthew* made – it was going to be an expensive and complex production, and b4 it

---

1 There is a colourized version of *The Gospel According To Matthew*, but it's shorter (running at 91 minutes, compared to the 142 minutes of the standard version). The film was intended to be around 150-165 minutes.

was filmed it was already viewed with suspicion in the public arena (E. Siciliano, 26). The movie took a long time to prepare, but that probably worked in its favour (movies of this scale are made in pre-production, as everyone knows).

Some in the Italian industry (and in the Catholic Church) thought that Alfred Bini, Pier Paolo Pasolini *et al* were crazy in taking on the *Gospel*s. Crucially, *The Gospel According To Matthew* was originated by Pasolini – it didn't come from a producer/ writer/ production company/ studio, etc (Pasolini took the idea to Bini, and Bini loved it straight away, jumping out of his chair). However, *The Gospel According To Matthew* is also a product of its time: more religious movies were made in the 1950s and 1960s than any other time in film history.

We have to remember that the Italian film industry was churning out a huge number of ancient world movies and Biblical movies during one of its busiest periods – copycat versions of Hollywood spectaculars like *Cleopatra, Ben-Hur, Alexander the Great et al*, the *Hercules* craze (begun in 1958), which included loads of Ancient Greek and mythological flicks, and plenty of historical films, including Ancient Roman and mediæval films. Everybody in the Italian film industry, it seems, was in a toga, gladiator armour, or the long robes of Ancient Palestine.

Pier Paolo Pasolini – and his crew – would've been very conscious of all of those movies coming out of Rome and Cinecittà (indeed, many in the crew of *The Gospel According To Matthew* worked on them). So you can see how *The Gospel According To Matthew* was conceived very much *in opposition*[2] to the schlocky, melodramatic historical movies, to *Hercules* flicks and to Biblical movies, the bread and butter of the Italian film business at the time.

✦

The Gospel According To Matthew was a film of

---

2 *Contempt* (1963) is a Euro-art movie that's partly a commentary on the ancient world movie bonanza.

austerity, simplicity, lyricism and profundity. It is one of the greatest religious films (only one or two films are in the same league, such as *The Seventh Seal* and *The Passion of Joan of Arc*).

The *conception* of *The Gospel According To Matthew* is brilliant, quite, quite brilliant. The movie has an extraordinary self-assurance – it really knows what it's doing. It has something to say and it knows how to say it (I mean, it *really* has something to say). The combination of music, images, acting, casting and action is inspired and inventive – it's miraculous like a sacred act in itself.

Atom Egoyam said that Pier Paolo Pasolini 'is one of the few directors who have communicated the true nature of transcendent experience on film', and cited the 'brilliant depiction of Christ' in *The Gospel According To Matthew* as an example.[3]

As that opening quote illustrates, Pier Paolo Pasolini plus the *Gospels* was a perfect match: 'Philosophically, nothing that I have ever done has been more fitted to me than *The Gospel According To Matthew* because of my tendency always to see something sacred, mythical and epic quality in everything'. *The Gospel According To Matthew* is the perfect embodiment of Pasolini's notion of the cinema of poetry, and of poetic cinema. Consider any two-minute stretch of *The Gospel* movie and you can appreciate instantly how beautifully the filmmakers were suited to the material, and how the elements – the script, the cast, the acting, the music, the images, the sounds – plus of course that incredible story – all fit together.

A match made in heaven.

Made in Italy.

Same thing.

LOCATION HUNTING IN PALESTINE.

The documentary on *Il Vangelo Secondo Matteo*, *Sopraluoghi In Palestina* (1965, a.k.a. *Location Hunting In Palestine*), had come about when the

3 In J. Boorman, 1995, 65.

producers at Arco Film asked Pier Paolo Pasolini to put together the footage that had been filmed in the Middle East to show to distributors and Christian Democrats. It was produced by Alfredo Bini, with camerawork by Aldo Pennelli, Domenico Cantatore and Otello Martelli, and sound by Domenico Cantatore. *Sopraluoghi In Palestina* was shown at the Spoleto Festival in Summer, 1965. Pasolini provided a commentary to the footage that had been cut to 55 minutes without his supervision (PP, 73).[4]

When Pier Paolo Pasolini and don Andrea Carraro and his team went to Palestine in 1963, a cameraman (Aldo Pennelli) joined them – the idea at that point was to film some material as research for *Il Vangelo Secondo Matteo,* rather than with the intention of making a documentary.

As well as scenes of Pier Paolo Pasolini in his neat, white suit speaking to camera about his film project, there are also interviews with Andrea Carraro, the Italian priest who joined him on the trip.[5]

In the documentary, we see the River Jordan, Capernam, the hill of the Sermon on the Mount, Nazareth, Bethlehem, the Dead Sea, Mount Tabor and of course Jerusalem. Pasolini writing in a notebook. Pasolini studying a map in the car. Pasolini observing farmers at work. Pasolini greeting a bunch of kids. Donkeys. Camels. Roads. Small towns.

Location Hunting In Palestine is a rare item: nowadays, cameras following filmmakers around on set and elsewhere are familiar, and on television behind-the-scenes shows are common (turning every part of life into 'reality TV'). Back then, it was unusual to see a major film director visiting potential locations in this manner, and in this depth (many 'making of' films of the 1950s and 1960s were usually short, fluffy publicity pieces made for talk shows or as little info pieces for cinema, like extended trailers of 3 minutes. They might show a bit of filming, but not pre-production). Ah, if only there

4 Pier Paolo Pasolini was accompanied by Don Andrea Carraro, of Pro Civitate Cristiana, on the research trip to Israel.

5 The interviews do have a slightly stilted, rehearsed quality.

were similar documentaries showing F.W. Murnau discussing how he was going to make *Sunrise*, or D.W. Griffith visiting the colossal sets for *Intolerance*, or Orson Welles in the R.K.O. Studios for *Citizen Kane*...

Location Hunting In Palestine is in part a record of an essential aspect of filmmaking – searching for locations. For some filmmakers (such as Ken Russell), this is one of the most enjoyable parts of film production: it consists of driving around in a car with one or two colleagues, and a map, and stopping at suitable locations and visiting buildings and taking lots of photographs. The filmmakers are away from the city and the film studio, so the pressure is off a little, and they are seeking out places to make their movie (so they are imagining and planning scenes in their heads).

Indeed, most location scouting trips involve taking 100s of photographs – but bringing a movie camera along for the journey and filming the filmmakers is more unusual (tho' more common today with video). In this period, though, Pier Paolo Pasolini had made some documentaries, and was used to filming as he travelled about (for *Love Meetings,* for instance, in the same year – which was also in part another location scouting trip for the *Gospel* film).

By the time that Pier Paolo Pasolini recorded the narration for *Location Hunting In Palestine, The Gospel According To Matthew* had been produced. But even during the visit to Israel and Palestine in 1963, Pasolini had already realized that he couldn't make his movie of Jesus there. Altho' the terrain had the familiar deserts and mountains, it was altogether too built-up, too industrialized, and too heavily populated. Pasolini pointed out that the geography of the *Bible* was too small and too modest for the grander visions he had from reading the *Gospels*, and for his movie. (Locations such as Jerusalem, Bethlehem and the Dead Sea are not very far from each other).

Another consideration was the supply of suitable extras: Pier Paolo Pasolini was after a certain look, and planned to play much of the Christ movie off people's faces. Why? Because the *reactions* of people to Jesus and his ministry are absolutely fundamental to this movie – and to many religious movies. (Pasolini discusses Jews and Arabs in the documentary – in a way that some viewers have found racist).[6]

While most of the landscapes in Palestine were too domesticated and too modest for Pasolini's elevated vision for his Christ movie, the desert and hills near the Dead Sea possessed the requisite spectacle. In the end, *The Gospel According To Matthew* recreated the desert on the slopes of Mount Etna[7] and parts of Calabria. Which, as the documentary shows, are not as vast as the canyons, ridges, and rocky screes of the shores of the Dead Sea.

Professional location managers could probably have informed Pier Paolo Pasolini beforehand that filming in Palestine and Israel wouldn't be a great idea for a feature film, but the trip was useful in many other ways. Such as: visiting the real places where the fantastical events in the *New Testament* occurred; thinking about the events and how to film them; and meeting the people who lived in those places (and contemplating how they might relate to the people who lived 2,000 years ago, something that concerned Pasolini. He was fascinated by the idea that people today were related to their ancestors hundreds or even thousands of years ago).

THE PRODUCTION.

Il Vangelo Secondo Matteo was dedicated to the memory of Pope John XXIII (Angelo Roncalli, 1881-1963). Pier Paolo Pasolini (then 40) had been invited to Assisi by Pro Civitate Cristiana, along with other filmmakers and artists, to discuss Jesus.[8] Pasolini had read the *Gospels* in his hotel while visiting Assisi, as a

---

6 For instance, Pasolini explains that he doesn't want Arab extras, because they come from a pre-Christian, pagan culture.
7 Mount Etna became a favourite spot for Pier Paolo Pasolini. The volcano pops up in all sorts of places – footage of the eruptions appeared in *Star Wars: Revenge of the Sith* (2005), for example.
8 Pro Civitate Christiana regarded cinema as potentially a modern form of sacred art.

guest of the Citadella. The idea for *The Gospel According To Matthew* grew steadily, Pasolini explained, as he read the *Bible*, eventually overwhelming all of the other ideas he was contemplating. He chose Matthew's *Gospel*, rather the others, because it had a 'national-popular epic' quality, and 'Mark's seemed too crude, John's too mystical, and Luke's sentimental and bourgeois' (1964, 297).

Pier Paolo Pasolini described in February, 1963 how the film production came about:

> One day the Pope arrived in the city. The whole place was in a ferment. I didn't fancy going out in all that confusion and decided to stay in my room. Not knowing how to pass the time, I picked up a copy of St Matthew's Gospel. I was remarkably impressed and enthusiastic.
> When I returned to Rome, I spoke to producer Alfredo Bini about it. I told him I wanted to make a film out of the Gospel. He was so excited about the project that he jumped out of his seat.[9]

Pope John XXIII was famous for inaugurating the Second Vatican Council (1959-1964); he was elected Pope in 1958;[10] and for updating (*aggiornamento*) some of the Church's activities and ideas (and introducing liberalization). The links to Popes (the movie is dedicated to Pope John XXIII) and Pro Civitate Cristiana gives *The Gospel According To Matthew* surprising connections to distinctly right-wing and conservative institutions. You can't get much more establishment and traditional than the Catholic Church,[11] can you?[12] Yet Pier Paolo Pasolini and the film movement of the European New Wave is usually thought of as radical and non-conformist and left-wing (it would be associated

9 P. Pasolini, in *Scene*, Feb 19, 1963.
10 If Pope Pius XII (1939-58) had lived on for another 3 or 4 years, Pier Paolo Pasolini said he would never have been able to make *Il Vangelo Secondo Matteo* (PP, 75).
11 *The Gospel* is a wholly Catholic movie – of course. Protestantism didn't really exist in the same way as it does in Northern Europe (PP, 46).
12 As Sam Rohdie put it, Pasolini was now working with 'the Father, the Pope, the Church, Authority, Society' (1995,156).

with the man-the-barricades idealism and political activism of the years leading up to 1968, for instance). And Pasolini's previous movies *Accattone, Curd Cheese* and *Mamma Roma* had irritated right-wing political groups.

> I want to create a pure work of poetry [Pasolini wrote to his producer, Alfredo Bini], risking even the periods of æstheticism (Bach and Mozart as musical accompaniment; Piero della Francesca and in part Duccio for pictorial inspiration; the basically prehistory and exotic reality of the Arab world as background and setting). (1964, 20)

Sam Rohdie suggested that one of the inspirations for Pier Paolo Pasolini to make the film was Orson Welles, who had narrated *King of Kings* (released in the early 1960s), and who had appeared in Pasolini's *Curd Cheese,* which had depicted Christ's Passion (1995, 25).

Many filmmakers have ached to make a film of Christ but didn't – Carl Theodor Dreyer, Paul Verhoeven, Ken Russell and Orson Welles (it's possible that Welles might've discussed his Jesus film with Pasolini). While we might lament that we never got to see Dreyer's *Christ* or Welles' modern version of the life of Jesus, we do have *The Gospel According To Matthew*. And, in a way, *The Gospel According To Matthew* does many of the things that modern directors were keen to do, or something approximating to them. (There's more than one director who has looked at *The Gospel According To Matthew* and admitted, darn it, I was going to do that!).

The Gospel According To Matthew examines the ideals and values of Pier Paolo Pasolini's youth, according to Enzo Siciliano – as if Pasolini is exploring what it means to him to live by (Christian) values.

The budget of *The Gospel According To Matthew* was small, the actors mostly amateurs, yet the film, which could easily have been disastrous (there are many things that could've gone wrong), is magnificent. Pier Paolo Pasolini explained his thinking behind the casting in 1969:

> I was obliged to find everything – the characters
> and the ambience – in reality. And so the rule that
> dominated the making of the film was the rule of
> analogy. That is, I found settings that were not
> reconstructions, but were analogous to ancient
> Palestine.[13]

So Pier Paolo Pasolini and co. picked peasants from
Southern Italy's rural communities, and the disciples
from the ruling classes. Danilo Donati dressed Herod's
men as Knights Templar, soldiers from Paolo Uccello
paintings, and fascist hoodlums. (Pasolini remarked that
he was very happy with the cast of *The Gospel
According To Matthew;* it is a production that meticulously selected the actors).

The disciples in this version of the *Gospels* are:
Peter, Simon, Judas, Andrew, Thaddeus, John, James,
James son of Alphæus, Philip, Thomas, Bartholomew,
and of course Matthew. The casting of the disciples
presents a range of faces and types; many are in their
twenties or thirties; they are working class people (in
the main), not intellectuals, scribes or poets.

The Apostles are not given much characterization
beyond what the actors themselves bring to the part.
Some have more to do than others, and many have only
one or two lines in the film. The daily lives of the
disciples are not depicted – in most scenes they are
following Jesus (tho' there are domestic scenes, such as
a moment when they buy some food and eat it).

The decision to let the text speak for itself, and to
avoid psychology and conventional characterization,
suits this film very well, and reinforces the concept that
this is an 'anti-Hollywood' interpretation of the
Christian story. (However, in many Hollywood versions
of Christ's life, Jesus remains a mysterious figure,
ultimately unknowable).

Enzo Siciliano (who played Simon) recalled that
Pier Paolo Pasolini was tireless in directing *The Gospel*

13 In J. Leyda, 346. True, but there is some material filmed in the studio.

According To Matthew, and they worked all day (ES, 274). Pasolini didn't want 'acting', and told his cast to just use their normal expressions (relying on the process of cinema to do the rest of the work. Because for Pasolini cinema was *already a dream.* The actors thus didn't need to 'do' anything – the magical apparatus of cinematography would do it all).

Low budget *The Gospel According To Matthew* might have been (by Hollywood terms),[14] but it had a large cast, a huge number of locations, hundreds of costumes, a welter of props and practical effects, animals, and other expensive items. Historical films are usually more costly to produce than those set in contemporary times. And shooting on location can be more expensive than shooting in the studio: all of those actors and extras, for instance, had to be bussed out to the locations, put in costume, and fed (and some would stay in hotels). Had it been made within the Hollywood system at the time, *The Gospel According To Matthew* would have cost millions – *The King of Kings* of 1961 would be a budgetary comparison for a Christ movie, as would *The Greatest Story Ever Told* of 1965. (You can see that some of those locations were probably difficult to reach – the crew would've had to schlepp heavy gear up the volcano at Mount Etna, for instance, by hand. No Hollywood helicopters on this shoot. Mount Etna is in Sicily, near Messina and Catanbia. It's 10,912 feet (3,350m) high).

THE CAST AND THE CREW.

Among the cast were Margherita Caruso as the young Mary, and Susanna Pasolini as the elder Mary;[15] Marcello Morante[16] (Elsa Morante's brother) was Joseph; Mario Socrate was the Baptist;[17] Settimio Di

14 One wonders what Pier Paolo Pasolini might've done with a colossal budget – something with the $$$$ of Cecil B. De Mille or the epic movies of the 1960s.
15 Susanna Pasolini is probably too old – if Mary was in her late teens (in movie terms) when she had Jesus (in the *Bible*, she is 14 or 15), she would in her late forties when the adult Jesus is encountered.
16 Morante was dubbed by Gianni Bonagura.
17 Socrate was dubbed by Pino Locchi.

Porto was Peter; Otello Sestili[18] was Judas; Ferruccio Nuzzo was Matthew;[19] Giacomo Morante was John; Amerigo Bevilacqua was Herod I; Francesco Leonetti[20] was Herod II; Alfonso Gatto was Andrew; Luigi Barbini[21] was James; Giorgio Agamben was Phillip; Elio Spaziani was Thaddaeus; Enzo Siciliano was Simon; Guido Cerretani was Bartholomew; Rosario Migale was Thomas; Marcello Galdini was James, son of Alphaeus; Juan Rodolfo Wilcock was Caiaphas; Alessandro Clerici was Pontius Pilate; Franca Cupane was Herodias; Paola Tedesco was Salomé; Rossana Di Rocco was the Angel of the Lord; Renato Terra was the Possessed One; Eliseo Boschi was Joseph of Arimathea; Natalia Ginzburg was Mary of Bethany (her real husband, Gabriele Baldini, played her husband); and Ninetto Davoli was a Shepherd.[22] Released: October 2, 1964. 142m.

Some of the cast of *The Gospel According To Matthew* were played by intellectuals and authors that Pier Paolo Pasolini knew: Giorgio Agamben (Phillip) was a philosopher, Enzo Siciliano[23] (Simon) and Alfonso Gatto (Andrew) were writers, and Natalia Ginzburg (Mary of Bethany) and Juan Rodolfo Wilcock (Caiaphas) were poets.[24]

Many of the actors in *Il Vangelo Secondo Matteo* only appeared in this film and in no others (such as Margherita Caruso). It is truly a cast of unknowns – even if you watch Italian television and movies, you won't have seen most or any these actors before.[25] Or since. Only Pier Paolo Pasolini and producer Alfredo Bini are familiar names in this production (but even many

18 He was an extra in *Accattone*. Pier Paolo Pasolini said he cast an intellectual to play Matthew.
19 Matthew is cast as a young man (perhaps to tie in with the date of the *Gospel*'s composition, many decades later).
20 Playwright Leonetti was a regular in the Pasolini Circus – he's the crow's voice in *The Hawks and the Sparrows*, Laius' servant in *Oedipus Rex*, and in *Che Cosa Sono la Nuvole?* he's the puppet-master.
21 Barbini pops up in later Pasolini films – he's the youth that Massimo Girotti stares at in Milan station in *Theorem*, for instance.
22 Pasolini put Davoli in as 'kind of screen-test' (PP, 103).
23 Enzo Siciliano is Pasolini's brilliant biographer.
24 But the minor characters were played by the agricultural proletariat of Southern Italy, as Pasolini described them (PP, 77).
25 Many of the extras were hired from where the movie was shot (as usual in movies) – in places like Barile, Matera and Massafra.

Italians wouldn't haven't heard of Pasolini or Bini at the time of the movie's theatrical release). And many actors didn't do much at all in movies afterwards (Morante, Irazoqui, etc). This is quite common when employing non-actors: they appear in just one movie, and in nothing else (because they're not interested in acting). And sometimes, when they are so good, it's a pity. Margherita Caruso (the young Virgin), for instance, has a face that could launch a thousand movies, and she is stunning as the Madonna, but I think her only appearance on celluloid is *Il Vangelo Secondo Matteo.*

Using a cast of total unknowns (and proper unknowns, not like the 'unknowns' of North American and European movies, who aren't 'unknowns' at all, but just happen to have appeared in TV and movies already, and have agents and/ or managers), works for one simple reason: the story, the characters, the themes, the settings – in short, the everything – in *The Gospel According To Matthew* are so well-known. The story of Jesus, Mary, Joseph, and the twelve disciples and all the rest don't need a guest star as Joseph or the older Mary, because it is all so familiar. (There is only one star in *The Gospel According To Matthew* – and that's the director, Pasolini. And, after the film was released, Enrique Irazoqui, perhaps. But, in truth, the true star is the movie itself).

The acting in *The Gospel According To Matthew* ranges from Enrique Irazoqui's histrionic, gestural style (no doubt encouraged by the maestro – Pier Paolo Pasolini would be keen to elicit the right sort of performance from Irazoqui), to the minimal expressions of the non-professional extras (the *sensei* seems to have told them to simply stand there and look in this direction; if an actor or extra breaks the fourth wall and glances at the camera, it only adds to the verisimilitude of the film – and several do). On a production like this, with such a large cast, and so many people to organize in the frame, and in so many locations, the assistant directors do a lot of the work: the A.D.s were Maurizio Lucidi, Paolo Schneider and Elsa Morante.

As well as Tonino Delli Colli, another important Italian cinematographer worked on *The Gospel According To Matthew*: Giuseppe Ruzzolini (as camera operator). With so many shots featuring the camera shifting around the actors very intimately, Ruzzolini can he regarded as a key contributor to the film. (Ruzzolini acted as DP for some of Pasolini's later films).

The crew on *The Gospel According To Matthew* also included: Luigi Scaccianoce, production designer, Andrea Fantacci, set decorator, Dante Ferretti, assistant production designer, costumes by Danilo Donati, Manolo Bolognini, production manager, editing by Nino Baragli, sound by Mario Del Pozzo, sound mixing by Fausto Ancillai, make-up by Marcello Ceccarelli, hair by Mimma Pomilia, and script girl Lina D'Amico (many in the crew worked often with Pasolini).

On a historical movie like this, hair and make-up are absolutely vital – not only for the principals, but to organize hair and make-up assistants to dress and prepare all of those extras.

Most of *The Gospel According To Matthew* is filmed during the day, including night scenes (such as the Agony in the Garden). Because night shoots are more expensive, and some would be logistically tough in some of those locations (like lighting large outdoor areas far away from electricity supplies).

CASTING CHRIST.

Casting Christ is a daunting task. Christ in *The Gospel According To Matthew* was played by a young Spanish[26] student from Barcelona, Enrique Irazoqui (born July 5, 1944, Barcelona), that Pier Paolo Pasolini found by chance. As a student, Irazoqui had read Pasolini's *Ragazzi di vita* (unusual – but that would endear Irazoqui to Pasolini); Irazoqui asked to meet Pasolini when he was visiting Rome. As soon as the maestro saw Irazoqui, he was cast in the role of a

26 Irazoqui's mother is Italian, however.

lifetime. Pasolini recalled:

> And then one day I came back to the house and
> found this young Spaniard, Enrique Irazoqui,
> sitting here waiting to see me and as soon as I saw
> him, even before he had a chance to start talking, I
> said: 'Excuse me, but would you act in one of my
> films?' – even before I knew who he was or any-
> thing. He was a serious person, and so he said 'no'.
> But then I gradually won him round. (PP, 78)

Following his portrayal of Jesus, Irazoqui had his
passport confiscated, his career at university suspended
for a year, and spent 15 months in the National Service.[27]

Pretty remarkable, though, isn't it? Enrique
Irazoqui had little acting experience, is only 20 years-
old, and next minute he's playing Jesus in a big Italian
movie! And he does a brilliant job: and Christ, as actors
have found over the years, is a tough acting gig on many
levels. (And Irazoqui was Spanish, and probably one of
the few Spaniards in this Italian production).

It was a huge risk – casting a non-actor in a lead
role is a big deal; added to that was the large and
complex production, plus it was a prestige production
by a famous director. As if that wasn't pressure enough,
this was also the story of Christ – a formidable subject,
and a very challenging role for any actor.

Enrique Irazoqui wasn't Max von Sydow or Jeffrey
Hunter, who also played Jesus in films of this period;
they were established actors who'd worked in some
important movies directed by masters (John Ford,
Nicholas Ray, Ingmar Bergman, etc). Irazoqui had to
trust Pasolini's faith in him.

Enrique Irazoqui was dubbed by Enrico Maria
Salerno,[28] an Italian actor: so Irazoqui's performance is a
double act (by two Enriques/ Enricos); it's not only
Irazoqui alone. Indeed, in the scenes where Christ is a

27 Following *The Gospel According To Matthew*, Irazoqui appeared in
Noche de vino tinto (José María Nunes, 1966, Spain), *Dante no es
únicamente severo* (Jacinto Esteva and Joaquim Jordà, 1966, Spain) and
A la soledat (2008, José María Nunes, Spain). Rather than acting,
Irazoqui became a lawyer.
28 He had appeared in *A Violent Life.*

figure off in the distance, it's Salerno we're listening to, not Irazoqui we're watching. Salerno is vitally important to the success of *The Gospel According To Matthew* – if this were an animated movie, audiences would be applauding Salerno for his performance as the voice of Christ.

Thus, Jesus was *not* wholly an unknown, non-professional actor – because he is voiced by Enrico Maria Salerno. When they hired Enrique Irazoqui, Bini and Pasolini knew they would be replacing his voice (and they probably had Salerno in mind).

Enrico Salerno (1926-1994) appeared in numerous films and TV series, and also directed films and plays. He worked for many well-known Italian directors, such as Fellini, Zeffirelli, Argento, Bolognini, Monicelli, Rossellini, Risi and Magni. (Salerno voiced many other characters in Italian cinema, including dubbing Clint Eastwood in the Spaghetti Westerns, and Richard Basehart for Federico Fellini). Salerno's films included: *Three Nights of Love, Six Days a Week, Casanova 70, Le Masque de Fer, Escape By Night, Seasons of Our Love, The Strange Night, Candy, The Bird With the Crystal Plumage, The Swinging Confessors, The Sicilian Checkmate, The Assassination of Trotsky, City Under Seige, Gambling City, Dianry of a Passion,* and *An Ideal Adventure.*

✦

Christ was initially going to be African, part of Pier Paolo Pasolini's modernization of the myth, with Christ as 'the true 'savage father'' (Pasolini had visited Africa several times in the early 1960s, and the idea, the culture and the reality of Africa subsequently remained fundamental to his art).

Then Pier Paolo Pasolini considered using a poet or an intellectual to play Christ – after going through all the poets Pasolini came up with Jack Kerouac and Yevgeny Yvetushenko (one can't help thinking that Kerouac would have been disastrous). The movie demonstrates that to *play* a *poetic* Christ, you don't need to have an *actual* poet (let's face it, writers make some really bad actors – even worse than directors!). At another time, Pasolini had considered using a German actor. He also said that he had spent more than a year looking for the right person to play Jesus (PP, 78).

Why didn't Pier Paolo Pasolini choose Franco Citti, probably the obvious choice at the time? Dunno. In *Accattone*, Pasolini and Citti had already explored Christ-like themes. Probably one reason was to have an unknown – even though an untried actor is a big gamble, and the role is very demanding – and very physical. Also, Citti had played anti-social characters in Pasolini's films – a pimp and a thief. (It can't have been an age issue, as Citti was 26 at the time).

As well as casting Christ, there are so many other roles in *The Gospel According To Matthew* to fill: and *The Gospel According To Matthew* is much bigger than some Jesus movies, which focus on the Holy Family, the disciples, and secondary figures. *The Gospel According To Matthew* took in temple elders, Pharisees, Sadducees, priests, courtiers, soldiers, people to be healed... the list is endless. So part of the decision of where to shoot must take that into consideration: where you film the life of Christ, you need *a lot* of extras (and you need a *choice*, too, not just one actor for each role).

Thus, the casting director on *Gospel* was hugely important (Pier Paolo Pasolini's name overshadows all of the other collaborators in *The Gospel According To Matthew*, and the casting director[29] is seldom cited in film criticism. But when you've done some casting yourself (as I have), you realize how vital the role is. The film crew didn't just roll up in Matera and grab some people out of the onlookers nearby and throw them into a scene!).

PASOLINI THE UNBELIEVER.
Certainly Pier Paolo Pasolini was an unusual film director to decide to make a film of Jesus. As everyone

---

29 There is no credit for the casting director on *The Gospel According To Matthew* – Pier Paolo Pasolini said he chose all of the extras himself – but they were ordinary people from the area, not film extras (PP, 40). Of course, assistants would've helped.

discussing the production has noted, he was an atheist and a Marxist (and a radical). Pasolini's personality contained seemingly contradictory ingredients for a director who would be dealing with Christian themes and the story of Christ. But if you know about Pasolini's previous movies, and his poetry, and his views, it isn't so surprising.

Of *The Gospel According To Matthew*, Pier Paolo Pasolini said he did not believe in the divinity of Christ, and the film was not a practising Catholic's film (in fact, it was 'an unpleasant and terrible work, at certain points outright ambiguous and disconcerting, particularly the figure of Christ'). However, it was religious; Pasolini said the film fitted philosophically into his 'tendency always to see something sacred and mythic and epic in everything, even the most humdrum, simple and banal objects and events' (PP, 77).

> I've never been religious unless you can count a
> very ridiculous religious crisis at fourteen years of
> age, I was still very innocent. Then from one day to
> the next, I didn't believe anymore. I was born
> Catholic by mere chance because I was born in Italy,
> but I was never particularly Catholic and I came to
> my criticism of the Church as every Italian
> intellectual has. I had a very agnostic upbringing;
> this led me to Marxism so therefore I arrived at it in
> the most obvious and natural way. The Church in
> Italy has always been an instrument of power but I
> don't think it's an ideological power as opposed to
> its practical power, as any influence over the Italian
> peasant. An Italian's not religious. I don't want to
> say pagan because that would be generic but he's
> pre-Catholic in as much as he's remained in the
> state in which Catholicism found him, above all, in
> the South. It is a superficial cross over the Italian
> people and I believe it would only take a strong
> confrontation to destroy these ideals. (1971)

'I don't believe in God,' P.P. Pasolini stated, as if it was necessary to remind everyone. But he did believe in the cult of love of Christianity, or at least, reckoned that the Christian form of love was going to crop up in his films inevitably.

Externally, Pier Paolo Pasolini said, *The Gospel According To Matthew* may have been a Catholic film, but internally it was aligned with his mythic, sacred view of the world ('making *The Gospel* was to reach the maximum of the mythic and the epic' [ibid.]). Pasolini did not believe Christ was the Son of God. He was not interested in reconstructing the history of Christ; as he was not a believer, he did not want to turn Christ's life into that of one of the thousands of saints preaching in Palestine at the time (PP, 83). But he was concerned with transmitting his view of life as sacred and mythic.

Pier Paolo Pasolini said, however, that he did not want to deconsecrate Christ: 'this is a fashion I hate, it is *petit bourgeois*. I want to re-consecrate things as much as possible, I want to re-mythicize them' (PP, 83). My Christ, Pasolini explained, would take into account two thousand years of Christian mythicizing and history. 'My film is the life of Christ plus two thousand years of storytelling about the life of Christ' (ibid.). And Pasolini acknowledged that the two thousand years of Christianity were his heritage and culture: 'I know that in me there are two thousand years of Christianity'.

No need to point out the elements of persecution in the story of Jesus as presented in *The Gospel According To Matthew* and how that relates to Pier Paolo Pasolini's own life at the time. In this early 1960s era, the notoriety of Pasolini grew, and he seemed to draw attention and trouble to himself with an unconscious skill. It's an era of several court cases and accusations – against Pasolini as a sexual predator as well as a filmmaker who irritated the authorities (and neo-fascist groups) in Italy with controversies like *La Ricotta* and *Mamma Roma*. (Lesser filmmakers might've been put off making a movie of the *Gospels*, or to shelve it for a few years until the memories of the controversies faded. Not Pasolini!).

A CONFIDENT MOVIE.

In *The Gospel According To Matthew,* the filmmakers have clearly relied a good deal upon the audience already knowing the story in detail (you could follow *The Gospel According To Matthew* without knowing anything about Christianity or the story of Christ, but I would imagine that most of the people who've seen the movie would know something about Christianity. Certainly the initial main audience for the movie – Italy – partly defined how the movie was produced; this is an Italian movie – made by Italians, in Italy and in Italian – speaking first of all to fellow Italians).

Hence the filmmakers could employ the *tableau*-style of presentation within scenes (as to staging), and could emphasize those *tableaux* with montages of close-ups of faces. Or, to put it another way: *The Gospel According To Matthew* could have been edited, like any movie, many different ways. But the two approaches – montages of *tableaux* and more conventional dramatic scenes– fused perfectly with the material.

The movie is long – 142 minutes – that is, it's long compared to the average Italian flick of the period (but *not* long compared to movies in the 21st century, when going over two hours is commonplace, resulting in too many bloated, saggy movies). However, for a religious or historical epic movie, this was *not* long: historical epics, including the Biblical flicks, often went over two hours (and some, such as *Ben-Hur* and *The Ten Commandments*, were famously very long, up to three hours). Audiences accepted the long running times – these movies were often prestige films or they were super-productions, where everything is big, big, big. (However, most Italian films of the period were not prestige productions, and had regular running times).

But *The Gospel According To Matthew* does not out-stay its welcome, as too many movies of today do. There's no padding in here, no unnecessary scenes, and no scenes that drift on aimlessly. It's a pacey film; it doesn't meander or linger. In *The Gospel According To Matthew,* the filmmakers have got something important to say, and they say it (very different from so many contemporary movies, which have little to say, and no idea how to say it).

The Gospel According To Matthew is a masterful piece of cinema: you are in the hands of great artists, who really know what they're doing. It's confident, too: Pier Paolo Pasolini and his team must have been feeling *very* confident to take on this big subject.[30] Consider, for instance, that up to this time (1964), Pasolini had only made three theatrical features: *Accattone* (1961), *Mamma Roma* (1962) and *Comizi d'Amore* (1964 – though this was a documentary), and some shorter pieces, such as *The Anger* (1963), the *Curd Cheese* segment of *RoGoPaG* (1963), and *Location Hunting In Palestine* (1964). And certainly those films and documentaries are much more modest in scale and scope than *The Gospel According To Matthew* (some, like *The Anger*, are editing jobs done by someone else). To leap from two fiction features into a Biblical epic production seems especially bold.

Even Jean-Luc Godard, for me one of the two or three most significant filmmakers of the period from 1960 to the present day, felt humbled and unsure about filming the life of the Virgin Mary in his 1985 movie *Hail, Mary*. In *The Gospel According To Matthew*, you've got an actor who's impersonating Jesus and you're recreating events from the *Bible*. And that isn't easy. You've got to be feeling self-assured to be able to do that, and to know what you're doing.

FILMING THE DIVINE.

The film does not question Christ's divinity, as some later films have done. Whatever the filmmakers may personally believe, *The Gospel According To Matthew* presents a divine Jesus: this is a man who walks on water and performs miracles. For Pier Paolo Pasolini, Jesus was divine – that is, as a supreme manifestation of humanity: 'in him humanity is so lofty, strict, and ideal as to exceed the common terms of humanity', as Pasolini put it in his letter to Lucio S.

---

30 A really successful film has to have everyone in each department working at their best (or at least appearing to do so).

Caruso of the Pro Civitate Christiana of Assisi (ES, 270).

Pier Paolo Pasolini wrote to Lucio S. Caruso in February, 1963:

> My idea is to follow the *Gospel According to St Matthew* point by point, without making a script or adaption of it. To translate it faithfully into images, following its story without any omissions or additions. The dialogue too should strictly be that of St Matthew, without even a single explanatory or connecting sentence, because no image or inserted word could ever attain the poetic heights of the text. (P. Pasolini, 1964)

How do you make a film from one of the *Scriptures*? Have a look at the text of *The Gospel According To St Matthew* and ask the basic questions:

Where is this going to take place?

Who are you going to cast in the lead roles?

What will the actors wear?

What will they look like?

What will they say?

How will the characters relate to each other?

How much exposition is required?

How will you depict an angel?

How does an angel interact with a human being?

What will the dialogue be?

What is divinity?

How do you portray it on film?

And so on and on. The questions are endless (they are the sorts of questions that are fired at a film director continuously during pre-production and on set). In short, creating the script and concept of *The Gospel According To Matthew* was not simply a case of transcribing the *Gospel* into cinema. You don't carry the *Bible* onto the set and yell, 'action!'

Certainly, as Pier Paolo Pasolini stated above, the film was on the whole 'faithful' to the text of *St Matthew's Gospel* – but as numerous commentators have noted, and many filmmakers have found out, being 'faithful' to a text is not only not desirable most of the time, it's not even possible.

Yet *The Gospel According To Matthew* gives the *impression* of being a 'faithful' representation in images and sounds and music of the text of *The Gospel of St Matthew* written two thousand years ago. That's the trick – and a mighty, mighty trick it is, too.

Cinema is entirely fakery and lies, as everyone knows, but the skill is to persuade the audience to believe in the world of the movie for two hours. It's all lies in cinema, as the Japanese director Hayao Miyazaki stated in 1979, it's all a fabrication of something that the filmmakers want the audience to believe is real:

> Even if the world depicted is a lie, the trick is to make it seem as real as possible. Stated another way, the animator must fabricate a lie that seems so real viewers will think the world depicted might possibly exist.[31]

Audiences *want* to believe, of course. They *yearn* to think that some fantasy world can really exist. And they want to go there.

Or put it like this: *The Gospel According To Matthew* is a highly stylized, highly artificial movie made in the mid-1960s in a particular place and time, under particular financial and labour conditions, using a particular cast and crew, with a particular form of technological equipment, within a particular social and political context, based on a script by an Italian poet-turned-director that was in turn based on a text written two thousand years ago that was originally perhaps written in Aramaic but later translated into Greek (and Pasolini presumably used an Italian translation), and the original text was written many years after the extraordinary events that may or may not have happened.

In other words, the 1964 movie *The Gospel According To Matthew* is a highly stylized and self-conscious production subject to countless constraints

31 H. Miyazaki, *Starting Point, 1979-1996*, tr. B. Cary & F. Schodt, Viz Media/ Shogakukan, San Francisco, CA, 2009, 21.

and social contexts, and what it purports to be about is something that is both historical and religious, that might have happened, but might not (whatever the 'truth' of a historical event, we are *very* far from it here). So the trick is make what happens in front of the camera in *The Gospel According To Matthew* seem as if it's really happening, even though the audience knows it is a trick upon a trick upon a stylization upon a cliché upon a literary text upon multiple translations upon events that may or may not had some basis in history or reality.

We always need to remind ourselves that *everything* in movies is technological, everything is fake, everything is a highly sophisticated cultural form created by humans for mass entertainment.

And Christianity, like civilization and technology, is constantly evolving. For instance, the Catholic Church has had an ambiguous attitude towards the Madonna, as Julia Kristeva commented in her outstanding 1977 essay on the Virgin Mary, "Stabat Mater":

> Mary's function as guardian of power, later checked
> when the church became wary of it, nevertheless
> persisted in popular and pictural representation,
> witness Piero della Francesca's impressive
> painting, *Madonna della Misericordia,* which was
> disavowed by Catholic authorities at the time. And
> yet, not only did the papacy revere more and more
> the christly mother as the Vatican's power over
> cities and municipalities was strengthened, it also
> openly identified its own institution with the
> Virgin: Mary was officially proclaimed Queen by
> Pius XII in 1954 and *Mater Ecclesiæ* in 1964.
> (1986, 170)

So as recently as 1954 and 1964, the Vatican has altered its official stance on the Virgin Mary: thus *The Gospel According To Matthew* was being produced in a political atmosphere where issues that might seem to be 'eternal' and 'fixed' were still being negotiated.

Not many Biblical films explored the early life of

the Madonna. One is *The Gospel According To Matthew*; the other one is *Jesus of Nazareth*, the all-star, blockbuster TV series of 1977, which depicts the young Virgin and her life with Joseph (an Italian production from R.A.I. TV).

There have been further TV shows about the Madonna. For instance, the Italian company Lux Vide has produced a *Bible Collection* of TV movies centred on figures such as Jesus, Mary Magdalene, Judas, Simon, etc. The Hollywood *Nativity Story* (2006), distributed by New Line Cinema, depicted the early life of Mary in detail. And the *Da Vinci Code* (2006) phenomena, plus the surprise success of *The Passion of the Christ* (2004), has spearheaded renewed, millennial interest in Christian themes in movies (production of Christian movies reached a high in 2006). New outlets such as direct to DVD/ video, online/ streaming, and satellite/ cable TV have encouraged film companies, too.

The Italian film and TV industry has a long tradition of producing religious/ Biblical/ Christian works. Recently, from the 1990s onwards, companies such as Lux Vide and Five Mile River films have been active in religious movie production. Lux Vide, for example, made a film about St Paul, which had been one of Pasolini's long-cherished projects.

POETRY AND POLITICS IN *THE GOSPEL ACCORDING TO MATTHEW*.

Il Vangelo Secondo Matteo is described as having a Marxist approach. The combination of Marxism and Catholicism, Communism and Christianity, makes for a fascinating mix. Yet, *The Gospel According To Matthew* isn't a Marxist movie in any way, really: any Marxist politics it contains seems to derive more from the perception of Pier Paolo Pasolini as a Marxist artist. A purist Marxist approach would presumably be thoroughly materialist, and would debunk any religious or spiritual aspects; it would analyze the events in social and political terms. There would be no miracles in a purist's Marxist interpretation of the *Gospels*, would there? The spiritual elements would be ignored, or rationalized into nothing.

The director might be a Marxist (but many in the crew probably were, too – though not as out-spoken as Pasolini!), but the resultant movie isn't Marxist (Pasolini often downplayed his Marxism). It doesn't want to be. There is an emphasis on *materiality*, certainly, on the physicality of the ancient world, but that sensuality is not seen in Victorian, industrial, Marxist terms (or in modern Marxist or Communist terms, either).

As to the ideology and the politics[32] within *The Gospel According To Matthew*, one could just as well see them as *radical* and *anarchist* as *Marxist*. The individuality, the poetry, the sensuality and artistic aspects of Pier Paolo Pasolini's cinema also seem to me to come out triumphant above politics and ideology, Marxist or otherwise. Pasolini is a mass of contradictions, which's partly what makes him such a fascinating filmmaker to study (and his Christ is 'not bad in fact, he is just full of contradictions' [PP, 87]).

Pier Paolo Pasolini's Christ fights against the establishment like a political activist: he is an angry, passionate Christ, a fiery, Southern, Mediterranean peasant rebel, a social reformer, a world away from the pale, passive Anglo-Saxon Jesuses of Hollywood cinema (where Jesus is usually cast from white, American or European actors – whereas the historical Jesus was a Jewish man from the Middle East). But Christ's polemical ferocity is tempered by the 1964 film's incredibly tender lyricism. Jesus in *The Gospel According To Matthew* isn't always storming about yelling about baptisms of fire and inciting his disciples to use the sword ('Think not that I am come to send peace on earth: I came not to send peace, but a sword' [*Matthew,* 10: 34]); clearly a political firebrand, Pasolini's Jesus also has plenty of scenes of contemplation and gentleness.

32 Because it used analogy, rather than direct historical reconstruction, Pier Paolo Pasolini said, 'I have left out objectively important political and social factors' (PP, 82).

✦

Martin Scorsese wrote that Pier Paolo Pasolini's film 'really worked beautifully, the film is so joyous: he was a great poet' (M. Scorsese, 138). Scorsese wrote of the miracles:

> I love the way Pasolini did the miracles; for example, when Jesus cures the leper, with the Leadbelly steel guitar on the soundtrack. Just a simple cut, and it's so shocking and beautiful: he's looking into the eyes of Christ, who says, 'Go now yourself to the high priest.' (ib., 136)

Pier Paolo Pasolini's Jesus was for the sacred and the poetic, in the midst of the profane and the banal. Pasolini emphasized the rebellious aspect of Christ because for him Christ had been crucified by the fathers, the State, the Pharisees and Philhistines. Christ was instrumental in the revolution against the Law of the Father which was part of Pasolini's project.

> The fathers who killed Christ had killed Oedipus, had tried to kill Pasolini's poetry. Christ crucified therefore was a revolutionary sign of the sacred against the profane of authority. It was the idea made fact and made flesh.

as Sam Rohdie put it (1995, 164). Pier Paolo Pasolini's Christ appears 'revolutionary',[33] something of an agitprop or radical leader. Pasolini maintained that this 'revolutionary' character was not something he added or exaggerated: it was already there in Matthew's *Gospel*.

The quiet self-assurance of Jesus in *The Gospel According To Matthew* is striking – how he walks up to Simon and Peter hauling in their fishing nets on a beach and says simply, 'follow me'. There is never a question of doubt – either for Jesus, but also not for his disciples. They simply leave right away, as if they've always been

---

[33] 'Christ going round Palestine is really a revolutionary whirlwind: someone who walks up to a couple of people and says 'drop your nets and follow me' is a total revolutionary' (PP, 95)

waiting for him. This Jesus doesn't command, or persuade, or implore, he simply says – and quietly – what must be said, and what must be done: 'follow me'.

THE GOSPEL AS A BIBLICAL MOVIE.

The Gospel According To Matthew is a commentary on the religious film genre, of course, and it employs many New Wave and modernist cinematic techniques, and it has elements of Marxism and radical politics – but aside from all of that, *The Gospel According To Matthew* is a very traditional movie. It has all of the elements of the conventional religious movie: deserts, low, one-storey stone buildings, horses and donkeys, palm trees, hordes of extras in Biblical dress, and plenty of choral music.

The Baptism, for example, takes place in one of those shallow riverbeds, with rocks in the water, and onlookers dotted around the bank. While the Baptist may be angrier than previous incarnations of the role, the scene itself is very traditional, complete with the initiates looking up to Heaven after they've been baptized.

The visual aspects of *The Gospel According To Matthew* are instantly recognizable as belonging to the Biblical or religious movie. It's often in the *invisible elements* of movie-making that *The Gospel According To Matthew* reveals its modernism, its departure from the conventional religious movie. The editing, for instance, and the music. The simple decision of putting modern blues music like Blind Willie Johnson on the soundtrack was far-reaching, and automatically distances *The Gospel According To Matthew* from your average sword-and-sandal flick. Similarly, and also part of post-production, was the editing, the use of jump cuts, irregular parts of shots, and rapid montages.

It's as if Pier Paolo Pasolini and his team thought, well, you've seen a Biblical movie before, but we are going to do it in a very different way. Because the more you contemplate what Pasolini and co. are doing in *The Gospel According To Matthew*, you realize how startlingly different it is from what had gone on before. The French New Wave and Neo-realist approach had been taken with other subjects (such as the crime genre in *Breathless*, or the romantic comedy drama in *Jules et Jim*), but not in the religious movie genre.

RECEPTION.

The Gospel According To Matthew was premiered at the Venice Film Festival on September 4, 1964 (where earlier Pasolini-directed films, like *Accattone* and *Mamma Roma,* had made such an impact). However, neo-fascist groups once again attempted to disrupt the screening (insulting the audience, throwing leaflets, and attacking the film critic Palo Valmarana and painter Renato Guttuso). The critical response was inevitably strong, and divided (it's a film that demands you have an opinion), but the movie immediately drew support, and won the Grand Jury Prize in Venice (and 3 Nastro d'Argento Awards).

Il Vangelo Secondo Matteo was awarded a prize by the Ufficio Cattolico Internazionale del Cinema. The jury praised its simplicity and Pier Paolo Pasolini's humility, making it 'far superior to earlier, commercial films, on the life of Christ. It shows the real grandeur of his teaching stripped of any artificial and sentimental effect'.[34] It was nominated for 3 Oscars. It has subsequently been praised by religious organizations, including official Vatican publications, and regularly appears in top ten lists of films and religious films.

In Italy, according to Pasolini, *The Gospel According To Matthew* was perceived as a

> disconcerting and scandalous novelty, because no one expected a Christ like that, because no one had read Matthew's *Gospel*. (PP, 79)

Critics objected to the Marxism of *The Gospel According To Matthew*; its avoidance of the living conditions of Ancient Israel; the 'haughty, prophesying

---

34 Museo Nazionale del Cinema, Turin.

and violent transgression' translated onto Jesus (N. Greene, 78). Not 'Marxist' enough, then! Or the 'wrong kind' of 'Marxism'!

Pier Paolo Pasolini changed his mind about the film. Sometimes he thought the compound of styles – *cinema vérité*, handheld camera, zooms, long lenses, and so on – was a hotch-potch but worked (it *is* an uneven mix of cinematic styles). At other times, he found *The Gospel According To Matthew*

> a violently contradictory film, profoundly
> ambiguous and disconcerting, particularly the
> figure of Christ – at times he is almost embarrass-
> ing, as well as being enigmatic. (PP, 87)

But it's almost impossible to make a film about Christ without falling into embarrassment or awkward-ness at some point, and not a single one of the greatest religious films have avoided that completely.

When Pier Paolo Pasolini saw the picture after he'd finished it, he wondered if perhaps it did, in the end, have a stylistic unity – which derived from 'my own unconscious religiousness, which came out and gave the film its unity'. So, Pasolini mused, 'therefore I probably do believe after all' (PP, 87).

The miracles Pier Paolo Pasolini later found (in the 1969 interviews) 'repellent', 'disgusting pietism', because they were faked. Pasolini wanted them to be real, but the artificial aids made the fakery obvious (PP, 90). Pasolini wondered if he should have invented 'completely new miracles', such as

> the sense of miraculousness each of us can
> experience watching the dawn, for example:
> nothing happens, the sun rises, trees are lit up by
> the sun. Perhaps for us this is what a miracle is. (PP,
> 91)

I think that Pier Paolo Pasolini is being too hard on himself, or on his movie, which is an authentic masterpiece, almost a miracle in itself. (Besides, all of cinema is fakery, and the miracles in the 1964 movie are just one kind of fakery out of 1,000s. Computer-aided imagery and green screen visual effects look just as fake today as any other effects in film history).

But then, many filmmakers have been doubtful about their achievements. To take one example: one of Pier Paolo Pasolini's key influences, Jean-Luc Godard, for my money one of the two or three most significant filmmakers of the 1960-2010 period (Ingmar Bergman and Akira Kurosawa would be the others), often remarked that he didn't think his movies were that good:

> John Cassavetes, who was more or less my age – now he was a great director. I can't imagine myself as his equal in cinema. For me he represents a certain cinema that's way up above. (2000)

And Godard told Andrew Sarris in 1994 that he didn't think he'd

> succeeded in making any really good films. There are moments, scenes, whole movements that sing. It has all added up to a cinema of sorts, even though I'm still learning my art. (1994)

And this is the man who wrote and directed films such as *Breathless, Pierrot le Fou, Weekend, Contempt, Vivre Sa Vie, Hail Mary, Passion, Masculin/ Féminin, La Chinoise, Tout Va Bien, Alphaville, Two or Three Things I Know About Her, Histoire(s) du Cinéma, Notre Musique, Éloge de l'Amour* and *Bande à Part*!

One thing's for sure about *The Gospel According To Matthew*: anyone contemplating a movie based on the *Gospels* has to see it. And they have: Mel Gibson, Martin Scorsese, Atom Egoyam and Abel Ferrara are among many who have cited *The Gospel According To Matthew* as an influence (there must be 100s more filmmakers). But how can you *not* be influenced by *The Gospel According To Matthew* if you've seen it? The picture has such an impact, it's impossible to ignore it.

CRITICS.

For David A. Cook in *A History of Narrative Film*, *The Gospel According To Matthew* is a 'stark but brilliant work', and 'stands today as the most dynamic version of the gospel story ever filmed' (1990, 632).

Pamela Grace calls *The Gospel According To Matthew* 'spare, laconic, almost ritualistic in form... demanding and profoundly moving' (105). Greg Way (in *Movietone News* in 1976) found the film's pace breakneck and uncompromising, and very unexpected in a Jesus film. The viewer hurries to keep up with Jesus like the camera does.

Bosley Crowther, film critic for the *New York Times* (and tough to please), raved about *The Gospel* when it opened in Gotham in 1966, praising its 'extraordinary blending of black-and-white reality and the literalness of St Matthew's Gospel'; 'it is neither transcendent nor mundane, neither extravagant nor banal' (Feb 18, 1966).

THE LOOK AND THE STYLE

THE LOOK.

Jesus in *The Gospel According To Matthew* is depicted in a white robe (white pops out of the wilderness landscapes of much of the movie – many of the characters wear white), with bare feet and a black hood and cloak made from coarse[35] material. His hair is pulled back and shoulder length. He sports stubble which at times becomes a stubbly beard. Jesus's look is right out of Renaissance paintings: he might've stepped out of an altarpiece by Piero della Francesca[36] or Albrecht Dürer.

As for colour, Pier Paolo Pasolini said there were

[35] Many of Danilo Donati's costumes are about texture and weave – for this and other Pasolini movies.

[36] *Histoire(s) du Cinéma,* directed by Jean-Luc Godard, puts Pasolini together with Piero della Francesca on screen (a portrait of Pasolini is combined with part of Piero's *Legend of the True Cross*).

too many colours in real life (PP, 63), and he chose particular locations because they eliminated the many colours he didn't need (as with Morocco for *Oedipus Rex*). The black-and-white in *Il Vangelo Secondo Matteo* does seem to fit its stark, earthy, austere interpretation of the Christian story[37] (interestingly, the other time Pasolini staged the Passion story, in *La Ricotta*, was in lurid Technicolor made to look trashy. That is, if he was going to use colour, Pasolini seemed intent on deliberately exaggerating the colour).

In developing the shooting style for *The Gospel According To Matthew*, the filmmakers started off principal photography by using the reverential technique of *Accattone*. This did not work for the theme and subject of the *Gospels*, so they jettisoned that approach.

During the filming of the Baptism scene (near Viterbo and Orte), DP Tonino Delli Colli and Pier Paolo Pasolini began using zooms, and different camera movements which were 'not reverential, but almost documentary' (PP, 84). Thus, Pasolini and his team were mixing Godardian and *cinema vérité* techniques with a traditional, religious subject.[38] It worked. The combination of filmic styles did not make for a stylistic unity, as Pasolini said: 'the unity comes from a mixture of styles' (PP, 87). The false continuity shots and many zooms, Pasolini said, recalled Jean-Luc Godard.

Pier Paolo Pasolini spoke of using the zoom lens to achieve close-ups from a distance, with the zoom set on 250mm, so they looked like Masaccio's paintings (i.e., a flattened sense of space and perspective). (And of course zooms are cheaper – and quicker – to set up than a tracking shot).

There is a significant advance, however, in terms of the handling of the camera, from Pier Paolo Pasolini's first two features to *The Gospel According To Matthew*:

37 But that's easy to say, because there isn't a colour version of *The Gospel According To Matthew* to compare it with. Actually there was a colourized version (a version was released on DVD in 2007).
38 Pasolini: 'the style in *The Gospel* is very varied: it combines the reverential with almost documentary moments, an almost classic severity with moments that are almost Godardian' (PP,84).

Pasolini and Tonino Delli Colli step away from using the standard 50mm lens, for instance, and use much longer focal lengths. They also employ wide angle lenses, much fancier camera angles, and tracking shots. (However, the camera is most often on a tripod, or handheld – dolly shots are used minimally).

The early days of Christ's ministry are depicted with handheld shots following just behind Jesus, as if the camera takes the viewpoint of one of the disciples. Meanwhile, Jesus looks over his shoulder as he leads the way, speaking urgently.

The costumes (by Danilo Donati) are the first examples of what would become a staple of Pier Paolo Pasolini's historical cinema: coarse textures that can be read by the camera, clothing that seems handmade by the wearer, and many out-of-period elements, such as mediæval/ Renaissance outfits for some groups of characters (such as Herod's henchmen), and of course the mandatory giant hats which Donati and Pasolini were very fond of (used for the Pharisees). With so many officials, soldiers, courtiers and priests to dress, the costuming is not all of the era (the approach was the same with the settings).

PHOTOGRAPHIC STYLE.

Il Vangelo Secondo Matteo was lensed (by Pier Paolo Pasolini's regular cameraman Tonino Delli Colli and camera operator Giuseppe Ruzzolini) in a Neo-realist/ New Wave style – a documentary style, with handheld camera, natural lighting and much camera movement (yet much of the film is also very straightforward, with a camera on a tripod with a standard (50mm) lens and no camera movement). The miracles (the curing of the lepers, the loaves and the fishes, the raising of the dead) are done with straight cuts by editor Nino Baragli (some of them are match cuts and some are jump cuts, straight out of Jean-Luc

Godard's cinema, which jolt the viewer).[39] Healing a man's disfigured face, for example, is achieved with a cut from Jesus to the leper (wearing special make-up by Marcello Ceccarelli to distort the nose and eyes), his face now healed, accompanied by a leap into an African spiritual song. The moment is from *Matthew* 8:1-4:

> When he was come down from the mountain, great multitudes followed him. And, behold, there came a leper and worshipped him, saying, Lord, if thou wilt, thou canst make me clean. And Jesus put forth his hand, and touched him, saying, I will; be thou clean. And immediately his leprosy was cleansed. And Jesus saith unto him, See thou tell no man; but go thy way, shew thyself to the priest, and offer the gift that Moses commanded, for a testimony unto them.

The miracles were transparently 'false' (or self-consciously theatrical), as with the other visual effects, in which the mechanisms of cinema were deliberately exposed.[40]

The straight cut works so well, though, doesn't it? It's as if you don't want to see how it was done, how Jesus might have healed a leper. Excessive (and expensive) movie trickery, of the Hollywood kind (digital effects, for instance, which could blend a Before and After face together slowly), wouldn't be nearly so effective and *right* as a simple cut. That fits, because a god healing someone instantly, in a millionth of a second, seems correct.[41]

There are two sorts of close-ups in *Il Vangelo Secondo Matteo*: those of the by-standers and crowds, filmed with long lenses that pan from face to face or linger over them (with the camera zoomed in from

---

39 I say out of Godard's cinema – but Godard and editor Agnès Guillemot did not invent the jump cut, of course. However, in *The Gospel According To Matthew* the editing techniques draw heavily on the French New Wave.

40 S. Rohdie, 1995, 8.

41 It doesn't matter a jot, either, that the continuity here is up the spout: when the leper walks towards Jesus, he's on his own, with nobody around him. But when he's healed, he runs into a throng of celebrating onlookers.

further away, so it isn't physically right in the face of the non-professional actors, which can be off-putting for newbies). Shots are left in by the editor (Nino Baragli) where the camera operator (Giuseppe Ruzzolini) searches for a face in a group, and occasionally the focus slips, as the focus puller struggles to keep the shots sharp.[42] *The Gospel According To Matthew* keeps coming back to this cinematographic device: actors are blocked in loose rows or semi-circles, and the camera searches for them in medium close-ups. The technique emphasizes the concept of seeing these people for the first time (as the viewer discovers them with the lens).

The second type of C.U. is usually handheld, with the camera very close to the actors. This approach is typically employed for dramatic scenes, and most memorably for the scenes where Jesus is speaking to his disciples (very effective in the Sermon on the Mount sequence).

Another technique the filmmakers employed was having the camera follow Jesus as if it were one of the disciples, walking behind him, while he turns his head and talks over his shoulder into the lens. That helps to give the film its hurried pace. As Martin Scorsese put it, Irazoqui 'doesn't act walking, he is walking; it's not self-conscious and yet it's very determined' (1990, 136). It's surprising just how many of the sayings of Jesus are delivered in this manner, over-the-shoulder, with Christ in quarter-profile, to his disciples (but we don't see the reverse angles much).

The handheld technique gave *The Gospel According To Matthew* an immediacy and *casualness* that was entirely lacking in religious movies and in particular films about Christ up until that time, when Jesus was *always* filmed reverentially,[43] and never *casually*, as if he just happened to be walking down

42 Parts of these shots would be instantly discarded by a conventional editor. One wonders if Ruzzolini was happy with having what appear to be mistakes left in the film.
43 Pier Paolo Pasolini wondered if he'd been too stylized and too reverential in his filmic approach to *Il Vangelo Secondo Matteo* (PP, 83). Some viewers who found the film irreverent and too casual would say the opposite.

some steps in Jerusalem and talking to his disciples over his shoulder (and then he will stride ahead of them, still declaiming).

The Gospel According To Matthew delivered a Jesus as a flesh-and-blood man, part of the real world, not a distanced, aloof, obviously divine personality. In *The Gospel According To Matthew,* Christ was really there, saying those things, walking that way.

The typical shot in *The Gospel According To Matthew* is a handheld shot of Enrique Irazoqui's Christ walking through stony hills, all the time declaiming rapidly from the *Scriptures*, followed by his disciples. Although he *acts* in a naturalistic or realistic manner (as well as a highly stylized manner), the look of Jesus is conventional: for example, the costumes that Jesus wears are traditional ones, instantly recognizable from all of cinema's previous Biblical, epic movies. So Jesus has the flowing robes, the hood or cowl (dark-hued), the long hair, the beard, etc. He might have stepped out of a fresco by Duccio or Massacio.

Of his general cinematic technique, Pier Paolo Pasolini said he tried to emphasize frontality; symmetry; characters moving against a background: these æsthetics derive from painting. When a tracking shot or pan was employed, for example, Pasolini said it referred to the camera moving over a canvas. There were few tricky dolly shots in *The Gospel*, and no characters entering or exiting the frame. Pasolini said (*pace Mamma Roma*) that he was trying for a Renaissance painterly approach. Pasolini was much impressed by Masaccio and the Quattrocento painters: background not landscape, figures on a background, not an empty field or landscape.

The Gospel According To Matthew, though, employs plenty of cinematic techniques, including dolly shots, handheld shots, long lens shots, overhead shots, jump cuts, zooms, crash zooms, rapid montage, film library footage (such as buildings collapsing), and practical effects such as fire, wind and smoke.

And there are many formal shots, including wide

angle, establishing shots filmed from a tripod, where the camera doesn't move, and many shots where the actors are arranged within the frame formally. The tracking shots are also generally formal. For obvious reasons, in many locations where laying dolly tracks isn't possible (such as atop Mount Etna), movement is often captured with a handheld camera.

PAINTING AND *THE GOSPEL ACCORDING TO MATTHEW.*

The visual style of *Il Vangelo Secondo Matteo* alluded, as so often in Pier Paolo Pasolini's cinema, to painters such as Paolo Uccello (the battle scenes, opulent robes and the large hats), Masaccio, Piero della Francesca (the use of static *tableaux,* the pregnant Madonna, and the Pharisees' costumes), Byzantine icons, and Georges Rouault[44] (for Christ's face).[45]

The references to painting may have been obvious, Pier Paolo Pasolini remarked, but that didn't detract from the film. Painting was an important element of *The Gospel According To Matthew* for Pasolini's view of the *Gospel*, because in the Italian cultural tradition painting contributed much to Christianity, and Pasolini wanted to make 'the story of Christ plus two thousand years of Christianity' (PP, 91). And of course painting – and Renaissance painting in particular – was central to the *Curd Cheese* episode in *RoGoPaG*.

Pier Paolo Pasolini was also aware that the references to painting could unbalance the narrative:

whenever I realized from behind the camera that something might recall the composition of a painting, I destroyed it immediately. I sought to do

44 Like Lovis Corinth, James Ensor, Egon Schiele and Emil Nolde, Georges Rouault was an Expressionist artist who explored Christian themes, producing anguished, modern versions of Christian icono-graphy. Rouault's *Crucifixion* (*c.* 1918, collection: H.P. McHenny, Philadelphia), for instance, is a moving, stained glass-like picture in bright colours, marked out by the thickest black outlines in Expressionism.
45 For Sam Rohdie, *Il Vangelo Secondo Matteo* drew not from reality but from art – it was Masaccio, Piero della Francesca, Giotto *et al* who formed the inspirations for the world of *Il Vangelo Secondo Matteo,* not the real world (1995, 60).

everything the most cinematographically possible. Naturally there are some painterly echoes – there's Duccio, there's Mantegna – but certainly not a precise painting or school, simply generic references.

The conscious effort to avoid painting on Pier Paolo Pasolini's part, and in particular Renaissance and mediæval painting, of course reveals his deep immersion in art, and in religious art, and also the pitfalls of wanting to relate cinema too closely to painting. As Pasolini acknowledges, some allusions to painting seem inevitable. Pasolini recognizes that in the West audiences have been aware of how the Christian story has been portrayed visually for centuries – and by some of the greatest artists. Pasolini realizes that cinema is a late addition to Christian art, and is inevitably inflected by the thousands of images that have preceded it.

But *The Gospel According To Matthew* does not feel like it is bogged down by the references to paintings at all: it is not overly self-conscious, and does not show off its painterly allusions like other movies (the films of Peter Greenaway, Derek Jarman and Martin Scorsese come to mind).

THE SETTINGS AND LOCATIONS.

Instead of modern Palestine, which did not evoke Ancient Palestine for Pier Paolo Pasolini and the team, the director and producer chose to film in modern Calabria, in which the Biblical past (or an equivalent for it) was still alive. 'Calabria now contains the sacred of the Gospel which the modern had obliterated in Palestine and would obliterate again in Calabria', Pasolini said in *Location Hunting In Palestine*.[46] At first, Pasolini had thought that modern Israel, which was where Jesus had preached, would be ideal, but there was 'something too modern, too industrial in the countryside' (it was also a turbulent time in the Middle East, and not the easiest (nor the most financially viable)

46 In S. Rohdie, 1995, 164.

time to produce the movie). Using Southern Italy enabled the production to 'remake the Gospel by analogy', without having 'to reconstruct it either archæologically or philologically' (PP, 82). His research film *Sopralluoghi In Palestina* came to be used for documentation – the production team had already decided to use Southern Italy.

The use of found locations in *The Gospel According To Matthew* is stunning, easily as accomplished as in any film ever made (and would have required weeks of location scouting – this is a production that filmed in many, many different places. The cast and the crew would be constantly getting in and out of cars and vans, and riding in cars and vans all over Southern Italy). Mary's village; the hill town near Jesus's home; Herod's palace; the coastal town, with its ruined castle (Aci Castello, Sicily), where the Baptist is held captive; Golgotha, overlooking the hill town (which doubles for Jerusalem); the plains of Massafra in Puglia; and the rocky hills in the desert (filmed in Calabria, up in the Sila massif, tho' avoiding the huge forests, of course).

Every time I watch *The Gospel According To Matthew* I am struck by how modern and 20th century many of the locations are: they *look* old, from a distance, but on closer inspection they clearly display many modern features (iron railings on a staircase, for instance, or concrete blocks, and the houses use cement and building materials in a modern fashion. (True, the Ancient Romans had forms of concrete and cement, but not used in this way.)

But it works. You forget about the very contemporary-looking locations for many reasons: the story is utterly compelling, the filmmaking is so brilliant, the performances are so engrossing, and there's so much going on. Even tho' the art directors might've taken down a few TV aerials, and covered up a shop sign with a sheet, or hung a rug in front of a glass doorway (for the scenes where Christ walks thru a town), it doesn't matter.

The Baptism was the first scene to be shot (in

Spring, 1964), near Orte and Viterbo (the Fosso Castello Waterfalls, Soriano nel Cimino); the Mount of Olives (staged near Hadrian's Villa and Tivoli) was next; then Matera[47] and Crotone (the two towns formed Capernaum). Satan's temptation was staged on Mount Etna (using the familiar black, volcanic earth which crops up in a few Pier Paolo Pasolini movies).[48] Bethlehem was filmed in Barile, Apulia. Some of the locations (such as Matera, Massafra and Crotone) had been discovered during the filming of the documentary *Love Meetings.* Other locations included: Potenza, Basilicata; Aci Castello, Acireale, Catania in Sicily;[49] and Canale Monterano, Rome.

Bethlehem in *The Gospel According To Matthew* is a cluster of dwellings built into the hillside, virtually like caves, modest, small, and lit by fires only – very different from the usual Biblical movie setting of freestanding buildings, where Joseph, Mary and Jesus live in relative comfort (filmed in Barile, Apulia). Of course, people have been living in caves for at least three million years (depending on what you class as 'human').

It's striking how much of *The Gospel According To Matthew* is set by the ocean: Jesus is often filmed against the sea, and there are many scenes staged on beaches: the loaves and the fishes, Jesus walking on water, the castle (the exterior of Herod's palace), and of course the scenes where Jesus finds Peter and Andrew. (Calabria is only twenty miles across in some parts, so the Ionian Sea and the Tyrrhenian Sea are never far away, and it's well-known for its memorable coastal spots. And the sea doesn't date or age! – if you point a camera at the ocean, it probably looks the same as it did 2,000 years ago).

The Gospel According To Matthew was not all

47 Matera is famous for its *sassi*, the buildings constructed in tiers in a ravine. Now mainly abandoned, they were populated by the poorest of the poor, living in squalor that Carlo Levi's sister compared to Dante's *Inferno.* Matera was also used for *The Passion of the Christ* (2004).
48 Another filmmaker was fond of the black soil of volcanoes – Akira Kurosawa. To the point where the *sensei* staged entire battles with horses and soldiers on Mount Fuji – such as in the incredible 1985 epic *Ran.* Kurosawa's films also influenced *The Gospel.*
49 The castle on the beach.

filmed on location – the cell for the Baptist, for instance, is a set, and parts of the *Sermon On the Mount* sequence were filmed in the studio (in Incir De Paolis Studios in Roma).

The settings in *The Gospel According To Matthew* are simple, earthy, dusty, and mainly found rather than constructed sets. The settings are not only presumably cheap (as they had to be), they also suit the pared-down visual style (one of the reasons big budget, Hollywood epics look unreal is because of their over-elaborate sets, or, more accurately, the way that those sets are lit and filmed). Some of the settings are anachronistic, and clearly mediæval (and some have elements, such as doors, which are 19th or 20th century).

At the same time, the locations in *The Gospel According To Matthew* were also obviously art directed (props were added, but also taken away: many of the settings would have had to be cleared of material that wasn't analogous with the ancient world). The art department (Luigi Scaccianoce, Andrea Fantacci and Dante Ferretti) created a wholly convincing ancient look, that appeared lived-in, dusty, dirty, and real. It was a world of old stone walls, uneven and worn steps, mats and low tables. Everything looked ancient and well-used. (For some filmmakers, such as Ken Russell, that's a mistake when recreating a historical period on celluloid: those times and places would have often been relatively new: instead of a crumbling, mediæval castle, if a castle had been recently built, it should look new. That was the approach that Russell and his team took with *The Devils* (1971), for instance).

There is a wonderful sense of landscape in *The Gospel According To Matthew*; the film contains many panoramic shots of mountains, rocks, fields, the camera drifting slowly to the right, accompanied by the sound of wind, or birds (that particular sound of the breeze crops up in many films of Federico Fellini too – it seems to be a sound effect that many Italian filmmakers employed at the time. Maybe it was the only wind sound effect they had at Cinecittà).

MUSIC.

Besides keeping the imagery earthy and simple (like Ingmar Bergman and Andrei Tarkovsky), *The Gospel According To Matthew* employed highly emotive music: Johann Sebastian Bach,[50] 1685-1750 (used more than any other composer in *The Gospel*),[51] Sergei Prokofiev, Wolfgang Amadeus Mozart, Anton Webern, the Congolese *Missa Luba*, spirituals ("Sometimes I feel like a motherless child"), Russian revolutionary songs, and Blind Willie Johnson.

The pieces of music in *The Gospel According To Matthew* include:

• Johann Sebastian Bach: *St Matthew Passion* (1727).[52] Number 78: *Wir setzen uns mit Tränen nieder* and number 47: *Erbarme Dich*.

• Johann Sebastian Bach: C*oncerto For Violin and Oboe In D Minor* (BWV 1060). Number 2: *Adagio*.

• Johann Sebastian Bach: *Fugue (Ricercata), A 6,* Number 2 (arranged by Anton von Webern). From *Das Musikalische Opfer* (BWV 1079).

• Johann Sebastian Bach: *High Mass* (BWV 232). *Agnus Dei (Dona nobis pacem)*.

• Johann Sebastian Bach: *Concerto For Violin In E Major* (BWV 1042). Number 2: *Adagio*.

• Wolfgang Amadeus Mozart: *Maurerische Trauermusik In C Minor* (KV 477). *Quartet For Two Violins, Altviolin and Cello, Number 19 In C major.*

• Wolfgang Amadeus Mozart: *Dissonant-Quartet* (KV 465).

• Sergei Prokofiev: *Cantate 'Alexander Nevsky', Number 1.*

• *Gloria* from the *Missa Luba* (a Congolese work by Father Guido Haazen, 1958).

• Odetta: "Sometimes I feel like a motherless child".

• Blind Willie Johnson: 'Dark Was the Night, Cold Was the Ground' (1927).

---

50 Jean-Luc Godard commented that you can put Bach's music with anything and it works.

51 Orchestrated by Carlo Rustichelli.

52 The *St Matthew Passion* (1727/ 79), like the *B Minor Mass* and the *Goldberg Variations*, was composed in Leipzig, where Bach moved in 1723 (where he was the Cantor of St Thomas's Church).

The score of *The Gospel According To Matthew* is a library score, an off-the-shelf score. It is nearly all found music. As such, it also one of the finest found or bought scores in all cinema.

However, there is some incidental music composed and arranged specially for the movie (by Luis Bacalov), and some of the existing pieces were orchestrated by Carlo Rustichelli.

Billie Holiday is sometimes wrongly credited on the soundtrack of *The Gospel According To Matthew* – the confusion perhaps comes from the song "Sometimes I feel like a motherless child", which is sung by Odetta not Holiday. Odetta (1930-2008) was known as 'the Queen of American folk music' (as Martin Luther King called her).

"Sometimes I feel like a motherless child" is used a couple of times in *The Gospel According To Matthew* – over the Nativity scene with the three Kings, and during the Baptism. It is a Negro spiritual song that has been covered by everybody from Paul Robeson to Prince:

Sometimes I feel like a motherless child
Sometimes I feel like a motherless child
Sometimes I feel like a motherless child
Long way from my home

Sometimes I wish, I could fly
Like a bird up in the sky
Oh, sometimes I wish, I could fly
Fly like a bird up in the sky

Sometimes I wish, I could fly
Like a bird up in the sky
Little closer to home

Nina Power, in a 2013 article ("Subversive Pasolini"), commented:

This spiritual can be read in the film as a comment on Jesus of course, albeit with the roles reversed – the virgin birth makes him a "fatherless child" in a human, though not divine, sense – but as a comment on slavery and the diasporic nature of the lives of black people kidnapped into work, Odetta's refrain is stark, and the dissonance between the modernity of the recording and the historical legacy of slavery fused with the gospel is, to my mind, one of the most striking things about the film. (2013)

Some observers have confused Blind Willie Johnson with Leadbelly (the slide guitar perhaps adds to the confusion). Johnson (1897-1945) was a Texan bluesman best-known for 'Jesus Make Up My Dying Bed', 'John the Revelation', 'It's Nobody's Fault But Mine' and the song used here, 'Dark Was the Night, Cold Was the Ground'. Johnson has influenced and been covered by Bob Dylan, Led Zeppelin, Tom Waits, Eric Clapton and Fairport Convention.

Luis Bacalov was the music arranger of *The Gospel According To Matthew*, as well as the composer of some pieces (for Salomé's dance, for example, and some of the folky flute music). So although P.P. Pasolini is credited as the grand *auteur* of this masterpiece of 1964 (Pasolini's contribution to his movies tends to overshadow everyone else's efforts), Bacalov's input was vital – when we're not hearing famous classical music by Bach or Mozart, we are hearing Bacalov's music. (Also, Elsa Morante helped with selecting music – she discussed the music at length with her friend Pasolini, and her choices of J.S. Bach, W.A. Mozart, Leos Janácek, etc).

Italian-Argentian Luis Bacalov (1933-2017) was a veteran composer of numerous movies and TV shows. He scored movies such as *City of Women, Blood and Diamonds, The Sicilian Cross, Seduction, The Man Called Noon, Catch As Catch Can, Django, Sea of Dreams, The Postman, Mother Theresa, Woman On Top, The Love Letter, Polish Wedding* and *The Truce,* and many TV series and TV movies.

One of many great touches in *The Gospel According To Matthew* is the use of music within scenes (diegetic music), played by youths on flutes and pipes[53] (for

53 Tho' dubbed, of course.

instance, as the boats row out on the water, there's a piper playing). The boys who play music on the edge of a scene in Pier Paolo Pasolini's cinema might've stepped out of a painting by Michelangelo da Caravaggio.

Music is also used in *The Gospel According To Matthew* to enlarge scenes – folk music (often with choral vocals), is heard, not as accompaniment or mood music, but to suggest that people are singing off-screen. Like the spot sound effects (horses neighing, bird calls, sheep), they expand the scope of the picture.

The mix of music works brilliantly. The soundtrack of *The Gospel According To Matthew* is simply remarkable. Combined with the filmmakers' extraordinary feeling for faces (faces which are so individual and direct, faces which recall those painted by Hieronymous Bosch, Rembrandt van Rijn, Albrecht Dürer and Francisco de Goya), and the passionate music, the result is tremendous.

In fact, the first time you see *The Gospel According To Matthew* and *hear* the African spiritual and "Sometimes I feel like a motherless child" by Odetta in the early section of the movie, the effect is staggering. Because this sort of music had *never* been deployed in a Biblical movie before. You could say that the use of the music is an even more striking departure from the usual kind of Christian movie than many other elements in *The Gospel According To Matthew* – like portraying an angry Christ, or the use of extras and faces, or the desacralizing, *cinéma verité* approach.

I'm sure some people would've found the music difficult to accept, because up until that time, scoring accompanying Christ on screen was always reverential, slow, solemn music. And the opening credits play with Johann Sebastian Bach, which audiences would've found very suitable. Imagine, for example, that *The Gospel According To Matthew* had *opened* with "Sometimes I feel like a motherless child" (but there is an African spiritual song also in the opening credits).

In its radical deployment of music, particularly

laying modern popular music such as Willie Johnson on top of traditional, religious scenes, *The Gospel According To Matthew* reminds me of *Scorpio Rising* (1963), Kenneth Anger's cult movie which makes an instant impression with its combination of bikers, leather, homosexuality, hints of S/M, and the outrageous fusion of 1960s pop songs with religious movies. (It's like a flashy, American version of a Pasolini film).

Scorpio Rising is a classic cult movie in every sense: it displays anti-establishment and rebellious attitudes, acute fashion-consciousness, an exploration of subcultures (Hell's Angels and biker culture), and a terrific soundtrack (which includes Elvis Presley, the Randells, the Angels, Bobby Vinton, Ray Charles, the Crystals, Kris Jensen, Claudine Clark, Gene McDaniels, the Surfans and Little Peggy March). If you made a list of the elements that a cult movie should have, *Scorpio Rising* has them in spades. (Certainly the mix of pop music and visuals was influential: Martin Scorsese and David Lynch have been influenced by *Scorpio Rising*, for Andy Medhurst, in pictures such as *GoodFellas, Mean Streets* and *Blue Velvet*).[54]

Using Sergei Prokofiev's music for *Alexander Nevsky* (1938) inevitably gives the 'Massacre of the Innocents' scene in *The Gospel According To Matthew* a specific cultural context. That Pier Paolo Pasolini would cite the cinema of Sergei Eisenstein seems inevitable, Eisenstein being a firm favourite with critics and filmmakers, and *Alexander Nevsky* has inspired many subsequent filmmakers.[55] (*Alexander Nevsky* is ideologically problematic, tho', being a State-endorsed production, made at the height of the repressive regime of Joseph Stalin's administration; the same goes for much of Eisenstein's cinema and its alignment with Stalin and the Soviet authorities. Maybe the *Alexander Nevsky* music works ideologically, despite being a quote from another movie, because it grew out of the period of Communism when it had fascistic under-pinnings – and

54 A. Medhurst, in J. Romney, 1995, 75.
55 *Ivan theTerrible* is in there, too.

the act of King Herod ordering the death of children who threaten his rule is supremely fascistic).

EDITING.

Pier Paolo Pasolini said he did all his own editing, with the technical help of Nino Baragli. '[Baragli] is full of good sense, and he is a Roman, so he has a sense of irony, so I use him to keep a rein on some of my excesses' (PP, 139).

The editing in *The Gospel According To Matthew* is such an important ingredient to its overall success. Yes, this is true of many movies, but in a movie like *The Gospel According To Matthew,* film critics tend to always emphasize the visuals, and it's true that visually *The Gospel According To Matthew* is stunning. But it requires the editing of Nino Baragli to maintain the pacing, knowing when to move on and when to linger, when to introduce a montage of shorter shots, and when to stay on a lengthier shot.

But because editing is invisible, very few critics remark upon it. But it's editing that dictates how the images unfold, how one scene relates to the one coming next and the one before it, and how the story is told.

In spite of its occasional radical innovations, *The Gospel According To Matthew* is actually cut in the usual shot-reverse-shot manner. For instance, scenes often open with a simple establishing shot. Or that other favourite device of editors: a close-up of a symbolic object, before going wider and back to regular continuity editing.

There *are* more unconventional editing choices, such as jump cuts and rapidly repeated shots – which pop out more because of the context of a religious movie about Christ. When Christ walks on the water, for ex, Nino Baragli cuts in several crash zooms, from the Apostles' point-of-view. (The jump cuts that occur in *Breathless*, released four years earlier, for instance, seem more part of the piece, the genre (gangsters), and the loose, handheld approach. But *Breathless* made the old device of jump cuts seem startling again).

More radical than jump cuts in *The Gospel According To Matthew*, however, in terms of editing, are the montages – particularly the Sermon on the Mount montage, and the *Psalms* sequence. To chop up the speeches of Jesus Christ seems a more drastic departure from the conventional cinematic techniques of a religious movie.

Meanwhile, the two trials of Jesus do away with the expected close-ups, to cross the distance between the onlookers (such as the disciples Peter and Matthew), and the Saviour and the officials in the distance. Precisely when the agony that Christ is suffering is intensifying, the 1964 movie does something very unexpected and, for some viewers, probably very frustrating, by staying back (especially when for much of the time the camera has been right next to Jesus).[56]

ADAPTING THE *GOSPEL.*

There is plenty of material in the *Gospel* authored by St Matthew that was left out of the Italian, 1964 production – most of the parables, for instance: in the *Scriptures*, Jesus tells many parables. A movie, even one that's two hours and 22 minutes long, just doesn't have time for all of those stories (it's striking just how much Jesus is a storyteller). Some of the parables are simply summed up in a sentence or two. Not all of the quotations are from St Matthew's *Gospel*; some are from *Isaiah.*

Who was (St) Matthew? He was famously a tax collector, one of Jesus's disciples, who supposedly wrote the *Gospel* in 60-65 A.D. (some say later, 80-85 A.D.) – 30 or 50 years after the events, then. *The Gospel According To St Matthew* was the first *Gospel* to be written, and it opens the *New Testament.*

Pier Paolo Pasolini said he preferred *The Gospel of John*, but 'I thought Matthew's was the best for making a film' (P, 95). However, a TV mini-series of *The Gospel of John* was produced in 2003 (it was an attempt at a 'faithful' interpretation (impossible to achieve) of the

56 The device was employed in the 'trilogy of life' movies.

Bible).[57] A film based on *The Gospel of Luke* was produced in 1979. Matthew's *Gospel* has also been used for stage musicals (such as *Godspell*, which opened Off Broadway in 1971[58]).

The Gospel According To Matthew doesn't adapt all of St Matthew's *Gospel*, either: the opening chapter involves one of those long lists of 'so-and-so begat so-and-so':

> And Judas begat Phares and Zara of Thamar; and Phares begat Esrom; and Esrom begat Aram; (4) And Aram begat Aminadab; and Aminadab begat Naasson; and Naasson begat Salmon; (5) And Salmon begat Booz of Rachab; and Booz begat Obed of Ruth; and Obed begat Jesse; (6) And Jesse begat David the king; and David the king begat Solomon of her that had been the wife of Urias; (7) And Solomon begat Roboam; and Roboam begat Abia; and Abia begat Asa; (8) And Asa begat Josaphat; and Josaphat begat Joram; and Joram begat Ozias; (9) And Ozias begat Joatham; and Joatham begat Achaz; and Achaz begat Ezekias...

There's a lot of begetting in the *Bible*.

Scenes filmed but dropped from *Il Vangelo Secondo Matteo* included some of the miracles, and the possessed people, which were taken out 'because it was really horrible', Pasolini said (PP, 97).[59]

The Gospel According To Matthew follows the chronology of the *Gospel* of St Matthew pretty much, but not entirely. For instance, there are a few switches from the main story of Jesus and his ministry to John

57 Directed by a 73 year-old Brit (Philip Saville (d. 2016) – he had helmed the rival production of *Oedipus Rex*, in 1968), *The Gospel of John* was produced by Garth Drabinsky and Chris Chrisafis and executive producers Sandy Pearl, Joel B. Michaels, Myron Gottliel and Martin Katz for Think Film and Visual Bible, Inc, a Canadian company who had previously produced word-for-word versions of *The Gospel of Matthew* and the *Acts of the Apostles*. It was written by John Goldsmith, with Henry Ian Cusick as Jesus, and narrated by Christopher Plummer (who had been Oedipus in 1968).

58 *Godspell*'s book was by John-Michael Tebelak, with music and lyrics by Stephen Schwartz. *Godspell* was filmed in 1973, and opened on Broadway in 1976.

59 He used some students, Pier Paolo Pasolini recalled, 'but you could see they were students from the film school, the reality came out, it was awful, so I got rid of it' (PP, 97).

the Baptist in prison. The scenes with the Baptist are only brief, but they serve to remind the viewer of this parallel plot. In the scriptural text, the Baptist and his fate is important – Jesus discusses the Baptist at length, for instance. *The Gospel According To Matthew* brings together Jesus and the Baptist with the scenes on the beach, in front of the fortress of Aci Castello in Sicily: Jesus discusses the Baptist with his disciples, and also talks to the Baptist's followers. *The Gospel According To Matthew* also includes the scene where Jesus, hearing of John's death, leaves: 'When Jesus heard of it, he departed thence by ship into a desert place apart' (14: 13).

And notice how the fate of the Baptist stops Jesus in his tracks: up to this point, in movie terms, he has been a force of nature, a charismatic leader. As he contemplates the Baptist's fate, he is depicted sitting, dejected.

One character familiar from many film adaptations of the *Gospels* is featured only briefly in *The Gospel According To Matthew*: Mary Magdalene. In St Matthew's *Gospel,* the Magdalene is only mentioned three or so times, as one of the women who tended to Christ after the Crucifixion (she plays a larger role in the apocryphal *Gospels*).

The world of *The Gospel According To Matthew* is thoroughly patriarchal; the movie contains only two women with prominent roles: Mary and Salomé (Herodias has a minor role as Salomé's mom). Later film versions of the Christian story sometimes try to bump up the presence of women in key parts (the Magdalene, for instance), for obvious reasons. (However, in non-speaking roles, there are many women in *The Gospel According To Matthew*, as onlookers).

DIALOGUE.

The dialogue in *The Gospel According To Matthew* is straight out of the Evangelists[60] (in many ways,

---

60 The dialogue comes straight out of the *Gospel*, with Salomé's dance from the *Gospel* of Mark.

despite its modernist, New Wave techniques and loose, apparently improvisatory approach, *The Gospel According To Matthew* is a very traditional film). The dialogue is of course very famous, and there are numerous sequences in *The Gospel According To Matthew* which quote the well-known phrases of the *Bible*. You will recognize these phrases:

Man shall not live by bread alone. (4:4)

I will make you fishers of men. (4:19)

Blessed are the poor in spirit: for theirs is the kingdom of heaven. (5:3)

Love your enemies. (5:44)

Give us this day our daily bread. (6:11)

Lead us not into temptation, but deliver us from evil. (6:13)

Where your treasure is, there will your heart be also. (6:21)

Ye cannot serve God and mammon. (6:24)

Consider the lilies of the field, how they grow; they toil not, neither do they spin: And yet I say unto you, that even Solomon in all his glory was not arrayed like one of these. (6:28)

Seek ye first the kingdom of God, and his righteousness; and all these things shall be added unto you. (6:33)

Judge not, that ye not be judged. (7:1)

Ask, and it shall be given you; seek, and ye shall find; knock, and it shall be opened unto you. (7:7)

Strait is the gate, and narrow is the way, which leadeth unto life, and few there be that find it. (7:14)

By their fruit ye shall know them (7:20)

I can not to send peace, but a sword. (10:34)

He that is not with me is against me. (12:30)

Be of good cheer; it is I; be not afraid. (14:27)

O thou of little faith, wherefore didst thou doubt? (14:31)

Get thee behind me, Satan. (16:23)

Let him deny himself, and take up his cross, and follow me. (16:24)

Except ye be converted, and become as little children, ye shall not enter into the kingdom of heaven. (18:3)

Thou shalt love they neighbour as thyself. (19:16)

It is easier for a camel to go through the eye of a needle, than for a rich man to enter into the kingdom of God. (19:24)

My house shall be called the house of prayer; but ye have made it a den of thieves. (21;13)

Many are called, but few are chosen. (22:14)

Before the cock crow, thou shalt deny me thrice. (26:34)

My God, my God, why hast thou forsaken me? (27:46)

With so many wonderful speeches and phrases to include in the film, it's no wonder that at times Jesus in the 1964 movie speaks rapidly, in order to cover them all,[61] particularly during the Sermon on the Mount episode (which incorporates many of those famous phrases), and when he's talking to his disciples.

You'll notice, too, that the Virgin Mary does not speak in *Il Vangelo Secondo Matteo* – neither as a young woman, nor as an older woman (and neither does Herodias in the scenes with Salomé. Indeed, how many women have speaking parts in *The Gospel*? One or two speak when Christ returns home). And neither does Joseph speak. Indeed, a great deal of *Il Vangelo Secondo Matteo* is accomplished without dialogue. Of course, it's Christ who has the most dialogue in *Il Vangelo Secondo Matteo*, and sometimes he is rattling off many pages of the script (as in the Sermon on the Mount sequence). This is a Jesus who is never lost for words, and he can argue with the best of them (yet there are also segments where he is silent and withdrawn).

That comes from partly from the *Gospels*, which gives Jesus lengthy monologues, but little or nothing to Mary or Joseph (one of the challenges that Jean-Luc Godard set himself when he tackled the Christian story in his 1985 movie *Hail Mary* was to imagine what Mary and Joseph would have said to each other).[62]

The sound teams of Pier Paolo Pasolini's movies

---

61 As you have to with William Shakespeare's plays, if you want to include all of the lines.

62 Myriem Roussel watched *The Gospel According To Matthew* in preparation for playing the Virgin in *Hail Mary* in 1985, at Godard's behest, and also a film Godard loved, *The Passion of Joan of Arc*.

preferred to dub the dialogue of the actors, rather than use direct sound (common practice in Italian cinema, and in nearly all of Pasolini's movies). Although it wasn't as 'naturalistic' as synchronized sound, it could be more 'realistic'. For Pasolini, dubbing 'enriches a character; it is part of my taste for pastiche; it raises a character out of the zone of naturalism' (PP, 39). It can be off-putting at first (when you can see that the extras in *The Gospel* are clearly mouthing different dialogue), but, as with the work of Federico Fellini, one soon gets used to it.

On set, the sound of the takes in *The Gospel According To Matthew* would have included Pier Paolo Pasolini directing the actors, sometimes beat for beat. You can tell in some scenes that the actors, many of whom had never appeared in front of a camera before, are being cued and guided by the director. As in the films of Federico Fellini, Pasolini would direct the actors from near to the camera, asking them to move over there, or look this way. Directors had been doing that since the origins of cinema, and all through the silent movie era.

The sound in *The Gospel According To Matthew* (by Mario Del Pozzo and Fausto Ancillai), skilfully employs off-screen sound to enlarge the cinematic space:[63] horses, sheep, goats, dogs, birds (swifts and swallows), cockerel's cries (for dawn scenes), and the sound of the breeze and high wind. The spot sound effects are judiciously employed: horses, for instance, in the scenes in King Herod's palace (the horses are nearby), but suggesting wealth and military power. Loud gale noises for the forty days in the desert. Birdsong (with swifts prominent) over many of the early scenes of Mary and Joseph (as if the parents are part of the natural order of things, and as if Jesus's early life took place in a kind of Paradise or Eden). The quality of the soundtrack, however, can be a little rough: you can hear the scratches on the vinyl records used for the music, for instance (but olde schoole musos might find that even

---

[63] And more imaginatively than in some of Pier Paolo Pasolini's later films, where the sound design can be pedestrian.

that enhances the piece).

FACES.

The Gospel According To Matthew is a film of faces: it's one of the great films of faces in cinema – the wizened, wrinkled faces of the peasants and onlookers; the sweet, pure lines of the young Virgin Mary, straight out of the Renaissance art of Sandro Botticelli or Fra Filippo Lippi; the youthful, beguiling charm of Salomé; the haunting eyes of the beautiful, androgynous archangel Gabriel; Joseph's bewildered, tender expression; the aged Madonna's agony; the craggy, grizzled faces of the older disciples; the cute faces of grinning children; the haunted look of the ill and the disabled; and of course Jesus's intensity and poetry.

The filmmakers filmed the expressive faces using simple close-ups, often with a long lens, lingering on them as they stood still and looked silently at the scenes unfolding before them. In a lesser director, these static, simple shots of Italian peasants and extras might appear dull; but in the hands of this group of filmmakers, they are full of mystery, and so moving.

There is a huge variety of human life portrayed in *The Gospel According To Matthew*, from babies, through children and youths, to older folk. The 1964 movie is particularly strong on aged men and women, faces with lifetimes of experience etched into them. And just as important are the groups of children which the production surrounds Jesus with many times. It's a reminder of how life is lived out on the streets and in the open in warmer climes, in Mediterranean and Middle Eastern countries. It's a totally different kind of society from Northern communities, where everyone scurries home as soon as possible, and the place's dead after four or five p.m.

The extras and non-professionals are not used in a condescending fashion in *The Gospel According To Matthew*, but are filmed with a deep sense of empathy and respect. The close-ups of extras take up a far larger proportion of screen time than one would expect from many another filmmaker (and for a story which has so many events to pack in): it's as if the filmmakers assumed that the audience would have a pretty good idea about what was going on from moment to moment, because each event in the *Scriptures* was so well-known. Thus, the filmmakers spend as much time showing the *reactions* of onlookers to what Christ and his disciples are doing, rather than the events themselves (and if you want to show that something is amazing, scary, funny or whatever, the easiest option is to cut to observers reacting appropriately).

The typical approach to each scene in *The Gospel According To Matthew* is a *tableau* form – editorially as well as visually. That is, the scene frequently begins with a montage of close-ups of extras before moving into the dramatic or narrative segment of the scene. The *tableau* approach derives in part from painting, of course. The scenes are often deliberately (and stubbornly) *static*: the filmmakers have arranged the extras and lead actors in *tableaux*, flat spaces of figures against backgrounds. The lengthy close-ups of the actors and extras are filmed with either one close-up cut in after another, or with the camera wandering from face to face (sometimes in a deliberately loose fashion – shots which many another producer and director would reject from the rushes).

It's as if the film is taking its time, and is looking at everyone involved in the scene before beginning the dramatic action. And it's as if the landscape of this particular movie is the human face as well as the desert or the mountains or the dusty towns and villages of Palestine and Israel.

And no one is saying anything in these close-ups of extras and actors, and often the montages have no music. *The Gospel According To Matthew* exists in a special space cinematically, very different from your average movie. For Pasolini, faces were enough, and the act of photographing a face was enough in a movie:

...a tree photographed is poetic, a human face

photographed is poetic because physicity is poetic in itself, because it is an apparition, because it is full of mystery, because it is full of ambiguity, because it is full of polyvalent meaning, because even a tree is a sign of a linguistic system. But who talks through a tree? God, or reality itself. Therefore the tree as a sign puts us in communication with a mysterious speaker.

Pier Paolo Pasolini's cinema was not one of long takes. Pasolini associated the long take with Neorealism and naturalness, which he hated. He did not like having people acting out everyday interchanges in lengthy takes. Thus, Pasolini did not use master shots of a whole scene, but had each actor say their piece to the camera. Pasolini's is thus a montage cinema, a poetic heap of broken images, rather than a chain of Wellesian sequence shots. One supposes that many of the scenes were filmed in one or two takes.

MULTITUDES.

In the *Bible*, there are many multitudes – not just crowds, but always 'multitudes' (such as on the shore, listening to Jesus, whole multitudes stood on the shore (*Matthew*, 13:1)). If you're a god, maybe you can speak to thousands of people at the same time (maybe they all heard Jesus speaking inside their minds). In realistic situations, it's more difficult, if Jesus was a man with a regular human voice – and some filmmakers have explored how to portray that.

In *The Gospel According To Matthew*, the solution is very simple: there are no casts of thousands listening to sermons or parables (as in many Hollywood versions). There are hundreds of extras, of course, but in most of the scenes where Christ is addressing a crowd, the crowd is not huge. In the loaves and fishes episode, for instance, there is no multitude of five thousand sitting on the grass.

And when it was evening, his disciples came to him, saying, This is a desert place, and the time is now past; send the multitude away, that they may go into the villages, and buy themselves victuals. But Jesus said unto them, They need not depart; give ye them to eat. And they say unto him, We have here but five loaves, and two fishes. He said, Bring them hither to me. And he commanded the multitude to sit down on the grass, and took the five loaves, and the two fishes, and looking up to heaven, he blessed, and brake, and gave the loaves to his disciples, and the disciples to the multitude. And they did all eat, and were filled: and they took up of the fragments that remained twelve baskets full. And they that had eaten were about five thousand men, beside women and children. (14: 15-21)

However, in some of the last scenes where Christ is preaching, the crowds have become very large: the shots are composed like Renaissance paintings, and make use of verticality and perspective, for the simple reason that when you have a large crowd you either get up high to see them from above (the most extreme solution being the famous images in *Intolerance* from the special crane built to film the Gates of Babylon), or you range them across slopes or tiers or bleachers.

Thus, in some images, the filmmakers and the assistant directors (Maurizio Lucidi, Paolo Schneider and Elsa Morante) spend some time arranging the extras across hillsides, with the camera lower down, looking up at them. Meanwhile, Christ is way off in the distance, preaching his heart out, and everybody listens quietly.

STAGING *THE GOSPEL*.

The staging of scenes and the blocking of actors in *The Gospel According To Matthew* often uses simple vertical symmetry: Christ is often in the middle of the frame, with people grouped around him. The camera is often below shoulder level, looking up at Jesus. And *The Gospel According To Matthew* employs the traditional set-up of Jesus standing separate from his followers – either walking ahead of them, or turning to address them. In this treatment of the life of Christ, the Saviour is always shown walking ahead of his disciples, always in the lead, never lagging behind them. This is a dynamic Jesus, striding ahead, and often addressing his followers over his shoulder (so that they have to struggle to keep up).

The tactic is used time and again in *The Gospel According To Matthew*, and it gives the religious *Scriptures* a real feeling of urgency. It's as if Jesus has thought of what he's going to say right at that moment, and doesn't wait to stop and talk to his disciples in a formal fashion, so that they can all hear him (or debate the issues). Instead, he calls over his shoulder, looking past the camera. It really is as if, as some commentators have noted, that the cameras were right there, capturing the events as they occurred, and followed Jesus as he rattles off parables and psalms and pithy phrases.

The problem is, the middle section of the *Gospel* text of Matthew (and the other *Gospels*), can be interpreted *dramatically* as a series of conversations: Jesus talks... his disciples listen... Putting Jesus in motion like this is a dynamic motif that activates the whole movie.

Nobody bursts into song, and nobody (except Salomé) dances, but much of *The Gospel According To Matthew* is actually staged and blocked like a musical movie. The minimal dialogue, the *tableau* staging, the central characters surrounded by crowds, it looks like a stage musical. (That *Jesus Christ Superstar* turned up seven or so years later seems inevitable. *Jesus Christ Superstar* opened in Gotham on Oct 12, 1971, and was controversial, with demonstrations outside the Mark Hellinger Theater).

There are millions of ways of staging the Christian story: one absolutely key decision, as far as the visual approach went, was to keep Jesus in motion in many scenes. That automatically separates *The Gospel According To Matthew* not only from previous interpretations of the Christian story, but also from the history of art. It's as if the filmmakers decided to celebrate one of the things that cinema can do, often more compellingly than painting or sculpture: show people in motion.

✛

Pier Paolo Pasolini and the team didn't construct the 1964 film as a conventional piece of drama, with the components of a traditional film script: rising action, cause and effect, sub-plots, foreshadowing, pay-offs, motivations, back-story and the like. Instead, the scenes from Matthew's *Gospel* are portrayed pretty much as they appear in the text; in other words, there are no conventional transitions between scenes or sequences, and characters disappear and reappear in a non-dramatic fashion.

There is some back-story, but it's largely scriptural – that is, it comes from references to earlier events, such as those referenced in the *New Testament* (often by Jesus). There is some foreshadowing, of course: Jesus in the latter part of the film points out those who will betray him, and those who will deny him. And there are some minor sub-plots, though they are not the conventional ones: the fates of Judas and Peter, for instance, following Christ's capture, are kind of sub-plots, but not really, as they are functions of the central plot.

However, altho' the filmmakers relied on the audience knowing the story very well and in detail, they *did* construct a conventional film script from the *Gospels*. You can't carry the *Bible* onto the set and just start shooting. Scenes need to be staged, shots planned, actors rehearsed, etc.

The story of Christ in the *Gospels* is for some people *the* story, it's the Ultimate Story. For J.R.R. Tolkien, for instance, it was the ultimate story, and it was true, and every other story was in imitation, a pale reflection of the original story.

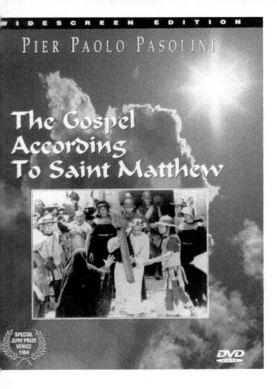

The Gospel According To Matthew (1964).
This page and over.

Making The Gospel According To Matthew.
This page and over.

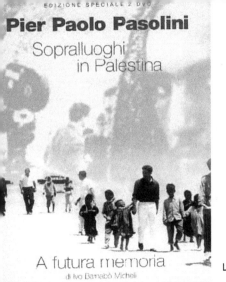

EDIZIONE SPECIALE 2 DVD

Pier Paolo Pasolini

Sopralluoghi
in Palestina

A futura memoria
di Ivo Barnabò Micheli

DVD

RHV

Location Hunting In Palestine(1965).

2

SCENES IN *THE GOSPEL ACCORDING TO MATTHEW*

THE BEGINNING.

'In the Beginning was... the Movie'. Many Biblical epics and sword and sandal flicks of this period opened with a prologue, or captions, or a voiceover (from Orson Welles, say, or Chuck Heston), to set the scene, to act as a bridge between the audience coming into the theatre, settling down in their seats, and the story itself. Sometimes maps would be used, or a montage of shots (taken from later scenes in the movie), to illustrate the historical context (and also to act as teasers for what's coming later). Filmmakers have employed every sort of opening to an ancient world movie, to make the transition from the audience sitting in an auditorium to immersing themselves in the movie.

In *The Gospel According To Matthew*, the lengthy credits do that, to a degree. The usual black-lettering-on-white titles of a Pier Paolo Pasolini movie have Johann Sebastian Bach's sublime music played over them, plus an African spiritual. In those days, movies often had the major production and cast credits at the beginning, so that at the end, there is simply the title card: 'FINE'. Great – now we can get a drink!

These days, it's the other way around: on many North American movies (and American-financed foreign movies), there's just the studio logo[1] followed by the title card, and the story starts. Meanwhile, the credits at the end run on *forever* (until the Last Judgement, it seems, when the Archangel Michael materializes in a flurry of angels' wings and slices the celluloid with a giant sword).

The Gospel According To Matthew departs from your typical historical or Biblical movie from the beginning: because after the credits, there is no prologue, no scene-setting, no solemn voiceover intoning, 'Two thousand years ago, in the land of Galilee…' etcetera.

Instead, the 1964 movie cuts directly to a medium shot of the Virgin Mary, which runs for twelve feet. The movie assumes – rightly – that the audience knows the story. It's some time b4 any words are spoken. When they are, they come from an Angel: 'Joseph, fear not to take Mary as your wife…' (That the first words are those of God, via an archangel, gives us a hint of how this movie is going to depart from convention. There's no dialogue, in fact, between Mary and Joseph at all; not in this scene, nor in any subsequent scene. They are together, but their relationship is one of quiet, sombre companionship).

But the filmmaking in *The Gospel According To Matthew* is so lyrical and descriptive, it doesn't need any dialogue or voiceover to explain anything. And of course, dialogue isn't necessary: silent cinema took on the Christ story without dialogue, in films such as *Intolerance* and *King of Kings*.

THE OPENING SCENE.

There is little exposition, little dialogue describing to the audience what is going on in *Il Vangelo Secondo Matteo*. The filmmakers assume (rightly) that the audience knows the famous story, one of the central legends/ myths/ tales of Western civilization. So they strip away all the pomp and padding which classical Hollywood narration uses. There are many moments of

---

1 Or several companies.

silence: the film opens so magically with the young Mary (Margherita Caruso) and the older Joseph (played by lawyer Marcello Morante, brother of Pasolini's friend Elsa Morante) staring at each other. There is a cut to Joseph, watching in silence; a cut to Mary, staring back at him. It is hypnotic, deep, resonant.

Il Vangelo Secondo Matteo has one of great opening sequences in all cinema: a cut to the woman, then a cut to the man. No elaborate opening title sequence, no painted captions, no animated letters sliding across the screen, just the simple mechanics of cinema: shot/ reverse shot. No establishing shots of the Holy Land, either, no cuts from vistas of hills to villages and then to Mary's home. No – it's straight into Mary in close-up.

The filmmakers decided not to use explanations, exposition, or inter-titles. The story was already very well-known. However, voiceover is used in *The Gospel According To Matthew* – and it is no less than voice of God (that is, the quotes from the *Bible* use God's own speech (and when Jesus speaks, the use of the subjective, the 'I', is also God's).[2] The narration is used sparingly, however – just enough to fill the audience on the background (but you don't *really* need the voice-over).

But the filmmakers were right in this respect: when Mary stands beside Joseph and a donkey outside their home, there is no need to explain to the viewer in dialogue or captions that this is the beginning of the flight into Egypt (well, the Angel has told Joseph in the previous scene that he must take his family to Egypt).

OPENING SCENE: SHOT-BY-SHOT BREAKDOWN.

The opening sequence of *The Gospel According To Matthew* runs like this:

Titles: single title, of the film, with black letters on white (as usual in Pier Paolo Pasolini's cinema).

2 The narrator was likely played by Francesco Leonetti. There is a second voice, too.

Producer Alfredo Bini has a credit as 'Alfredo Bini presents' (Bini and Pasolini receive the largest size names in the credits, with the next in the hierarchy being the DP, Tonino Delli Colli).

Shot 1: fade up out of black to a C.U. of the Virgin Mary, standing in front of a run-down stone arch (a reference of course to Renaissance painting).[3] Near-silence. 8 seconds. (This is her home).

Shot 2: C.U. of Joseph. 4 secs.

Shot 3: as shot 1. Mary looks down meekly. 4 secs.

Shot 4: as shot 2. Joseph moves slightly. 8 secs.

Shot 5: M.S. of Mary, fully pregnant,[4] shot against the arch. 6 secs.

Shot 6: M.S. Joseph; he walks away, down some steps (which lead out of the courtyard of the house); the camera tracks to the left. 11 secs.

Shot 7: L.S. The Virgin Mary walking out of her dwelling, seen from the direction of Joseph. Quiet, religious singing is heard, and birdsong. Her relations, some older women and a child,[5] come to the doorway behind her. 21 secs.

Shot 8: Joseph walking away from the camera, into the distance, on a rocky road. 8 secs.

Shot 9: M.C.U. on Mary looking after him. 8 secs.

Shot 10: L.S. Joseph on the road, same view, but seen slightly closer in, using a long lens. 8 secs.

Shot 11: C.U. of Mary; she looks down pensively. 8 secs.

Shot 12: the next scene, in a new location. Joseph arrives at a hill town; a handheld shot, starting on Joseph's head in the foreground; he walks away from the camera. 3 secs. (Pier Paolo Pasolini often put actors really close to the camera, and he does so many times in *The Gospel According To Matthew*).

Shot 13: L.S., handheld, panning around the town,

3 In particular the flattened perspectives of the Early Italian Renaissance. The Madonna is the Church symbolically.

4 A painterly reference here to the pregnant Madonna might be the *Madonna del Parto* by Piero della Francesca.

5 Putting a baby in the scene is simple but effective foreshadowing.

showing people, donkeys, children playing. The first loud sounds in the film. The sounds are mixed loud because their disappearance announces the arrival of the Angel. (No blasts of arc lights, clouds of smoke, wind machines, and trilling choirs to evoke the Angel's introduction. The opposite – the sound dips out).

Shot 14: M.S. Joseph, looking at the scene; he rests on the ground, leaning his head on his hands by a wall.

Shot 15: children playing.

Shot 16: M.S. as shot 14, on Joseph.

Shot 17: as shot 15.

Shot 18: C.U. of Joseph asleep. Sound of the children playing stops abruptly, Joseph wakes, looks up, at:

Shot 19: L.S. of an Angel, in a white dress, with long hair and an intense expression.[6]

Shot 20: the Angel in C.U. The Angel[7] says the first words of the film (the first words are thus divine in origin): 'Joseph, fear not to take Mary as your wife...'

Shot 21: C.U. of Joseph, as the Angel tells him to go back to the Virgin.

Shot 22: L.S. zoom towards Mary's village, with African spiritual music suddenly heard (the burst of music accompanies the first aggressive camera movement in the movie, emphasizing the sudden eruption of spiritual energy).

Shot 23: L.S. Joseph on the road, with a voiceover from the *Gospel*: 'the virgin shall be with child'.

Shot 24: M.S., handheld, Joseph, from behind, on the road.

Shot 25: Mary coming out of her house (similar to shot 7).[8]

Shot 26: C.U. Mary.

Shot 27: M.S. Joseph entering the courtyard (similar to shot 6).

Shot 28: as shot 26. Mary smiles.

---

6 Martin Scorsese said of the actor chosen to play the Archangel Gabriel, Rossana Di Rocco: her 'face is so extraordinary, like Botticelli' (1990, 143)

7 Rocco was dubbed by Emanuela Rossi.

8 These scenes would've been filmed on the same day.

Shot 29: C.U. Joseph; he smiles; no sound in these scenes.

Shot 30: as shot 26; Mary still smiling.

✢

Shot 31: the next scene, showing a busy town by day. (This is another marvellous scene, full of details. It's also one of the finest scenes in Pier Paolo Pasolini's cinema of a bustling market[9] – they were a fundamental element of the 'trilogy of life' pictures, for instance. The film re-uses this scene later. You can spot some of Danilo Donati's famous hats and helmets in this scene).

✢

We are now about three and a half minutes into the 1964 film.

One sees how Pier Paolo Pasolini and the team build up the narrative of the 1964 film, which opens with simple, static, lengthy (8-second) shots of two people looking at each other, but saying nothing. Dialogue is completely superfluous here, in such evocative shots. Of Joseph meeting Mary, in that stunning opening sequence, Pasolini said he was trying to exaggerate the disproportion between the two human beings and their simple, earthy innocence, and the divine powers infusing them. He was intensifying the

> spiritual element there is in all innocence: any innocent young girl is full of mystery, all I tried to do was to multiply a thousandfold the mystery in this young girl. (PP, 94)

Like other filmmakers, Pier Paolo Pasolini realized that a single image taken from a film could assume a 'huge importance' (PP, 111). (It's fitting, too, that this film, probably the greatest film of the Christian story,[10] should open with a close-up of the Virgin Mary's face).

The list of shots from the opening sequence also reminds us of the significance of cinema's invisible but incredibly important element: *editing*. Critics have

9 The inspiration for this scene partly comes from Pier Paolo Pasolini's visit to Palestine the year before.
10 Certainly in the opinion of many viewers.

often remarked on Pier Paolo Pasolini's visual style, which's flamboyant and self-conscious (as with his contemporaries Luchino Visconti and Federico Fellini). But critics have seldom drawn attention to the cutting in Pasolini's cinema (but critics hardly ever talk about editing. Partly because they have no idea what it is or how it works). And cutting is of course one of Pasolini's signature ingredients: Pasolini's movies are edited in the European New Wave manner. Very Godardian. (The *rhythms* of the scene, for instance, the pattern of shots, would come very much from editor Nino Baragli).

In *The Religious Film*, Pamela Grace describes the scene thus:

> The film presents one of the most important events
> in the New Testament narrative – the Incarnation –
> in entirely human terms, and specifically as a sexual
> dilemma. (106)

ADAPTING THE *BIBLE*.

The Gospel According To Matthew does not add many new scenes to the story in the *Bible*, and does not introduce sub-plots, or characters which do not appear in the *Gospel* (which some religious films do). The basic spine of the *Gospel* is there, as are most of the characters. However, the movie *does* include all sorts of additions to the original *Scriptures*, which's inevitable in an adaptation of this kind. Even the most 'faithful' cinematic adaptation of a written text (impossible in itself, theoretically as well as practically), will involve additions to the text (and any adaptation or appropriation will alter the text anyway).

Thus, although *The Gospel According To Matthew* aims to be a 'faithful' and (reverential) interpretation of *The Gospel of St Matthew* in the *Bible*, it has to add numerous elements – from details such as costumes and hair and make-up (what did these people actually *look like*? is a question every filmmaker – or painter – has to ask) – to questions such as, how did they relate to each other? – to big questions such as: how to depict the miracles? How to illustrate the Agony in the Garden?

Take the opening sequence of *The Gospel According To Matthew*, which I discussed above. The text of the *Gospel of St Matthew* says very little about how Mary and Joseph got together, or how they were with each other, what they said, what they did, their attitudes, their lifestyle, etc:

> Now the birth of Jesus Christ was on this wise: When as his mother Mary was espoused to Joseph, before they came together, she was found with child of the Holy Ghost. Then Joseph her husband, being a just man, and not willing to make her a publick example, was minded to put her away privily. But while he thought on these things, behold, the angel of the Lord appeared unto him in a dream, saying, Joseph, thou son of David, fear not to take unto thee Mary thy wife: for that which is conceived in her is of the Holy Ghost. And she shall bring forth a son, and thou shalt call his name JESUS: for he shall save his people from their sins. Now all this was done, that it might be fulfilled which was spoken of the Lord by the prophet, saying,
>
> Behold, a virgin shall be with child, and shall bring forth a son, and they shall call his name Emmanuel, which being interpreted is, God with us.
>
> Then Joseph being raised from sleep did as the angel of the Lord had bidden him, and took unto him his wife: And knew her not till she had brought forth her firstborn son: and he called his name JESUS. (1: 18-25)

A movie adaptation, in translating this written text to the screen, has to answer 100s of questions, from casting to costume to lighting to setting to dialogue, etc (as well as many economic issues). The solutions that Alfredo Bini, Pier Paolo Pasolini and the team came up with seem so right and 'obvious' to us now, because they are presented with such clarity and poetry and skill (and we haven't seen the tests for costumes, make-up, etc, for instance, or the rehearsals, or the numerous discussions and meetings that occur in pre-production on any movie. It was in pre-production that *The Gospel*

According To Matthew was really made).

It must have been tempting to include material from the other *Gospels* (or from the apocryphal *Gospels*), which many other versions of the life of Christ have done (only a few have stuck to a single *Gospel*).

In other words: the *Bible* had to be *adapted*, and a *script* had to be written. The filmmakers couldn't simply chuck the *Bible* at the actors and say, 'there you go'.

THE VIRGIN MARY.

The viewpoint in the early scenes is often with the Virgin Mary. For instance, there are long cuts between Mary looking at Joseph as he walks away from her house, from her point-of-view. When Mary and Joseph leave for Egypt, there are mobile point-of-view shots as Mary looks back her home (little more than a cave in a hillside), where she has been her happiest.

Mary's childhood home is brought back in a scene where Jesus and his followers pass by – this comes after the scene where Jesus has rejected his mother. The same angles are selected – of the stony road, and the house: the aged Mary walks to the wall to watch her son pass, just as she had done b4, looking at Joseph. (This is great filmmaking – an example of how carefully the screenplay was worked out).

Notice that the Madonna does not speak in *The Gospel According To Matthew*. That partly allows the audience to fill in everything else, if they want to. It's the same with Joseph. Similarly, the way that Margherita Caruso plays Mary allows the viewer to add their own interpretations. Most film adaptations of the *Bible* add dialogue for Mary; it's too irresistible. Not this movie: there isn't speech for Mary in the *Gospel* of Matthew, so there isn't in the film.

THE NATIVITY.

The Nativity is a marvellous sequence in *The Gospel According To Matthew*, in which the plaintive, lulling blues song "Sometimes I feel like a motherless child" by Odetta is played throughout, with the local sound soon faded down. This is images plus music, an ideal (and idealized) state of cinema. The whole thing's staged in Christmas greetings card style (by way of thousands of Italian Renaissance paintings and sculptures), as a series of static *tableaux:* the three Kings[11] approach from above, from a hillside (a series of caves cut into the hill serve as their home); there is a crowd of smiling people, including many children wriggling about, surrounding the principals; they kneel before Mary and her child; Mary offers her baby to one of the Magi, who holds him up. (The previous scene depicted the wise men visiting King Herod in Jerusalem, with some dialogue about the birth of the Messiah, but omitted much of their journey, and of course that magical, shining star.)

> And when they were come into the house, they saw the young child with Mary his mother, and fell down, and worshipped him: and when they had opened their treasures, they presented unto him gifts; gold, and frankincense, and myrrh. (2: 11)

The Nativity scene, like so much in *The Gospel According To Matthew*, is deceptively simple. It employs a classical editing pattern, for instance, with long shots mixed with medium shots, and with the shots of Mary getting successively larger. The *joy* of the sequence is tangible, and Margherita Caruso as Mary, when she smiles, is very beautiful. Joy, joy, joy.

Though directed by a non-believer, a Marxist, and a radical poet, the Nativity nevertheless captures this moment of sheer ecstasy in the Christian story: it is perhaps the happiest moment in the whole of the *Gospels*. After all, when the three Kings visit the Christ Child in traditional theology, it is called the Epiphany, it is the moment when Christ's divinity is revealed to all (January 6th = Twelfth Night).

The flight into Egypt is a sweet interlude, depicting the happy family life of the young Jesus. There are

11 The scenes with the Kings play without dialogue. (The Kings don't include a black actor for Caspar).

charming scenes where Jesus is seen playing, and running towards Joseph's arms, while Mary looking on indulgently (this is among the last times we see the young Mary).

THE MASSACRE OF THE INNOCENTS.

The massacre of the innocents is from *Matthew* 2: 16-18:

> Then Herod, when he saw that he was mocked of the wise men, was exceeding wroth, and sent forth, and slew all the children that were in Bethlehem, and in all the coasts thereof, from two years old and under, according to the time which he had diligently inquired of the wise men. Then was fulfilled that which was spoken by Jeremy the prophet, saying,
>
> In Rama was there a voice heard, lamentation, and weeping, and great mourning, Rachel[12] weeping for her children, and would not be comforted, because they are not.

The sequence was shot with long lenses, mobile camerawork and many cuts, showing the babies being thrown around like dolls. The long shots are intercut with medium close-ups of dead children (but not *too* close, and the amount of blood and injury is held back. Blood and gore isn't needed here to evoke this obscene act of killing children). 'One of the most horrific scenes in cinema', remarked Howard Hughes in *Cinema Italiano* (74).

Staged on a hillside in daylight,[13] the massacre was cut to music: but before the music comes in and the massacre begins, there are moments of stasis, the calm before the storm: frontal close-ups of the soldiers[14] standing in a row nearby and sitting on their horses awaiting the signal to attack (these are the Pasolinian *ragazzi*, the working class guys from *Accattone* who're

---

12 The film, in voiceover, references Rachel.
13 A night scene might be more dramatic, but logistically would be much tougher.
14 They might've stepped out of a Caravaggio or Piero painting, with their felt caps and helmets.

once again the tools of dictators).[15]

When the opening strains of the *Alexander Nevsky* cue by Sergei Prokofiev are heard, the soldiers rush forward, coming upon the people from above and below; the movie employs a rapid montage to convey the chaos and agony of the genocide, the biggest scene of bloodshed in the film.

The Massacre of the Innocents scene captures the *senselessness* and *pointlessness* of such an act of violence (and notice, too, that all of the men folk are mysteriously absent from the village: it is women and children only, unable to defend themselves against King Herod's butchers. It's a dramatic choice, presumably made to enhance the obscenity of the scene. In reality, surely many fathers, brothers and uncles would be prepared to defend their relatives and children?).

THE DEATH OF HEROD.

Before the Nativity, King Herod I (Amerigo Bevilacqua) is depicted with his advisers, meeting the Three Kings. He is not given much characterization, other than a pleasant, officious demeanour; he might be a petty criminal elevated by chance to the stature of the King (there are only subtle hints at Herod's anxiety over the prophecy, and what he'll do to nix it[16]). The scene sets up the Massacre of the Innocents, and what seems to be divine justice (in movie terms), when it cuts back afterwards, to show the demise of the ruler.

In the *Bible*, the death of King Herod takes up a single sentence: 'But when Herod was dead' (2: 19). The 1964 movie rightly expanded that into a longer sequence, where Herod is writhing about on his bed, surrounded by courtiers, in his death throes (no one dares to come near or comfort him). Only when he's near gone do the old women move forward to tend to him. Yes – because the audience needs to see Herod dying in a longer sequence, because this guy ordered one of the

15 This is not a job a professional soldier would relish, is it? Killing defenceless babies? A side-story might explore some soldiers rebelling.
16 However, notice the cut to Herod's soldiers waiting in a courtyard, foreshadowing the massacre.

vilest acts in the Christian story. If there is a God – and in this movie there is – Herod should rot in Hell for eternity.

THE BAPTISM.

The Baptism takes place in a verdant valley with a shallow river running over rocks, right out of a picture book *Bible*.[17] Much of the scene is traditional, and very similar to previous renditions in cinema (including Hollywood versions). The Baptist (Mario Socrate, dubbed by Pino Locchi) is the usual grizzled firebrand,[18] yelling at the Pharisees and Sadducees (who just happen to be passing by).

> Then cometh Jesus from Galilee to Jordan unto
> John, to be baptized of him. But John forbad him,
> saying, I have need to be baptized of thee, and
> comest thou to me? And Jesus answering said unto
> him, Suffer it to be so now: for thus it becometh us
> to fulfil all righteousness. Then he suffered him.
> And Jesus, when he was baptized, went up straight-
> way out of the water: and, lo, the heavens were
> opened unto him, and he saw the Spirit of God
> descending like a dove, and lighting upon him:
> And lo a voice from heaven, saying, This is my
> beloved Son, in whom I am well pleased. (3: 13-17)

John the Baptist is depicted baptizing a few people before Jesus arrives, as in most other Christ movies, standing next to a pool in the middle of the river (the participants are an old woman, a younger woman and a child: they look up at the Heavens after they're baptized, as we all do).

This is the first introduction of the adult Jesus,[19] and our first look at Enrique Irazoqui, the non-actor chosen to play this very challenging role: the sound dips out; there's a close-up (over a dissolve) of Irazoqui walking towards the camera (which tracks backwards, as

17 But not like the real River Jordan which, as the *Location Hunting In Palestine* documentary showed, was actually a small, modest river.
18 We also meet some of the future disciples of Christ, who're the Baptist's assistants.
19 There is no indication of the intervening years, then: the last time we saw Christ, he was a young boy.

THE GOSPEL ACCORDING TO MATTHEW ✝ 220

if deferentially – nay, as if reverentially), looking offscreen at the Baptist. A slow, awed music cue fades up (here, music is providing the emotional context, making this a stunning and moving moment in *The Gospel According To Matthew*). The film cuts to the Baptist's dazed reaction.

This is one of the great close-ups in all of cinema.

Notice that the film simply cuts to a big close-up shot of Jesus, rather than, say, to images like feet walking, or the people on either side looking at him, which would build up the reveal of Christ (close-ups of feet occur a little later, with the introduction of Satan).

There's no need for anything fancy here, so a cut to a close-up does the job, with the change in the soundtrack cueing the new moment. Cutting to silence also occurred when the Angel appeared. (So, again, no choirs welling up, no spotlights, no halo effects, no swathes of dry ice).

The switching to a different soundscape is a much-used technique to shift the narration into a different mode: the use of silence then the slow orchestral music helps to cue the audience into the proper response, as does John's startled and respectful reaction. If you want to demonstrate that someone is powerful, or scary, or funny, or weird, a very good way of showing that to the audience is to have other people react to them appropriately within the scene. Thus, religious movies have always relied heavily on *reaction shots*, with the actors being persuaded to look Amazed and Awestruck.

CHRIST IN THE WILDERNESS.

Christ encountering Satan in the desert in *The Gospel According To Matthew* is beautifully staged: it begins with long, establishing shots of the rocky slopes and windswept hills[20] (the location is the slopes of a volcano, with black soil, at Mount Etna – the first appearance (of many) of Etna in Pier Paolo Pasolini's cinema); huge, cloudy skies; clouds casting shadows

20 Pier Paolo Pasolini, in the Palestine documentary, admitted that he wouldn't be able to replicate the epic, grand vistas of the wilderness he found in Israel.

which run rapidly over the ground; mist; the sound of the wind; Jesus is shown kneeling and praying, palms raised (a pose later taken up in the garden of Gethsemane); there are cuts from Jesus to his point-of-view: the sun behind clouds, a time-honoured but very effective trope of God and Heaven (in this scene, Jesus may be regarded as communicating with God silently – even tho' he is, also, God himself. It's such a *mystery*!).

The Devil (Renato Terra) approaches in long shot, from a distance, kicking up dust (close-ups focus on his feet), backlit, with the foreground in shadow, a shot also used in Westerns, Hong Kong action movies and Omar Shariff's famous entrance in *Lawrence of Arabia* (perhaps desert locations seem to suggest such long focal length shots). (Pier Paolo Pasolini and the casting director chose a middle-aged, white actor to play Satan (and he resembles Pasolini, as does one of the Kings). Renato Terra is credited as 'the possessed one'. His attitude is supercilious but not exaggeratedly so.[21] In fact, he's a rather affable Satan, compared to some in cinema!).

✦

The 1964 film then cuts to a number of different locations, showing Satan's temptations: the pair are seen standing before a Cathedral (they may be standing on a balcony on the West front of a Cathedral), and near a church, as they exchange theological arguments in close-up (again, anachronistic, of course: these Christian edifices were built over a thousand years after Christ. But it works: Satan is also showing Christ the future. Later Christ movies, such as the 1999 movie *Jesus: The Bible Collection,* explored putting Jesus into modern-day situations, such as a world war, and a refugee camp).

But the montage structure of the wilderness sequence in *The Gospel According To Matthew* enables the encounter between Jesus and Satan to take on a much larger significance than scenes of two people talking (which's what these scenes are, in part). Here, Jesus is

---

21 King Herod is also held back, and not typed as a movie villain.

supremely confident, and isn't tempted by the Devil at all. He counters Satan's every offer with a theological line: this Jesus knows his *Scriptures* better than any rabbi or theologian (and he delivers them in a cool, firm tone, which enhances his confidence). And this is how Jesus often reacts to confrontations, to attacks from authority figures, and to attempts to get the better of him – by arguing, by using rhetoric, by quoting from the sacred texts (indeed, Jesus turns to the *Scriptures* many times in this interpretation of his life – he is always trying to change how people think – especially people who have influence and power).22

As written in the text of *The St Matthew Gospel*, the wilderness episode is depicted thus:

> Then was Jesus led up of the spirit into the wilderness to be tempted of the devil. And when he had fasted forty days and forty nights, he was afterward an hungered. And when the tempter came to him, he said, If thou be the Son of God, command that these stones be made bread. But he answered and said, It is written, Man shall not live by bread alone, but by every word that proceedeth out of the mouth of God. Then the devil taketh him up into the holy city, and setteth him on a pinnacle of the temple, and said unto him, If thou be the Son of God, cast thyself down: for it is written,
>
> He shall give his angels charge concerning thee: And in their hands they shall bear thee up, Lest at any time thou dash they foot against a stone.
>
> Jesus said unto him, It is written again, Thou shalt not tempt the Lord thy God. Again, the devil taketh him up into an exceeding high mountain, and sheweth him all the kingdoms of the world, and the glory of them; and saith unto him, All these things will I give thee, if thou wilt fall down and worship me. Then saith Jesus unto him, Thou shalt worship the Lord they God, and him only shalt thou serve. Then the devil leaveth him, and, behold, angels came and ministered unto him. (4: 1-11)

22 Which's why we would love to hear how Jesus interacted with Pontius Pilate, and with the Temple authorities, in the trial scenes later on, which were covered with subjective shots from a distance.

Some cinematic interpretations of this battle between two gods employ visual effects[23] – the story of Christ lends itself to visual fx and cinematic trickery. And the duel between Satan and Jesus is certainly a place where visual effects can flourish. Instead, *The Gospel According To Matthew* relies on sleight-of-hand editing, in a rapid montage-style, which places the protagonists in a variety of situations. (But editing is not only about the cheapest and easiest 'effect' in cinema, it is also, as all filmmakers know, about the most effective).

And the performances of the actors Enrique Irazoqui and Renato Terra in the wilderness sequence are keep relatively low-key – this's no Satan who's going to shout and scream and turn halfway through into a giant demon.[24] Rather, the Devil's temptations are remarkably matter-of-fact.

So there is no real struggle,[25] and Jesus is never tempted once. So Satan turns on his heels, and walks away. Following this sequence, Jesus is filmed walking purposefully up in the mountains – now he is a man (a god) on a mission. Right after this, Christ is gathering followers.

THE APOSTLES.

The Apostles are encountered and invited to follow Jesus in further scenes of rapid storytelling. Psychology, motivation, thought, inner life and conventional characterization – all are dispensed with, and the sequence takes a picture book or *tableau* approach. We're on a beach, we meet the fishermen, we meet Peter, Andrew, Matthew *et al* very quickly, and then it's off we go – the feeling of decisive movement (from Christ) is beautifully portrayed.[26] Christ is flowing thru this and other scenes as an unstoppable, charismatic (yet enigmatic) force.

23 For instance, *Jesus* (1999) and *The Last Temptation of Christ* (1988).
24 Which he most definitely would in a Japanese animation version!
25 Hollywood cinema, meanwhile, especially in more recent years, never lets an opportunity pass for confrontation.
26 As is screen direction and continuity.

The subsequent section, detailing the first weeks of Christ with the Apostles, including the first miracles, is similarly compelling. The apparent simplicity of the filmmaking disguises just how subtle and intricate it is. Making Jesus a person with so much inner energy, and in constant motion, works so well – it seems as if he can accomplish anything. And he has charisma to spare: when he says, join me, off we go, with no second thoughts.

Jesus encounters some of the local authorities at this point: the priests (travelling in a group with ponies and drivers) complain about healing being done on the Sabbath (during the healing of a cripple). As soon as the issue is raised, Jesus comes back with a theological argument that silences the priests. He is portrayed as a brilliant politician. At the close of the scene, one of the clerics mutters that they must get rid of him.

Christ's ministry is filmed in a variety of ways: the most striking is the use of a handheld camera following Jesus as he walks thru towns or on the hills. The camera takes a subjective viewpoint, as if the audience is one of the disciples, walking right behind Jesus. He turns, talking to us over his shoulder (sometimes the camera is inches away from Irazoqui's face).

THE MIRACLES.

Deciding how to photograph and stage the miracles in the *Gospels* is, like the Resurrection, one of the key areas in which filmmakers have to acknowledge the divinity or supernatural powers of Jesus. The simple cut from a Before to an After stage is a beautiful way of stating: *it happened.* Yes, miracles do occur in this reading of the *Bible*: the first miracle is a disfigured, young man; there is a crippled boy, and a man on crutches – plus the leper colony. Again, there is no attempt at back-story or even much characterization: the faces, the movement, the light say it all (and the music, of course, is invisibly supplying everything you could possibly need. Music being one of the great miracles in human history).[27]

The staging is repeated for the miracles several times: Jesus steps forward; the victim moves towards him; the followers watch from a distance; the victim has relatives/ friends/ onlookers nearby. Following the match cut (for the Before and the After), there is a very big close-up of the eyes. Again, it is the *editing*, coupled with the *music,* the two invisible superpowers of cinema, that really sell these scenes.

Jesus doesn't 'do' anything especially demonstrative in performing the miracles. No hand waving or hieratic gestures. No smoke or bright light. This isn't *Harry Potter* or Hollywood Cheese. Jesus being there is enough. Jesus says, 'get up and walk', and the miracle has already happened.

THE SERMON ON THE MOUNT.

The Sermon on the Mount[28] in *The Gospel According To Matthew* is brilliantly staged, an absolutely stunning sequence, one of the highpoints in the film (and thus also in the history of religious cinema): the movie shifts gear and narration: it becomes an extended montage comprising a series of medium close-ups of Jesus, many handheld (often from slightly below), with Jesus looking slightly off-camera, addressing and looking at an unseen audience (which we imagine are gathered closely around him), as he recites the famous passages from *St Matthew's Gospel*. There are no reverse angles, no other voices (only the sound of the wind), and no cuts to faces in the listening crowd (a long shot at the beginning of the sequence establishes that Christ is addressing his followers on a hill; once again, we don't need any of that information, because we know this story inside-out. Plus, we too have seen thousands of movies, including films about Christ).

One shot follows after another, forcefully staged; some shots are seen against the sea, or hills, or in high

27 Ken Russell calls music the most miraculous event in history.
28 It starts at *Matthew* 5: 1-2: 'And seeing the multitudes, he went up into a mountain: and when he was set, his disciples came unto him; And he opened his mouth, and taught them'.

wind, or at night in a lightning storm[29] (this's when the Messiah recites the *Lord's Prayer*); there are jump cuts to a different part of the same shot; most shots are against the sky, at different times of the day;[30] the camera repeatedly pushes in slightly; Christ's appearance changes from shot to shot (his hood on, or off, and so on).[31] Johann Sebastian Bach's *aria* from *St Matthew Passion* comes in towards the end of the sequence (the go-to music in several works helmed by Pasolini at this time). Remarkable.

Some of these scenes were filmed in the studio in Rome. Pier Paolo Pasolini had struggled to shoot the *Beatitudes*. The solution seemed unsatisfying to the director, until it was edited into the movie as short shots and lightning flashes (ES, 274). Editing defines so much of the impact of *The Gospel* movie.

Thus, the Sermon on the Mount sequence in *The Gospel According To Matthew* is definitely one of the greatest instances of using jump cuts in cinema. The *context*, for a start, is way more profound than a gangster flick like *Breathless*, or even the celebrated Sergei Eisenstein pictures. The cutting (by Nino Baragli) is truly masterful, and it turns the Sermon on the Mount scene into a thrilling barrage of religious principles.

SALOMÉ'S DANCE.

Salomé's (Paola Tedesco) dance is filmed from King Herod's point-of-view, in tight, medium close-ups, with a telephoto lens, focussing on Salomé (her face, but not her body),[32] with reaction shots of Herod (there is no obvious hint of sexual desire, as in some other (usually

---

29 Preaching during a storm at night? It looks great, but it's unlikely.
30 In some scenes, the sun moving in and out of the clouds, forming light and shade across Jesus' face, which other filmmakers would automatically cut, is retained.
31 It looks as if the Sermon on the Mount shots would have been taken in each location the production visited, so if they happened to be up in the volcanic mountains, they would shoot a couple of Sermon on the Mount scenes, and days or weeks later, if they were in Massafra, say, they would do a couple more.
32 For some directors – Gene Kelly, Woody Allen, John Badham – this is how *not* to film dance.

Hollywood) depictions of the scene).[33] It's not one of the great dance scenes in cinema,[34] nor the finest interpretation of this famous episode (the well-known historical paintings of Salomé, Herod and the Baptist, for instance (Artemisia Gentileschi, Michelangelo da Caravaggio, Titian, Gustave Moreau, etc), far surpass this scene). Neither Salomé nor her mother Herodias (Franca Cupane) speak – such is the power of this movie[35] – but Salomé has her one famous line: 'bring me the head of John the Baptist'.

> But when Herod's birthday was kept, the daughter of Herodias danced before them, and pleased Herod. Whereupon he promised with an oath to give her whatsoever she would ask. And she, being before instructed of her mother, said, Give me here John Baptist's head in a charger. And the king was sorry: nevertheless for the oath's sake, and them which sat with him at meat, he commanded it to be given her. And he sent, and beheaded John in the prison. And his head was brought in a charger, and given to the damsel: and she brought it to her mother. And his disciples came, and took up the body, and buried it, and went and told Jesus. (14: 6-12)

When the guards arrive to behead the Baptist the same ominous music (from *Alexander Nevsky*) is used that was heard over the catastrophic scene of the massacre of the innocents. However, there is no scene of the head of the Baptist being delivered to Salomé and Herod (the subject of many Renaissance paintings).

Salomé is depicted as a young girl, maybe sixteen (the actress, Paola Tedesco, was 14 at the time of filming).[36] Dangerous, yes, but not the *femme fatale* of

33 No need to add sexual desire to what is essentially a political move (altho' that's what fascinates people – politics plus religion plus sexuality).
34 We have little idea what Salomé's dance looks like – the close-ups conveniently elide the body. On-set photographs show Pasolini directing Tedesco – this was a scene where a professional choreographer could've enhanced the movements.
35 They share a moment when Salomé is getting dressed in her chambers, again without dialogue.
36 About the only lapse in the costuming (by Danilo Donati) was to put Paola Tedesco in a white under-garment, a tunic dress that's just too reminiscent of a Sixties mini dress.

the art of Gustave Moreau[37] or the Symbolist artists. This Salomé is not the murderess of the history of art (like Judith with Holofernes or Delilah with Samson). This Salomé seems too young and too innocent to be demanding the head of John the Baptist on a platter (the way she hurries over to her mother Herodias, for instance, to be comforted, is like a little girl). But her request is instantly obeyed.[38]

JESUS AND HIS MOTHER.

The scene where Jesus renounces his mother (and her family), with tears in his eyes, speaking from a balcony, up some stairs, with his mother below, beside the disciples, looking up at him with her expressive face, is very moving. The cuts from the face of Pier Paolo Pasolini's real mother (Susanna Colussi) to Enrique Irazoqui are especially emotional. The scene also includes shots of Jesus turning his back to the camera – the staging again emphasizes the viewpoint of the followers standing behind Jesus, who can't believe that he is literally turning his back on his mother and relations (the film dwells on their dismayed reactions).

It's from *Matthew* 12: 46-50:

> While he yet talked to the people, behold, his mother and his brethren stood without, desiring to speak with him. Then one said unto him, Behold, thy mother and thy brethren stand without, desiring to speak with thee. But he answered and said unto him that told him, Who is my mother? and who are my brethren? And he stretched forth his hand

37 Gustave Moreau depicted Salomé many times – usually as a deadly *femme fatale* lost in a dream of her own power. Salomé is the ultimate castrating force. For Freudians, Salomé in Moreau's art is the return of the castrating mother. Moreau's famous *The Apparition* (1876) orchestrates in the most decorative and stylized manner, more mannered than Mannerist art, more baroque than Baroque art, more romantic than Romantic art, the anguish of fear and desire, the fear of rejection and loss, the craving for contact and sublimation.

38 In the version of Oscar Wilde's play *Salomé's Last Dance*, directed by Ken Russell in 1988, it takes a *long time* for King Herod to agree to the beheading. In amongst the camp surface, the in-jokes and the OTT costumes, jewellery and make-up, *Salomé's Last Dance* packs a strong, dramatic punch. Altho' Ken Russell is often derided for being vulgar and showy, *Salomé's Last Dance* is actually a tightly-plotted and carefully-scripted movie (with a superb cast).

toward his disciples, and said, Behold my mother and my brethren! For whosoever shall do the will of my Father which is in heaven, the same is my brother, and sister, and mother.

Later, Jesus and his followers pass his former home. The aged Madonna looks on longingly as Jesus glances back. In the scenes where Christ returns to his homeland,[39] the sceptical reception of the people is understated but very effective: Jesus's disappointment plays across Enrique Irazoqui's face as he's derided as being the carpenter's son, a local lad who got too big for his boots.

The Gospel According To Matthew doesn't depict onlookers and crowds as having the same reactions of undiluted awe as Jesus walks among them as everyone else. Some are mocking, and some are indifferent; some of the children run up to him and tug at his clothes; some beg to become followers (but are rejected); sometimes Jesus pushes thru the crowds (as on the beach, when he's distressed at the Baptist's death).

In this part of the 1964 movie, the encounter with the rich man of the parable is staged (on the stone stairs of Matera, a favourite location for many encounters in *The Gospel According To Matthew*; Pasolini is very fond of using staircases in his movies).[40] The famous dialogue –

It is easier for a camel to go through the eye of a needle, than for a rich man to enter into the kingdom of God. (19:24)

– is issued as a coldly angry response by Jesus to the merchant (played by an actor who seems to be in his early twenties). Note the blocking of the scene – Christ is below, the merchant is above, on the stairs, with his retinue of lackeys (the camera, taking Jesus's p.o.v., pans across them, ending up on the shiny vessels

39 Filmed at the same location, Matera, from the early parts of the movie.
40 And many scenes in *The Gospel According To Matthew* are staged on slopes and mountains – enabling *tableaux* to be arranged, with actors and extras placed front-to-back, above each other.

attached to the donkey). As soon as Jesus tells the rich man to sell his goods, the man simply departs, indifferent. It's the under-playing of the scene, like so many scenes in *The Gospel According To Matthew*, that helps to make it memorable. It's as if this is just happening on a street, a short conversation – it's a striking step away from the histrionics and solemnity of so many Biblical and Christ films. (In this scene, it's easy to see Jesus as a revolutionary in the manner of young, political activists of the 1960s who berated the wealthy and the authorities (the sort you see in the movies of Jean-Luc Godard of the Sixties). This is a very Pasolinian Christ who sees a complacent bourgeoisie flaunting his riches and aches to bring him down).

JERUSALEM.

Jesus informs his followers (twice), prior to Jerusalem, that he will be taken by the authorities. They don't believe it (they don't want to believe it). The moving scene where Christ singles out Simon Peter and talks about him being the keeper of the flame occurs here. The staging stays with the format of the disciples following behind Christ, so that he is always seen in isolation (often turning back to talk to the men). The camera often floats between their faces as Jesus talks, and sometimes it pan across from Jesus to someone else then back again.

There's an extraordinary, joyous entry into Jerusalem in *The Gospel According To Matthew*, with children madly waving palms and singing 'hosanna'. It's deliberately staged in a light-hearted, upbeat manner, because so much of the movie after this is sombre and gloomy.

> And the disciples went, and did as Jesus comm-
> anded them, And brought the ass,[41] and the colt, and
> put on them their clothes, and they set him thereon.
> And a very great multitude spread their garments in
> the way; others cut down branches from the trees,
> and strewed them in the way. And the multitudes

41 Even this minor detail of the *Gospel* was included.

that went before, and that followed, cried, saying,
Hosanna to the Son of David: Blessed is he that
cometh in the name of the Lord; Hosanna in the
highest. (21: 6-9)

It is the start of the descent in Christ's story. When
Christ overturns the stalls in the Temple, the film
employs rapid editing and crash zooms towards the
authorities gathering at the upper windows to see what's
going on (the setting that's been chosen is far from
looking like the historical Temple in Jerusalem. It's a
mediaeval structure, but it works as an equivalent for the
Temple).

The ending of the Temple episode is depicted once
again in *tableau*-style: Christ and his followers are
ranged on one side of a courtyard (in a flattened,
symmetrical pattern right out of Renaissance painting),
with the Pharisees on the other side.

A happier moment occurs when a group of children
gather b4 Christ, waving their palms vigorously. The
camera pans across each grinning, singing face.[42] When
Jesus looks down and smiles, it is genuinely sweet and
uplifting.

The following battle of wills between Christ and the
authorities of the Temple is also staged in a static,
tableau manner, with simple but very effective reverse
angles, cutting back and forth (the Temple scenes are
split in two). There's no action, no movement, no
embellishments to the scene, yet it is riveting. Jesus is a
brilliant orator, who knows his *Bible* inside-out (well,
you'd expect that of a god!); thus, he can run rings
around the Temple officials theologically and ethically
(he would make a powerful lawyer or judge. He has an
answer for everything, and is never, ever at a loss for
words). He also speaks in parables, where, given two or
more options by Jesus, the interlocutors always chose
the wrong one (sometimes Jesus is furious at their bad
choices).

The section of *The Gospel According To Matthew* in
42 They recall the singing angels in the art of Piero della Francesca.

Jerusalem, following the Temple episode, is a very lengthy series of scenes where Jesus is berating the assembled crowds in tones of recrimination and anger. The lines comes from *Matthew* 23:

> But woe unto you, scribes and Pharisees, hypocrites! for ye shut up the kingdom of heaven against men: for ye neither go in yourselves, neither suffer ye them that are entering to go in. Woe unto you, scribes and Pharisees, hypocrites! for ye devour widows' houses, and for a pretence make long prayer: therefore ye shall receive the greater damnation.

The camera in many of these scenes stays way back, framing the crowds in the foreground and Jesus off in the distance. If the images are static and somewhat cool, the way that Enrique Irazoqui delivers the speeches (and, just as significantly, how Enrico Maria Salerno voices them), often with a selection of Johann Sebastian Bach's choral music rumbling underneath, is full of fire. We are watching Irazoqui on the screen, but we also always listening to Salerno, sometimes yelling the dialogue. (It's a double whammy of Christian theological rhetoric – Christ's sermons, plus the choral music).

The editing pattern keeps the audience as one of the crowd: we are always viewing Jesus in the distance from behind onlookers. Only late in the sequence does the camera move in for a close-up,[43] and, yet again, it is that curious angle, right behind Jesus's head. Nobody else in the history of religious cinema has filmed a god so often from right behind their skulls!

And only at the very end of the episode does the camera shift around for a proper reverse angle, and we see Jesus in a medium shot.[44] Now he is the Messiah at the top of his powers, with hordes of devotees, and punters come to listen (including soldiers – the ones who'll capture him and string him up later. Their

---

43 There is a curious handheld shot approaching Jesus as he orates, like a fan sidling up to a celebrity for an autograph.

44 There is also a clumsy handheld shot where the camera lunges thru the crowd to get closer to the Saviour.

reaction to Jesus? Weary indifference – they have en-countered religious fanatics before).

The gatherings are also depicted as getting more'n more violent, with Jesus moving with difficulty thru the crowds, while the disciples manhandle the over-zealous folk on each side, just like bodyguards with a celebrity. (That aspect of celebrity culture had been depicted only a few years before in Italian cinema, in *La Dolce Vita* (1960), with its famous scenes of *paparazzi*). This is the point, of course, when Jerusalem's authorities decide to do something about Jesus (the film cuts back to the authorities contemplating their next course of action). Even before the Last Supper sequence, the film has singled out Judas many times amongst the disciples.

THE LAST SUPPER.

The Last Supper is a solemn affair (as it's usually portrayed), with music and looks predominating.

> And as they were eating, Jesus took bread, and blessed it, and brake it, and gave it to the disciples, and said, Take, eat; this is my body. And he took the cup, and gave thanks, and gave it to them, saying, Drink ye all of it; For this is my blood of the new testament, which is shed for many for the remission of sins.

It is beautifully staged, like most of the scenes in *The Gospel According To Matthew* – it *seems* 'simple', but of course it isn't. Sometimes scenes in *The Gospel* look as if they are 'just happening', as if the camera just happened to be there, recording the actors. But no, this is a meticulously arranged movie – the acting style appears 'naturalistic' only in certain areas, because in others, it is highly formal. Ditto with the filmmaking: the lighting, the blocking of the performers, the use of props, the editing structure, plus of course the music (here a plaintive cue) – it all amounts to a scene as carefully considered as the arrangements of the participants in a Renaissance altarpiece depicting the same scene.

This is the last time that Jesus smiles in *The Gospel According To Matthew* – in the final shots of the Last Supper sequence, before the movement into grimmer sections of the Passion.

THE AGONY IN THE GARDEN.

In the final act, *The Gospel According To Matthew*, if it were following the North American dramatic model, ought to be ramping up to a crescendo of action, emotion and reversals. Yet the Italian 1964 movie is still often slow and reflective. The Agony in the Garden scenes (mostly shot day for night, as such scenes often were at the time if they were filmed outdoors), are surprisingly loose and ponderous. Too much of the movie at this point consists of shots of either Jesus or Peter walking, walking, walking – walking thru the garden, or walking along alleys or trails in the city.[45] The film, in short, hasn't found a satisfying means of dramatizing the material: images of people walking are not sufficient to embody the life-and-death issues in play here. (Unfortunately, this cinematic deficiency crops up in many later movies from Pasolini – *Pigsty,* the 'trilogy of life' films, and even *Medea* and *Oedipus Rex*).

In this section of *The Gospel According To Matthew*, the drama and tension is not being sustained or accelerated, but is often diffused. The prayers in Gethsemane, for example, though moving, are far less emotive than similar scenes in the rest of the movie, such as the forty days in the wilderness, or the Sermon On the Mount (and they are very short prayers, too – other film interpretations of Christ's turmoil in the garden really milk the scene for all of its emotion).

The disciples disappear somewhat here as the 1964 movie opts to focus on Peter: he stands in for all of the followers, and the film uses his close-ups to stand in for the audience's concern and empathy. The flabbiness of the sequence is partly due to editing – Nino Baragli cuts

45 In the Garden, Jesus walks a way and then kneels – the action is repeated, in which seems to be different takes of the same shot. The repetition seems unnecessary.

the movie at a contemplative pace. (The investiture of Peter was taken out by Pier Paolo Pasolini following the first edit, but then he put it back again [PP, 96]).

THE TRIALS OF CHRIST.

The two trials of Christ are from filmed from the disciples' point-of-view, as onlookers: the trial with the scribes and leaders is covered with a handheld camera, from Peter's (Settimio Di Porto) p.o.v., the camera, very mobile, peering through the heads and shoulders of the bystanders. There are reaction shots (reverse angles) of Peter's troubled face intercut in the scene. The movie follows Peter for quite a while in the interval between Christ's capture and the Cavalry scenes: the movie coalesces all twelve disciples into one, and uses Peter to observe the famous scenes and the react to them. (There are perhaps a few too many shots of actor Di Porto walking along the streets of Matera, before the trial starts).

Similarly, the scene with Pontius Pilate (Alessandro Clerici) is shot from a distance (with Matthew (Ferruccio Nuzzo), this time) tearfully witnessing the events (in this scene and in the subsequent scenes, Matthew, in deep, tearful distress, is prominent among the onlookers. So we are seeing events thru Matthew's eyes,[46] the Matthew who in later years would write the *Gospel* of this story, as the movie would have it).

Both scenes place the viewer in the crowd, as if they're one of the onlookers at the scene, unable to make out exactly what is being said, unable to see Pontius Pilate or the scribes clearly. It's as if a TV reporter or a documentarian were trying to get close to the action.

> And they that had laid hold on Jesus led him away to Caiaphas the high priest, where the scribes and the elders were assembled. But Peter followed him afar off unto the high priest's palace, and went in, and sat with the servants, to see the end. Now the chief priests, and elders, and all the council, sought false witness against Jesus, to put him to death; But

---

46 Seen in a several very big close-ups of his eyes.

found none: yea, though many false witnesses came, yet found they none. (26: 57-60)

The Gospel According To Matthew maintains the uncertain, limited, subjective viewpoint throughout these scenes, without a single cut crossing the space to the other side of the onlookers, no clarifying shots, and, most telling of all – no close-up shots of Christ, or of Pontius Pilate or the officials (however, the soundtrack favours the principal characters, rather than the crowd – and it's another reminder than in reality, if you were standing fifty feet away as an inquisition or trial took place, it might be hard to hear what was going on (and you'd hear the comments of the people next to you in the crowd). And what is 'going on' is contained in the dialogue, because the scenes're filmed again in the static, undemonstrative *tableau* manner drawn from paintings – it's the polar opposite of silent cinema, where actors were encouraged to make sure the audience could follow the story by using gesture, movement and expression. Certainly, silent filmmakers such as F.W. Murnau or Buster Keaton would *not* film Jesus's trials in this manner).[47]

This's a radical approach: the pressure to go in close is very strong, and certainly virtually no mainstream, Hollywood film of the 1960s (and definitely not today) would stay back throughout both trials, which, along with the miracles and the Crucifixion, are the dramatic highpoints of the Christian story (it's also risky, because it has the possibility of alienating the audience – putting them at a distance from the action at key moments, when they want to be close to it). It's as if the filmmakers, conscious of existing Biblical movies, opted to do something very different.

47 But D.W. Griffith, in *Intolerance*, kept the camera (operated by Billy Bitzer) at a respectful distance in the portrayal of the Christ section of *Intolerance* (partly because of the morality of the 1910s era, when even to make a movie featuring Jesus was deemed disrespectful for some.)

CAVALRY.

The Crucifixion scene in *The Gospel According To Matthew* is as sublime and heart-rending as cinema can be. As with *The Passion of Joan of Arc* (1928), the filmmakers relied on the expressiveness of the human face, often shot in close-up (as they had done throughout *The Gospel According To Matthew*).

A close-up of the aged Mary, Jesus's mother (played by Pier Paolo Pasolini's own mother, Susanna Colussi), opens the Passion sequence in *The Gospel According To Matthew* (she is with Matthew and others, as they watch the procession of Christ on the way to Golgotha. Indeed, the viewpoint of Mary is often taken from now on – Mary plus Matthew (the Mother and the Writer of the *Gospel*),[48] and they're aided by two women and Joseph of Arimathea. This group follows Jesus's fate to the end, the triumphant Resurrection).

The road to Calvary is a very noisy scene, with the Saviour surrounded by loud, jostling crowds and soldiers;[49] his mother is seen being supported by the disciples and relatives. The camera is often in amongst the mob, trying to get a clear view of Jesus carrying the Cross (which's handed to Simon of Cyrene). To some in the crowd, this is simply a spectacle, a jamboree, an excuse to skip work;[50] to the followers of Christ, and his mother, it is as traumatic as any experience could be.

Then there is a striking cut to silence, with J.S. Bach's music beginning, and handheld shots of Christ and the procession following him up to Golgotha (the change in the soundtrack, from noise to music, creates a powerful shift in the mood. *The Gospel According To Matthew* often relies *a lot* on music to convey what it can't put into images). As the crowd approaches the place of skulls and death,[51] the sound of the wind is

48 The relationship of Mary and Matthew has inevitable biographical resonances, as with Mary and Jesus, when Mary is played by the director's own mom.

49 The sound of the crowd is mixed high as extras swarm thru the frame, pushing and shoving.

50 Some of the extras are smiling – that's quite right, because to some people this would be a spectacle.

51 The setting is not, however, art-directed as the realm of skulls, as it is in some Renaissance paintings and Hollywood versions.

heard over a shot of grass in the foreground and the procession in the background, seen against the hill town (many shots are composed looking into the sun, but never including the sun, or much of the sky).

THE CRUCIFIXION.

The music builds;[52] a man is seen being nailed to a cross by soldiers on the ground at Golgotha; sound of hammers and his screams; handheld shots of the hammer and nails and the man's face; Mary and the relatives approach, standing apart from the crowd; Jesus is nailed to the Cross and hauled upright; the 1964 movie cuts between Jesus and his mother, as she continually collapses and is supported on each side by women.

> And when they had platted a crown of thorns, they
> put it upon his head, and a reed in his right hand:
> and they bowed the knee before him, and mocked
> him, saying, Hail, King of the Jews! And they spit
> upon him, and took the reed, and smote him on the
> head. And after that they had mocked him, they
> took the robe off from him, and put his own raiment
> on him, and led him away to crucify him. And as
> they came out, they found a man of Cyrene, Simon
> by name: him they compelled to bear his cross. (27:
> 29-32)

In the Crucifixion sequence, *The Gospel According To Matthew* repeatedly moves back and forth from Christ to the aged Mary). She collapses, and weeps, and raises her arms in pain. It was Pasolini's own *Stabat Mater*, for his own mother. There is no local sound, only Johann Sebastian Bach's music. The use of Bach raises the film to the spiritual heights. *The Gospel According To Matthew* is an astonishing film. The *aria* from Bach's *St Matthew Passion* is the key soundtrack of the piece, appearing some 8 or so times, just the instrumental section, before the solo voice comes in.

The Gospel According To Matthew uses the traditional, Catholic belief that the Virgin Mary suffered the

---

52 The same section of Johann Sebastian Bach's *aria* from *St Matthew Passion* is used twice (with a clumsy edit).

same agonies as her son on the Cross. The Virgin's slumped body recalls historical depictions of the Crucifixion, such as Rogier van der Weyden's profoundly moving painting *Descent From the Cross* (1439-43, Madrid),[53] or Petrus Christus's *Lamentation* (*c.* 1455, Metropolitan Museum, New York). Look at the way that the Madonna's body bends to one side – that comes directly from Renaissance art.

It is largely a traditional portrayal of the Crucifixion in *The Gospel According To Matthew*, with many of the elements familiar from Italian Renaissance and Early Netherlandish painting:

- the Flagellation;
- the Crown of Thorns;
- the road to Calvary;
- Golgotha;
- the three crosses;
- the Roman soldiers under the Cross;
- Jesus being offered vinegar in a sponge;
- Jesus's last words ('My God, why has thou forsaken me?');
- buildings collapsing and general tumult;
- Mary and her companions watching from a distance;
- the descent from the Cross;
- the lamentation;
- the Pietà;
- and the burial in the winding sheet.

(Director Pasolini, as an ardent student of Renaissance painting, and the other key members of the team,

53 The painting, in tempera, is housed in the Prado, Madrid, where it is undoubtedly one of the highlights of the museum (no mean feat in amongst the Prado's extraordinary collection of works by Titian, Diego Velásquez, Peter Rubens and El Greco, among many others). *The Descent From the Cross* is not especially large, either (220 x 262 centimetres), but it packs a lot into that area. *The Descent From the Cross*, in short, is one of the greatest religious paintings. Every aspect of the composition is necessary and adds to the central tragedy. Nothing is wasted, and nothing is left out either. *The Descent From the Cross* is one of those paintings that is simply *full*, simply full with the requisite colour, geometry, gesture, tone, architecture and form. It is one of those few paintings that require nothing else to make it a success: you couldn't add anything to improve it. *The Gospel According To Matthew* is like seeing one of the great Renaissance altarpieces coming to life.

would have seen hundreds of such images).

> And when they were come unto a place called
> Golgotha, that is to say, a place of a skull, They
> gave him vinegar to drink mingled with gall: and
> when he had tasted thereof, he would not drink. And
> they crucified him, and parted his garments, casting
> lots: that it might be fulfilled which was spoken by
> the prophet, They parted my garments among them,
> and upon my vesture did they cast lots. And sitting
> down they watched him there; And set up over his
> head his accusation written, THIS IS JESUS THE
> KING OF THE JEWS. Then were there two thieves
> crucified with him, one on the right hand, and
> another on the left. (27: 33-38)

After the series of intensely moving cuts between
Christ and his mother, there is a curious element added:
a fade to black. Over black leader, the narrator/ voice of
God recites from the *Gospel* (it's probably Francesco
Leonetti – Herod II in this film and the voice of the crow
in *The Hawks and the Sparrows*);[54] then back to the film
– and a C.U. of Jesus on the Cross and the famous line,
'my God, why hast thou forsaken me?' As he dies, the
1964 picture cuts to a number of locations, showing the
destruction[55] that occurred at Christ's death: newsreel
footage of buildings toppling into dust, flames
flickering in windows, drifting smoke, followed by
handheld shots sweeping across landscapes (the
montage recalls the forty days in the desert sequence
and the temptations of Satan).

> Jesus, when he had cried again with a loud voice,
> yielded up the ghost. And, behold, the veil of the
> temple was rent in twain from the top to the bottom;
> and the earth did quake, and the rocks rent; And the
> graves were opened; and many bodies of the saints
> which slept arose, And came out of the graves after
> his resurrection, and went into the holy city, and
> appeared unto many. (27: 50-53)

54 Lines of admonition.
55 These aren't the finest second unit shots, but they do the job. Whenever a film of Christ falls short in terms of budget, the viewer can fill in
the rest of this very famous story. (Some of the shots of buildings
collapsing are bought footage).

THE RESURRECTION.

The music for the ending of *The Gospel According To Matthew* is, as we can guess by now, the African spiritual, used again as a sudden eruption of religious joy. Once again, the narrative of the film follows the *Scriptures* beat for beat, with the Madonna, Matthew, Joseph of Arimathea and the followers[56] tending the sepulchre (bringing offerings of flowers).[57]

The Virgin Mary is the most prominent figure in the three days between the Crucifixion and the Resurrection. The Archangel Gabriel makes his final appearance, informing the followers that Christ has risen.[58] The inrush of energy provided by the African music (again, the movie relies very much on music to provide the emotional lift), is echoed by shots of the disciples hurrying to greet the Risen Lord (when the film wants to intensify the energy, it often uses images of people hurrying). The last words of *The Gospel According To Matthew* are those of Jesus, delivered as a smiling, positive statement spoken in partial voiceover.

> And Jesus came and spake unto them, saying, All power is given unto me in heaven and in earth. (19) Go ye therefore, and teach all nations, baptizing them in the name of the Father, and of the Son, and of the Holy Ghost: (20) Teaching them to observe all things whatsoever I have commanded you: and, lo, I am with you always, even unto the end of the world. Amen.

The 1964 movie thus ends on a note of immense hope, of ultimate hope. The sentiment − 'I will always be with you' − is, of all the ways in which this movie could close, a marvellous affirmation of life.

By the end of this picture, the viewer has to agree that they have seen one of the most remarkable stories put on screen in a truly extraordinary manner... And in a movie without a single star (or even any well-known

56 Mary Magdalene is notable by her absence.
57 The sleepy soldiers are perhaps a tribute to Piero della Francesca's famous *Resurrection*.
58 The apocalyptic motifs − the 'great earthquake' of the *Gospel* − are not included.

actors at all), a movie where a young, Spanish student with no acting experience plays Jesus, along with a host of non-professionals... A film with a distinctly unusual soundtrack, with many radical ingredients which depart from expected norms... A picture which sticks firmly (at times pedantically) to the actual words of the *Gospel of Matthew*... And a film which goes against all previous religious outings in depicting an angry, sometimes unforgiving Jesus, yet a tender Jesus, a smiling Jesus, and a divine Jesus...

APPENDICES

THE GOSPEL ACCORDING TO ST MATTHEW

From *The Bible*, King James version

(1) The book of the generation of Jesus Christ, the son of David, the son of Abraham. (2) Abraham begat Isaac; and Isaac begat Jacob; and Jacob begat Judas and his brethren; (3) And Judas begat Phares and Zara of Thamar; and Phares begat Esrom; and Esrom begat Aram; (4) And Aram begat Aminadab; and Aminadab begat Naasson; and Naasson begat Salmon; (5) And Salmon begat Booz of Rachab; and Booz begat Obed of Ruth; and Obed begat Jesse; (6) And Jesse begat David the king; and David the king begat Solomon of her that had been the wife of Urias; (7) And Solomon begat Roboam; and Roboam begat Abia; and Abia begat Asa; (8) And Asa begat Josaphat; and Josaphat begat Joram; and Joram begat Ozias; (9) And Ozias begat Joatham; and Joatham begat Achaz; and Achaz begat Ezekias; (10) And Ezekias begat Manasses; and Manasses begat Amon; and Amon begat Josias; (11) And Josias begat Jechonias and his brethren, about the time they were carried away to Babylon: (12) And after they were brought to Babylon, Jechonias begat Salathiel; and Salathiel begat Zorobabel; (13) And Zorobabel begat Abiud; and Abiud begat Eliakim; and Eliakim begat Azor; (14) And Azor begat Sadoc; and Sadoc begat Achim; and Achim begat Eliud; (15) And Eliud begat

Eleazar; and Eleazar begat Matthan; and Matthan begat Jacob; (16) And Jacob begat Joseph the husband of Mary, of whom was born Jesus, who is called Christ.

(17) So all the generations from Abraham to David are fourteen generations; and from David until the carrying away into Babylon are fourteen generations; and from the carrying away into Babylon unto Christ are fourteen generations.

(18) Now the birth of Jesus Christ was on this wise: When as his mother Mary was espoused to Joseph, before they came together, she was found with child of the Holy Ghost. (19) Then Joseph her husband, being a just man, and not willing to make her a publick example, was minded to put her away privily. (20) But while he thought on these things, behold, the angel of the Lord appeared unto him in a dream, saying, Joseph, thou son of David, fear not to take unto thee Mary thy wife: for that which is conceived in her is of the Holy Ghost. (21) And she shall bring forth a son, and thou shalt call his name JESUS: for he shall save his people from their sins. (22) Now all this was done, that it might be fulfilled which was spoken of the Lord by the prophet, saying,

(23) Behold, a virgin shall be with child, and shall bring forth a son, and they shall call his name Emmanuel, which being interpreted is, God with us.

(24) Then Joseph being raised from sleep did as the angel of the Lord had bidden him, and took unto him his wife: (25) And knew her not till she had brought forth her firstborn son: and he called his name JESUS.

Matthew 2

(1) Now when Jesus was born in Bethlehem of Judaea in the days of Herod the king, behold, there came wise men from the east to Jerusalem, (2) Saying, Where is he that is born King of the Jews? for we have seen his star in the east, and are come to worship him.

(3) When Herod the king had heard these things, he was troubled, and all Jerusalem with him. (4) And when he had gathered all the chief priests and scribes of the people together, he demanded of them where Christ should be born. (5) And they said unto him, In Bethlehem of Judaea: for thus it is written by the

prophet,

(6) And thou Bethlehem, in the land of Juda, art not the least among the princes of Juda: for out of thee shall come a Governor, that shall rule my people Israel.

(7) Then Herod, when he had privily called the wise men, inquired of them diligently what time the star appeared.

(8) And he sent them to Bethlehem, and said, Go and search diligently for the young child; and when ye have found him, bring me word again, that I may come and worship him also. (9) When they had heard the king, they departed; and, lo, the star, which they saw in the east, went before them, till it came and stood over where the young child was. (10) When they saw the star, they rejoiced with exceeding great joy.

(11) And when they were come into the house, they saw the young child with Mary his mother, and fell down, and worshipped him: and when they had opened their treasures, they presented unto him gifts; gold, and frankincense, and myrrh. (12) And being warned of God in a dream that they should not return to Herod, they departed into their own country another way.

(13) And when they were departed, behold, the angel of the Lord appeareth to Joseph in a dream, saying, Arise, and take the young child and his mother, and flee into Egypt, and be thou there until I bring thee word: for Herod will seek the young child to destroy him. (14) When he arose, he took the young child and his mother by night, and departed into Egypt: (15) And was there until the death of Herod: that it might be fulfilled which was spoken of the Lord by the prophet, saying, Out of Egypt have I called my son.

(16) Then Herod, when he saw that he was mocked of the wise men, was exceeding wroth, and sent forth, and slew all the children that were in Bethlehem, and in all the coasts thereof, from two years old and under, according to the time which he had diligently inquired of the wise men. (17) Then was fulfilled that which was spoken by Jeremy the prophet, saying,

(18) In Rama was there a voice heard, lamentation, and weeping, and great mourning,Rachel weeping for her children, and would not be comforted, because they are not.

(19) But when Herod was dead, behold, an angel of the Lord appeareth in a dream to Joseph in Egypt, (20) Saying, Arise, and take the young child and his mother, and go into the land of Israel: for they are dead which sought the young child's life. (21) And he arose, and took the young child and his mother, and came into the land of Israel. (22) But when he heard that Archelaus did reign in Judaea in the room of his father Herod, he was afraid to go thither: notwithstanding, being warned of God in a dream, he turned aside into the parts of Galilee: (23) And he came and dwelt in a city called Nazareth: that it might be fulfilled which was spoken by the prophets, He shall be called a Nazarene.

Matthew 3

(1) In those days came John the Baptist, preaching in the wilderness of Judaea, (2) And saying, Repent ye: for the kingdom of heaven is at hand. (3) For this is he that was spoken of by the prophet Esaias, saying,

The voice of one crying in the wilderness,

Prepare ye the way of the Lord, make his paths straight.

(4) And the same John had his raiment of camel's hair, and a leathern girdle about his loins; and his meat was locusts and wild honey. (5) Then went out to him Jerusalem, and all Judaea, and all the region round about Jordan, (6) And were baptized of him in Jordan, confessing their sins.

(7) But when he saw many of the Pharisees and Sadducees come to his baptism, he said unto them, O generation of vipers, who hath warned you to flee from the wrath to come? (8) Bring forth therefore fruits meet for repentance: (9) And think not to say within yourselves, We have Abraham to our father: for I say unto you, that God is able of these stones to raise up children unto Abraham. (10) And now also the axe is laid unto the root of the trees: therefore every tree which bringeth not forth good fruit is hewn down, and cast into the fire. (11) I indeed baptize you with water unto repentance: but he that cometh after me is mightier than I, whose shoes I am not worthy to bear: he shall baptize you with the Holy Ghost, and with fire: (12) Whose fan

is in his hand, and he will throughly purge his floor, and gather his wheat into the garner; but he will burn up the chaff with unquenchable fire.

(13) Then cometh Jesus from Galilee to Jordan unto John, to be baptized of him. (14) But John forbad him, saying, I have need to be baptized of thee, and comest thou to me? (15) And Jesus answering said unto him, Suffer it to be so now: for thus it becometh us to fulfil all righteousness. Then he suffered him. (16) And Jesus, when he was baptized, went up straightway out of the water: and, lo, the heavens were opened unto him, and he saw the Spirit of God descending like a dove, and lighting upon him: (17) And lo a voice from heaven, saying, This is my beloved Son, in whom I am well pleased.

Matthew 4

(1) Then was Jesus led up of the Spirit into the wilderness to be tempted of the devil. (2) And when he had fasted forty days and forty nights, he was afterward an hungred. (3) And when the tempter came to him, he said, If thou be the Son of God, command that these stones be made bread. (4) But he answered and said, It is written, Man shall not live by bread alone, but by every word that proceedeth out of the mouth of God. (5) Then the devil taketh him up into the holy city, and setteth him on a pinnacle of the temple, (6) And saith unto him, If thou be the Son of God, cast thyself down: for it is written,

He shall give his angels charge concerning thee:

And in their hands they shall bear thee up,

Lest at any time thou dash thy foot against a stone.

(7) Jesus said unto him, It is written again, Thou shalt not tempt the Lord thy God. (8) Again, the devil taketh him up into an exceeding high mountain, and sheweth him all the kingdoms of the world, and the glory of them; (9) And saith unto him, All these things will I give thee, if thou wilt fall down and worship me. (10) Then saith Jesus unto him, Get thee hence, Satan: for it is written, Thou shalt worship the Lord thy God, and him only shalt thou serve. (11) Then the devil leaveth him, and, behold, angels came and ministered

unto him.

(12) Now when Jesus had heard that John was cast into prison, he departed into Galilee; (13) And leaving Nazareth, he came and dwelt in Capernaum, which is upon the sea coast, in the borders of Zabulon and Nephthalim: (14) That it might be fulfilled which was spoken by Esaias the prophet, saying,

(15) The land of Zabulon, and the land of Nephthalim, By the way of the sea, beyond Jordan, Galilee of the Gentiles; (16) The people which sat in darkness saw great light; and to them which sat in the region and shadow of death light is sprung up.

(17) From that time Jesus began to preach, and to say, Repent: for the kingdom of heaven is at hand.

(18) And Jesus, walking by the sea of Galilee, saw two brethren, Simon called Peter, and Andrew his brother, casting a net into the sea: for they were fishers. (19) And he saith unto them, Follow me, and I will make you fishers of men. (20) And they straightway left their nets, and followed him. (21) And going on from thence, he saw other two brethren, James the son of Zebedee, and John his brother, in a ship with Zebedee their father, mending their nets; and he called them. (22) And they immediately left the ship and their father, and followed him.

(23) And Jesus went about all Galilee, teaching in their synagogues, and preaching the gospel of the kingdom, and healing all manner of sickness and all manner of disease among the people. (24) And his fame went throughout all Syria: and they brought unto him all sick people that were taken with divers diseases and torments, and those which were possessed with devils, and those which were lunatick, and those that had the palsy; and he healed them. (25) And there followed him great multitudes of people from Galilee, and from Decapolis, and from Jerusalem, and from Judaea, and from beyond Jordan.

Matthew 5

(1) And seeing the multitudes, he went up into a mountain: and when he was set, his disciples came unto him: (2) And he opened his mouth, and taught them,

saying,

(3) Blessed are the poor in spirit: for theirs is the kingdom of heaven.

(4) Blessed are they that mourn: for they shall be comforted.

(5) Blessed are the meek: for they shall inherit the earth.

(6) Blessed are they which do hunger and thirst after righteousness: for they shall be filled.

(7) Blessed are the merciful: for they shall obtain mercy.

(8) Blessed are the pure in heart: for they shall see God.

(9) Blessed are the peacemakers: for they shall be called the children of God.

(10) Blessed are they which are persecuted for righteousness' sake: for theirs is the kingdom of heaven.

(11) Blessed are ye, when men shall revile you, and persecute you, and shall say all manner of evil against you falsely, for my sake.

(12) Rejoice, and be exceeding glad: for great is your reward in heaven: for so persecuted they the prophets which were before you.

(13) Ye are the salt of the earth: but if the salt have lost his savour, wherewith shall it be salted? it is thenceforth good for nothing, but to be cast out, and to be trodden under foot of men. (14) Ye are the light of the world. A city that is set on an hill cannot be hid. (15) Neither do men light a candle, and put it under a bushel, but on a candlestick; and it giveth light unto all that are in the house. (16) Let your light so shine before men, that they may see your good works, and glorify your Father which is in heaven.

(17) Think not that I am come to destroy the law, or the prophets: I am not come to destroy, but to fulfil. (18) For verily I say unto you, Till heaven and earth pass, one jot or one tittle shall in no wise pass from the law, till all be fulfilled. (19) Whosoever therefore shall break one of these least commandments, and shall teach men so, he shall be called the least in the kingdom of heaven: but whosoever shall do and teach them, the same shall be called great in the kingdom of heaven. (20) For I say unto you, That except your righteousness shall exceed

the righteousness of the scribes and Pharisees, ye shall in no case enter into the kingdom of heaven.

(21) Ye have heard that it was said by them of old time, Thou shalt not kill; and whosoever shall kill shall be in danger of the judgment: (22) But I say unto you, That whosoever is angry with his brother without a cause shall be in danger of the judgment: and whosoever shall say to his brother, Raca, shall be in danger of the council: but whosoever shall say, Thou fool, shall be in danger of hell fire. (23) Therefore if thou bring thy gift to the altar, and there rememberest that thy brother hath ought against thee; (24) Leave there thy gift before the altar, and go thy way; first be reconciled to thy brother, and then come and offer thy gift. (25) Agree with thine adversary quickly, whiles thou art in the way with him; lest at any time the adversary deliver thee to the judge, and the judge deliver thee to the officer, and thou be cast into prison. (26) Verily I say unto thee, Thou shalt by no means come out thence, till thou hast paid the uttermost farthing.

(27) Ye have heard that it was said by them of old time, Thou shalt not commit adultery: (28) But I say unto you, That whosoever looketh on a woman to lust after her hath committed adultery with her already in his heart. (29) And if thy right eye offend thee, pluck it out, and cast it from thee: for it is profitable for thee that one of thy members should perish, and not that thy whole body should be cast into hell. (30) And if thy right hand offend thee, cut if off, and cast it from thee: for it is profitable for thee that one of thy members should perish, and not that thy whole body should be cast into hell. (31) It hath been said, Whosoever shall put away his wife, let him give her a writing of divorcement: (32) But I say unto you, That whosoever shall put away his wife, saving for the cause of fornication, causeth her to commit adultery: and whosoever shall marry her that is divorced committeth adultery.

(33) Again, ye have heard that it hath been said by them of old time, Thou shalt not forswear thyself, but shalt perform unto the Lord thine oaths: (34) But I say unto you, Swear not at all; neither by heaven; for it is God's throne: (35) Nor by the earth; for it is his footstool: neither by Jerusalem; for it is the city of the

great King. (36) Neither shalt thou swear by thy head, because thou canst not make one hair white or black. (37) But let your communication be, Yea, yea; Nay, nay: for whatsoever is more than these cometh of evil.

(38) Ye have heard that it hath been said, An eye for an eye, and a tooth for a tooth: (39) But I say unto you, That ye resist not evil: but whosoever shall smite thee on thy right cheek, turn to him the other also. (40) And if any man will sue thee at the law, and take away thy coat, let him have thy cloke also. (41) And whosoever shall compel thee to go a mile, go with him twain. (42) Give to him that asketh thee, and from him that would borrow of thee turn not thou away.

(43) Ye have heard that it hath been said, Thou shalt love thy neighbour, and hate thine enemy. (44) But I say unto you, Love your enemies, bless them that curse you, do good to them that hate you, and pray for them which despitefully use you, and persecute you; (45) That ye may be the children of your Father which is in heaven: for he maketh his sun to rise on the evil and on the good, and sendeth rain on the just and on the unjust. (46) For if ye love them which love you, what reward have ye? do not even the publicans the same? (47) And if ye salute your brethren only, what do ye more than others? do not even the publicans so? (48) Be ye therefore perfect, even as your Father which is in heaven is perfect.

Matthew 6

(1) Take heed that ye do not your alms before men, to be seen of them: otherwise ye have no reward of your Father which is in heaven. (2) Therefore when thou doest thine alms, do not sound a trumpet before thee, as the hypocrites do in the synagogues and in the streets, that they may have glory of men. Verily I say unto you, They have their reward. (3) But when thou doest alms, let not thy left hand know what thy right hand doeth: (4) That thine alms may be in secret: and thy Father which seeth in secret himself shall reward thee openly.

(5) And when thou prayest, thou shalt not be as the hypocrites are: for they love to pray standing in the synagogues and in the corners of the streets, that they

may be seen of men. Verily I say unto you, They have their reward. (6) But thou, when thou prayest, enter into thy closet, and when thou hast shut thy door, pray to thy Father which is in secret; and thy Father which seeth in secret shall reward thee openly. (7) But when ye pray, use not vain repetitions, as the heathen do: for they think that they shall be heard for their much speaking. (8) Be not ye therefore like unto them: for your Father knoweth what things ye have need of, before ye ask him. (9) After this manner therefore pray ye: Our Father which art in heaven, Hallowed be thy name. (10) Thy kingdom come. Thy will be done in earth, as it is in heaven. (11) Give us this day our daily bread. (12) And forgive us our debts, as we forgive our debtors. (13) And lead us not into temptation, but deliver us from evil: For thine is the kingdom, and the power, and the glory, for ever. Amen. (14) For if ye forgive men their trespasses, your heavenly Father will also forgive you: (15) But if ye forgive not men their trespasses, neither will your Father forgive your trespasses.

(16) Moreover when ye fast, be not, as the hypocrites, of a sad countenance: for they disfigure their faces, that they may appear unto men to fast. Verily I say unto you, They have their reward. (17) But thou, when thou fastest, anoint thine head, and wash thy face; (18) That thou appear not unto men to fast, but unto thy Father which is in secret: and thy Father, which seeth in secret, shall reward thee openly.

(19) Lay not up for yourselves treasures upon earth, where moth and rust doth corrupt, and where thieves break through and steal: (20) But lay up for yourselves treasures in heaven, where neither moth nor rust doth corrupt, and where thieves do not break through nor steal: (21) For where your treasure is, there will your heart be also. (22) The light of the body is the eye: if therefore thine eye be single, thy whole body shall be full of light. (23) But if thine eye be evil, thy whole body shall be full of darkness. If therefore the light that is in thee be darkness, how great is that darkness!

(24) No man can serve two masters: for either he will hate the one, and love the other; or else he will hold to the one, and despise the other. Ye cannot serve God and mammon. (25) Therefore I say unto you, Take no

thought for your life, what ye shall eat, or what ye shall drink; nor yet for your body, what ye shall put on. Is not the life more than meat, and the body than raiment? (26) Behold the fowls of the air: for they sow not, neither do they reap, nor gather into barns; yet your heavenly Father feedeth them. Are ye not much better than they? (27) Which of you by taking thought can add one cubit unto his stature? (28) And why take ye thought for raiment? Consider the lilies of the field, how they grow; they toil not, neither do they spin: (29) And yet I say unto you, That even Solomon in all his glory was not arrayed like one of these. (30) Wherefore, if God so clothe the grass of the field, which to day is, and to morrow is cast into the oven, shall he not much more clothe you, O ye of little faith? (31) Therefore take no thought, saying, What shall we eat? or, What shall we drink? or, Wherewithal shall we be clothed? (32) (For after all these things do the Gentiles seek:) for your heavenly Father knoweth that ye have need of all these things. (33) But seek ye first the kingdom of God, and his righteousness; and all these things shall be added unto you. (34) Take therefore no thought for the morrow: for the morrow shall take thought for the things of itself. Sufficient unto the day is the evil thereof.

Matthew 7

(1) Judge not, that ye be not judged. (2) For with what judgment ye judge, ye shall be judged: and with what measure ye mete, it shall be measured to you again. (3) And why beholdest thou the mote that is in thy brother's eye, but considerest not the beam that is in thine own eye? (4) Or how wilt thou say to thy brother, Let me pull out the mote out of thine eye; and, behold, a beam is in thine own eye? (5) Thou hypocrite, first cast out the beam out of thine own eye; and then shalt thou see clearly to cast out the mote out of thy brother's eye.

(6) Give not that which is holy unto the dogs, neither cast ye your pearls before swine, lest they trample them under their feet, and turn again and rend you.

(7) Ask, and it shall be given you; seek, and ye shall find; knock, and it shall be opened unto you: (8)

For every one that asketh receiveth; and he that seeketh findeth; and to him that knocketh it shall be opened. (9) Or what man is there of you, whom if his son ask bread, will he give him a stone? (10) Or if he ask a fish, will he give him a serpent? (11) If ye then, being evil, know how to give good gifts unto your children, how much more shall your Father which is in heaven give good things to them that ask him? (12) Therefore all things whatsoever ye would that men should do to you, do ye even so to them: for this is the law and the prophets.

(13) Enter ye in at the strait gate: for wide is the gate, and broad is the way, that leadeth to destruction, and many there be which go in thereat: (14) Because strait is the gate, and narrow is the way, which leadeth unto life, and few there be that find it.

(15) Beware of false prophets, which come to you in sheep's clothing, but inwardly they are ravening wolves. (16) Ye shall know them by their fruits. Do men gather grapes of thorns, or figs of thistles? (17) Even so every good tree bringeth forth good fruit; but a corrupt tree bringeth forth evil fruit. (18) A good tree cannot bring forth evil fruit, neither can a corrupt tree bring forth good fruit. (19) Every tree that bringeth not forth good fruit is hewn down, and cast into the fire. (20) Wherefore by their fruits ye shall know them.

(21) Not every one that saith unto me, Lord, Lord, shall enter into the kingdom of heaven; but he that doeth the will of my Father which is in heaven. (22) Many will say to me in that day, Lord, Lord, have we not prophesied in thy name? and in thy name have cast out devils? and in thy name done many wonderful works? (23) And then will I profess unto them, I never knew you: depart from me, ye that work iniquity.

(24) Therefore whosoever heareth these sayings of mine, and doeth them, I will liken him unto a wise man, which built his house upon a rock: (25) And the rain descended, and the floods came, and the winds blew, and beat upon that house; and it fell not: for it was founded upon a rock. (26) And every one that heareth these sayings of mine, and doeth them not, shall be likened unto a foolish man, which built his house upon the sand: (27) And the rain descended, and the floods came, and the winds blew, and beat upon that house; and it

fell: and great was the fall of it. (28) And it came to pass, when Jesus had ended these sayings, the people were astonished at his doctrine: (29) For he taught them as one having authority, and not as the scribes.

Matthew 8

(1) When he was come down from the mountain, great multitudes followed him. (2) And, behold, there came a leper and worshipped him, saying, Lord, if thou wilt, thou canst make me clean. (3) And Jesus put forth his hand, and touched him, saying, I will; be thou clean. And immediately his leprosy was cleansed. (4) And Jesus saith unto him, See thou tell no man; but go thy way, shew thyself to the priest, and offer the gift that Moses commanded, for a testimony unto them.

(5) And when Jesus was entered into Capernaum, there came unto him a centurion, beseeching him, (6) And saying, Lord, my servant lieth at home sick of the palsy, grievously tormented. (7) And Jesus saith unto him, I will come and heal him. (8) The centurion answered and said, Lord, I am not worthy that thou shouldest come under my roof: but speak the word only, and my servant shall be healed. (9) For I am a man under authority, having soldiers under me: and I say to this man, Go, and he goeth; and to another, Come, and he cometh; and to my servant, Do this, and he doeth it. (10) When Jesus heard it, he marvelled, and said to them that followed, Verily I say unto you, I have not found so great faith, no, not in Israel. (11) And I say unto you, That many shall come from the east and west, and shall sit down with Abraham, and Isaac, and Jacob, in the kingdom of heaven. (12) But the children of the kingdom shall be cast out into outer darkness: there shall be weeping and gnashing of teeth. (13) And Jesus said unto the centurion, Go thy way; and as thou hast believed, so be it done unto thee. And his servant was healed in the selfsame hour. (14) And when Jesus was come into Peter's house, he saw his wife's mother laid, and sick of a fever. (15) And he touched her hand, and the fever left her: and she arose, and ministered unto them.

(16) When the even was come, they brought unto

him many that were possessed with devils: and he cast out the spirits with his word, and healed all that were sick: (17) That it might be fulfilled which was spoken by Esaias the prophet, saying, Himself took our infirmities, and bare our sicknesses.

(18) Now when Jesus saw great multitudes about him, he gave commandment to depart unto the other side. (19) And a certain scribe came, and said unto him, Master, I will follow thee whithersoever thou goest. (20) And Jesus saith unto him, The foxes have holes, and the birds of the air have nests; but the Son of man hath not where to lay his head. (21) And another of his disciples said unto him, Lord, suffer me first to go and bury my father. (22) But Jesus said unto him, Follow me; and let the dead bury their dead.

(23) And when he was entered into a ship, his disciples followed him. (24) And, behold, there arose a great tempest in the sea, insomuch that the ship was covered with the waves: but he was asleep. (25) And his disciples came to him, and awoke him, saying, Lord, save us: we perish. (26) And he saith unto them, Why are ye fearful, O ye of little faith? Then he arose, and rebuked the winds and the sea; and there was a great calm. (27) But the men marvelled, saying, What manner of man is this, that even the winds and the sea obey him!

(28) And when he was come to the other side into the country of the Gergesenes, there met him two possessed with devils, coming out of the tombs, exceeding fierce, so that no man might pass by that way. (29) And, behold, they cried out, saying, What have we to do with thee, Jesus, thou Son of God? art thou come hither to torment us before the time? (30) And there was a good way off from them an herd of many swine feeding. (31) So the devils besought him, saying, If thou cast us out, suffer us to go away into the herd of swine. (32) And he said unto them, Go. And when they were come out, they went into the herd of swine: and, behold, the whole herd of swine ran violently down a steep place into the sea, and perished in the waters. (33) And they that kept them fled, and went their ways into the city, and told every thing, and what was befallen to the possessed of the devils. (34) And, behold, the whole city came out to meet Jesus: and when they saw him, they

besought him that he would depart out of their coasts.

Matthew 9

(1) And he entered into a ship, and passed over, and came into his own city. (2) And, behold, they brought to him a man sick of the palsy, lying on a bed: and Jesus seeing their faith said unto the sick of the palsy; Son, be of good cheer; thy sins be forgiven thee. (3) And, behold, certain of the scribes said within themselves, This man blasphemeth. (4) And Jesus knowing their thoughts said, Wherefore think ye evil in your hearts? (5) For whether is easier, to say, Thy sins be forgiven thee; or to say, Arise, and walk? (6) But that ye may know that the Son of man hath power on earth to forgive sins, (then saith he to the sick of the palsy,) Arise, take up thy bed, and go unto thine house. (7) And he arose, and departed to his house. (8) But when the multitudes saw it, they marvelled, and glorified God, which had given such power unto men.

(9) And as Jesus passed forth from thence, he saw a man, named Matthew, sitting at the receipt of custom: and he saith unto him, Follow me. And he arose, and followed him.

(10) And it came to pass, as Jesus sat at meat in the house, behold, many publicans and sinners came and sat down with him and his disciples. (11) And when the Pharisees saw it, they said unto his disciples, Why eateth your Master with publicans and sinners? (12) But when Jesus heard that, he said unto them, They that be whole need not a physician, but they that are sick. (13) But go ye and learn what that meaneth, I will have mercy, and not sacrifice: for I am not come to call the righteous, but sinners to repentance.

(14) Then came to him the disciples of John, saying, Why do we and the Pharisees fast oft, but thy disciples fast not? (15) And Jesus said unto them, Can the children of the bridechamber mourn, as long as the bridegroom is with them? but the days will come, when the bridegroom shall be taken from them, and then shall they fast. (16) No man putteth a piece of new cloth unto an old garment, for that which is put in to fill it up taketh from the garment, and the rent is made worse. (17)

Neither do men put new wine into old bottles: else the bottles break, and the wine runneth out, and the bottles perish: but they put new wine into new bottles, and both are preserved.

(18) While he spake these things unto them, behold, there came a certain ruler, and worshipped him, saying, My daughter is even now dead: but come and lay thy hand upon her, and she shall live. (19) And Jesus arose, and followed him, and so did his disciples.

(20) And, behold, a woman, which was diseased with an issue of blood twelve years, came behind him, and touched the hem of his garment: (21) For she said within herself, If I may but touch his garment, I shall be whole. (22) But Jesus turned him about, and when he saw her, he said, Daughter, be of good comfort; thy faith hath made thee whole. And the woman was made whole from that hour. (23) And when Jesus came into the ruler's house, and saw the minstrels and the people making a noise, (24) He said unto them, Give place: for the maid is not dead, but sleepeth. And they laughed him to scorn. (25) But when the people were put forth, he went in, and took her by the hand, and the maid arose. (26) And the fame hereof went abroad into all that land.

(27) And when Jesus departed thence, two blind men followed him, crying, and saying, Thou Son of David, have mercy on us. (28) And when he was come into the house, the blind men came to him: and Jesus saith unto them, Believe ye that I am able to do this? They said unto him, Yea, Lord. (29) Then touched he their eyes, saying, According to your faith be it unto you. (30) And their eyes were opened; and Jesus straitly charged them, saying, See that no man know it. (31) But they, when they were departed, spread abroad his fame in all that country.

(32) As they went out, behold, they brought to him a dumb man possessed with a devil. (33) And when the devil was cast out, the dumb spake: and the multitudes marvelled, saying, It was never so seen in Israel. (34) But the Pharisees said, He casteth out devils through the prince of the devils. (35) And Jesus went about all the cities and villages, teaching in their synagogues, and preaching the gospel of the kingdom, and healing every sickness and every disease among the people.

(36) But when he saw the multitudes, he was moved with compassion on them, because they fainted, and were scattered abroad, as sheep having no shepherd. (37) Then saith he unto his disciples, The harvest truly is plenteous, but the labourers are few; (38) Pray ye therefore the Lord of the harvest, that he will send forth labourers into his harvest.

Matthew 10

(1) And when he had called unto him his twelve disciples, he gave them power against unclean spirits, to cast them out, and to heal all manner of sickness and all manner of disease. (2) Now the names of the twelve apostles are these; The first, Simon, who is called Peter, and Andrew his brother; James the son of Zebedee, and John his brother; (3) Philip, and Bartholomew; Thomas, and Matthew the publican; James the son of Alphaeus, and Lebbaeus, whose surname was Thaddaeus; (4) Simon the Canaanite, and Judas Iscariot, who also betrayed him.

(5) These twelve Jesus sent forth, and commanded them, saying, Go not into the way of the Gentiles, and into any city of the Samaritans enter ye not: (6) But go rather to the lost sheep of the house of Israel. (7) And as ye go, preach, saying, The kingdom of heaven is at hand. (8) Heal the sick, cleanse the lepers, raise the dead, cast out devils: freely ye have received, freely give. (9) Provide neither gold, nor silver, nor brass in your purses, (10) Nor scrip for your journey, neither two coats, neither shoes, nor yet staves: for the workman is worthy of his meat. (11) And into whatsoever city or town ye shall enter, inquire who in it is worthy; and there abide till ye go thence. (12) And when ye come into an house, salute it. (13) And if the house be worthy, let your peace come upon it: but if it be not worthy, let your peace return to you. (14) And whosoever shall not receive you, nor hear your words, when ye depart out of that house or city, shake off the dust of your feet. (15) Verily I say unto you, It shall be more tolerable for the land of Sodom and Gomorrha in the day of judgment, than for that city.

(16) Behold, I send you forth as sheep in the midst

of wolves: be ye therefore wise as serpents, and harmless as doves. (17) But beware of men: for they will deliver you up to the councils, and they will scourge you in their synagogues; (18) And ye shall be brought before governors and kings for my sake, for a testimony against them and the Gentiles. (19) But when they deliver you up, take no thought how or what ye shall speak: for it shall be given you in that same hour what ye shall speak. (20) For it is not ye that speak, but the Spirit of your Father which speaketh in you. (21) And the brother shall deliver up the brother to death, and the father the child: and the children shall rise up against their parents, and cause them to be put to death. (22) And ye shall be hated of all men for my name's sake: but he that endureth to the end shall be saved. (23) But when they persecute you in this city, flee ye into another: for verily I say unto you, Ye shall not have gone over the cities of Israel, till the Son of man be come. (24) The disciple is not above his master, nor the servant above his lord. (25) It is enough for the disciple that he be as his master, and the servant as his lord. If they have called the master of the house Beelzebub, how much more shall they call them of his household?

(26) Fear them not therefore: for there is nothing covered, that shall not be revealed; and hid, that shall not be known. (27) What I tell you in darkness, that speak ye in light: and what ye hear in the ear, that preach ye upon the housetops. (28) And fear not them which kill the body, but are not able to kill the soul: but rather fear him which is able to destroy both soul and body in hell. (29) Are not two sparrows sold for a farthing? and one of them shall not fall on the ground without your Father. (30) But the very hairs of your head are all numbered. (31) Fear ye not therefore, ye are of more value than many sparrows. (32) Whosoever therefore shall confess me before men, him will I confess also before my Father which is in heaven. (33) But whosoever shall deny me before men, him will I also deny before my Father which is in heaven.

(34) Think not that I am come to send peace on earth: I came not to send peace, but a sword. (35) For I am come to set a man at variance against his father, and the daughter against her mother, and the daughter in law

against her mother in law. (36) And a man's foes shall be they of his own household. (37) He that loveth father or mother more than me is not worthy of me: and he that loveth son or daughter more than me is not worthy of me. (38) And he that taketh not his cross, and followeth after me, is not worthy of me. (39) He that findeth his life shall lose it: and he that loseth his life for my sake shall find it. (40) He that receiveth you receiveth me, and he that receiveth me receiveth him that sent me. (41) He that receiveth a prophet in the name of a prophet shall receive a prophet's reward; and he that receiveth a righteous man in the name of a righteous man shall receive a righteous man's reward. (42) And whosoever shall give to drink unto one of these little ones a cup of cold water only in the name of a disciple, verily I say unto you, he shall in no wise lose his reward.

Matthew 11

(1) And it came to pass, when Jesus had made an end of commanding his twelve disciples, he departed thence to teach and to preach in their cities.

(2) Now when John had heard in the prison the works of Christ, he sent two of his disciples, (3) And said unto him, Art thou he that should come, or do we look for another? (4) Jesus answered and said unto them, Go and shew John again those things which ye do hear and see: (5) The blind receive their sight, and the lame walk, the lepers are cleansed, and the deaf hear, the dead are raised up, and the poor have the gospel preached to them. (6) And blessed is he, whosoever shall not be offended in me.

(7) And as they departed, Jesus began to say unto the multitudes concerning John, What went ye out into the wilderness to see? A reed shaken with the wind? (8) But what went ye out for to see? A man clothed in soft raiment? behold, they that wear soft clothing are in kings' houses. (9) But what went ye out for to see? A prophet? yea, I say unto you, and more than a prophet. (10) For this is he, of whom it is written, Behold, I send my messenger before thy face, which shall prepare thy way before thee. (11) Verily I say unto you, Among them that are born of women there hath not risen a greater than

John the Baptist: notwithstanding he that is least in the kingdom of heaven is greater than he. (12) And from the days of John the Baptist until now the kingdom of heaven suffereth violence, and the violent take it by force. (13) For all the prophets and the law prophesied until John. (14) And if ye will receive it, this is Elias, which was for to come. (15) He that hath ears to hear, let him hear.

(16) But whereunto shall I liken this generation? It is like unto children sitting in the markets, and calling unto their fellows, (17) And saying, We have piped unto you, and ye have not danced; we have mourned unto you, and ye have not lamented. (18) For John came neither eating nor drinking, and they say, He hath a devil. (19) The Son of man came eating and drinking, and they say, Behold a man gluttonous, and a winebibber, a friend of publicans and sinners. But wisdom is justified of her children.

(20) Then began he to upbraid the cities wherein most of his mighty works were done, because they repented not: (21) Woe unto thee, Chorazin! woe unto thee, Bethsaida! for if the mighty works, which were done in you, had been done in Tyre and Sidon, they would have repented long ago in sackcloth and ashes. (22) But I say unto you, It shall be more tolerable for Tyre and Sidon at the day of judgment, than for you. (23) And thou, Capernaum, which art exalted unto heaven, shalt be brought down to hell: for if the mighty works, which have been done in thee, had been done in Sodom, it would have remained until this day. (24) But I say unto you, That it shall be more tolerable for the land of Sodom in the day of judgment, than for thee.

(25) At that time Jesus answered and said, I thank thee, O Father, Lord of heaven and earth, because thou hast hid these things from the wise and prudent, and hast revealed them unto babes. (26) Even so, Father: for so it seemed good in thy sight. (27) All things are delivered unto me of my Father: and no man knoweth the Son, but the Father; neither knoweth any man the Father, save the Son, and he to whomsoever the Son will reveal him.

(28) Come unto me, all ye that labour and are heavy laden, and I will give you rest. (29) Take my yoke upon

you, and learn of me; for I am meek and lowly in heart: and ye shall find rest unto your souls. (30) For my yoke is easy, and my burden is light.

Matthew 12

(1) At that time Jesus went on the sabbath day through the corn; and his disciples were an hungred, and began to pluck the ears of corn, and to eat. (2) But when the Pharisees saw it, they said unto him, Behold, thy disciples do that which is not lawful to do upon the sabbath day. (3) But he said unto them, Have ye not read what David did, when he was an hungred, and they that were with him; (4) How he entered into the house of God, and did eat the shewbread, which was not lawful for him to eat, neither for them which were with him, but only for the priests? (5) Or have ye not read in the law, how that on the sabbath days the priests in the temple profane the sabbath, and are blameless? (6) But I say unto you, That in this place is one greater than the temple. (7) But if ye had known what this meaneth, I will have mercy, and not sacrifice, ye would not have condemned the guiltless. (8) For the Son of man is Lord even of the sabbath day.

(9) And when he was departed thence, he went into their synagogue: (10) And, behold, there was a man which had his hand withered. And they asked him, saying, Is it lawful to heal on the sabbath days? that they might accuse him. (11) And he said unto them, What man shall there be among you, that shall have one sheep, and if it fall into a pit on the sabbath day, will he not lay hold on it, and lift it out? (12) How much then is a man better than a sheep? Wherefore it is lawful to do well on the sabbath days. (13) Then saith he to the man, Stretch forth thine hand. And he stretched it forth; and it was restored whole, like as the other.

(14) Then the Pharisees went out, and held a council against him, how they might destroy him. (15) But when Jesus knew it, he withdrew himself from thence: and great multitudes followed him, and he healed them all; (16) And charged them that they should not make him known: (17) That it might be fulfilled which was spoken by Esaias the prophet, saying,

(18) Behold my servant, whom I have chosen;

My beloved, in whom my soul is well pleased:
I will put my spirit upon him,
And he shall shew judgment to the Gentiles.
(19) He shall not strive, nor cry;
Neither shall any man hear his voice in the streets.
(20) A bruised reed shall he not break,
And smoking flax shall he not quench,
Till he send forth judgment unto victory.
(21) And in his name shall the Gentiles trust.

(22) Then was brought unto him one possessed with a devil, blind, and dumb: and he healed him, insomuch that the blind and dumb both spake and saw. (23) And all the people were amazed, and said, Is not this the son of David? (24) But when the Pharisees heard it, they said, This fellow doth not cast out devils, but by Beelzebub the prince of the devils. (25) And Jesus knew their thoughts, and said unto them, Every kingdom divided against itself is brought to desolation; and every city or house divided against itself shall not stand: (26) And if Satan cast out Satan, he is divided against himself; how shall then his kingdom stand? (27) And if I by Beelzebub cast out devils, by whom do your children cast them out? therefore they shall be your judges. (28) But if I cast out devils by the Spirit of God, then the kingdom of God is come unto you. (29) Or else how can one enter into a strong man's house, and spoil his goods, except he first bind the strong man? and then he will spoil his house. (30) He that is not with me is against me; and he that gathereth not with me scattereth abroad.

(31) Wherefore I say unto you, All manner of sin and blasphemy shall be forgiven unto men: but the blasphemy against the Holy Ghost shall not be forgiven unto men. (32) And whosoever speaketh a word against the Son of man, it shall be forgiven him: but whosoever speaketh against the Holy Ghost, it shall not be forgiven him, neither in this world, neither in the world to come. (33) Either make the tree good, and his fruit good; or else make the tree corrupt, and his fruit corrupt: for the tree is known by his fruit. (34) O generation of vipers, how can ye, being evil, speak good things? for out of the abundance of the heart the mouth speaketh. (35) A good man out of the good treasure of the heart bringeth forth

good things: and an evil man out of the evil treasure bringeth forth evil things. (36) But I say unto you, That every idle word that men shall speak, they shall give account thereof in the day of judgment. (37) For by thy words thou shalt be justified, and by thy words thou shalt be condemned.

(38) Then certain of the scribes and of the Pharisees answered, saying, Master, we would see a sign from thee. (39) But he answered and said unto them, An evil and adulterous generation seeketh after a sign; and there shall no sign be given to it, but the sign of the prophet Jonas: (40) For as Jonas was three days and three nights in the whale's belly; so shall the Son of man be three days and three nights in the heart of the earth. (41) The men of Nineveh shall rise in judgment with this generation, and shall condemn it: because they repented at the preaching of Jonas; and, behold, a greater than Jonas is here. (42) The queen of the south shall rise up in the judgment with this generation, and shall condemn it: for she came from the uttermost parts of the earth to hear the wisdom of Solomon; and, behold, a greater than Solomon is here. (43) When the unclean spirit is gone out of a man, he walketh through dry places, seeking rest, and findeth none. (44) Then he saith, I will return into my house from whence I came out; and when he is come, he findeth it empty, swept, and garnished. (45) Then goeth he, and taketh with himself seven other spirits more wicked than himself, and they enter in and dwell there: and the last state of that man is worse than the first. Even so shall it be also unto this wicked generation.

(46) While he yet talked to the people, behold, his mother and his brethren stood without, desiring to speak with him. (47) Then one said unto him, Behold, thy mother and thy brethren stand without, desiring to speak with thee. (48) But he answered and said unto him that told him, Who is my mother? and who are my brethren? (49) And he stretched forth his hand toward his disciples, and said, Behold my mother and my brethren! (50) For whosoever shall do the will of my Father which is in heaven, the same is my brother, and sister, and mother.

Matthew 13

(1) The same day went Jesus out of the house, and sat by the sea side. (2) And great multitudes were gathered together unto him, so that he went into a ship, and sat; and the whole multitude stood on the shore.

(3) And he spake many things unto them in parables, saying, Behold, a sower went forth to sow; (4) And when he sowed, some seeds fell by the way side, and the fowls came and devoured them up: (5) Some fell upon stony places, where they had not much earth: and forthwith they sprung up, because they had no deepness of earth: (6) And when the sun was up, they were scorched; and because they had no root, they withered away. (7) And some fell among thorns; and the thorns sprung up, and choked them: (8) But other fell into good ground, and brought forth fruit, some an hundredfold, some sixtyfold, some thirtyfold. (9) Who hath ears to hear, let him hear.

(10) And the disciples came, and said unto him, Why speakest thou unto them in parables? (11) He answered and said unto them, Because it is given unto you to know the mysteries of the kingdom of heaven, but to them it is not given. (12) For whosoever hath, to him shall be given, and he shall have more abundance: but whosoever hath not, from him shall be taken away even that he hath. (13) Therefore speak I to them in parables: because they seeing see not; and hearing they hear not, neither do they understand.

(14) And in them is fulfilled the prophecy of Esaias, which saith,

By hearing ye shall hear, and shall not understand;
and seeing ye shall see, and shall not perceive:
(15) For this people's heart is waxed gross,
and their ears are dull of hearing,
and their eyes they have closed;
lest at any time they should see with their eyes,
and hear with their ears,
and should understand with their heart,
and should be converted, and I should heal them.
(16) But blessed are your eyes, for they see: and your ears, for they hear. (17) For verily I say unto you, That many prophets and righteous men have desired to

see those things which ye see, and have not seen them; and to hear those things which ye hear, and have not heard them.

(18) Hear ye therefore the parable of the sower. (19) When any one heareth the word of the kingdom, and understandeth it not, then cometh the wicked one, and catcheth away that which was sown in his heart. This is he which received seed by the way side. (20) But he that received the seed into stony places, the same is he that heareth the word, and anon with joy receiveth it; (21) Yet hath he not root in himself, but dureth for a while: for when tribulation or persecution ariseth because of the word, by and by he is offended. (22) He also that received seed among the thorns is he that heareth the word; and the care of this world, and the deceitfulness of riches, choke the word, and he becometh unfruitful. (23) But he that received seed into the good ground is he that heareth the word, and understandeth it; which also beareth fruit, and bringeth forth, some an hundredfold, some sixty, some thirty.

(24) Another parable put he forth unto them, saying, The kingdom of heaven is likened unto a man which sowed good seed in his field: (25) But while men slept, his enemy came and sowed tares among the wheat, and went his way. (26) But when the blade was sprung up, and brought forth fruit, then appeared the tares also. (27) So the servants of the householder came and said unto him, Sir, didst not thou sow good seed in thy field? from whence then hath it tares? (28) He said unto them, An enemy hath done this. The servants said unto him, Wilt thou then that we go and gather them up? (29) But he said, Nay; lest while ye gather up the tares, ye root up also the wheat with them. (30) Let both grow together until the harvest: and in the time of harvest I will say to the reapers, Gather ye together first the tares, and bind them in bundles to burn them: but gather the wheat into my barn.

(31) Another parable put he forth unto them, saying, The kingdom of heaven is like to a grain of mustard seed, which a man took, and sowed in his field: (32) Which indeed is the least of all seeds: but when it is grown, it is the greatest among herbs, and becometh a tree, so that the birds of the air come and lodge in the

branches thereof.

(33) Another parable spake he unto them; The kingdom of heaven is like unto leaven, which a woman took, and hid in three measures of meal, till the whole was leavened. (34) All these things spake Jesus unto the multitude in parables; and without a parable spake he not unto them:

(35) That it might be fulfilled which was spoken by the prophet, saying,

I will open my mouth in parables;

I will utter things which have been kept secret from the foundation of the world.

(36) Then Jesus sent the multitude away, and went into the house: and his disciples came unto him, saying, Declare unto us the parable of the tares of the field. (37) He answered and said unto them, He that soweth the good seed is the Son of man; (38) The field is the world; the good seed are the children of the kingdom; but the tares are the children of the wicked one; (39) The enemy that sowed them is the devil; the harvest is the end of the world; and the reapers are the angels. (40) As therefore the tares are gathered and burned in the fire; so shall it be in the end of this world. (41) The Son of man shall send forth his angels, and they shall gather out of his kingdom all things that offend, and them which do iniquity; (42) And shall cast them into a furnace of fire: there shall be wailing and gnashing of teeth. (43) Then shall the righteous shine forth as the sun in the kingdom of their Father. Who hath ears to hear, let him hear.

(44) Again, the kingdom of heaven is like unto treasure hid in a field; the which when a man hath found, he hideth, and for joy thereof goeth and selleth all that he hath, and buyeth that field. (45) Again, the kingdom of heaven is like unto a merchant man, seeking goodly pearls: (46) Who, when he had found one pearl of great price, went and sold all that he had, and bought it.

(47) Again, the kingdom of heaven is like unto a net, that was cast into the sea, and gathered of every kind: (48) Which, when it was full, they drew to shore, and sat down, and gathered the good into vessels, but cast the bad away. (49) So shall it be at the end of the world: the angels shall come forth, and sever the wicked

from among the just, (50) And shall cast them into the furnace of fire: there shall be wailing and gnashing of teeth. (51) Jesus saith unto them, Have ye understood all these things? They say unto him, Yea, Lord. (52) Then said he unto them, Therefore every scribe which is instructed unto the kingdom of heaven is like unto a man that is an householder, which bringeth forth out of his treasure things new and old.

(53) And it came to pass, that when Jesus had finished these parables, he departed thence.

(54) And when he was come into his own country, he taught them in their synagogue, insomuch that they were astonished, and said, Whence hath this man this wisdom, and these mighty works? (55) Is not this the carpenter's son? is not his mother called Mary? and his brethren, James, and Joses, and Simon, and Judas? (56) And his sisters, are they not all with us? Whence then hath this man all these things? (57) And they were offended in him. But Jesus said unto them, A prophet is not without honour, save in his own country, and in his own house. (58) And he did not many mighty works there because of their unbelief.

Matthew 14

(1) At that tim e Herod the tetrarch heard of the fame of Jesus, (2) And said unto his servants, This is John the Baptist; he is risen from the dead; and therefore mighty works do shew forth themselves in him. (3) For Herod had laid hold on John, and bound him, and put him in prison for Herodias' sake, his brother Philip's wife. (4) For John said unto him, It is not lawful for thee to have her. (5) And when he would have put him to death, he feared the multitude, because they counted him as a prophet. (6) But when Herod's birthday was kept, the daughter of Herodias danced before them, and pleased Herod. (7) Whereupon he promised with an oath to give her whatsoever she would ask. (8) And she, being before instructed of her mother, said, Give me here John Baptist's head in a charger. (9) And the king was sorry: nevertheless for the oath's sake, and them which sat with him at meat, he commanded it to be given her. (10) And he sent, and beheaded John in the prison. (11) And his

head was brought in a charger, and given to the damsel: and she brought it to her mother. (12) And his disciples came, and took up the body, and buried it, and went and told Jesus.

(13) When Jesus heard of it, he departed thence by ship into a desert place apart: and when the people had heard thereof, they followed him on foot out of the cities. (14) And Jesus went forth, and saw a great multitude, and was moved with compassion toward them, and he healed their sick.

(15) And when it was evening, his disciples came to him, saying, This is a desert place, and the time is now past; send the multitude away, that they may go into the villages, and buy themselves victuals. (16) But Jesus said unto them, They need not depart; give ye them to eat. (17) And they say unto him, We have here but five loaves, and two fishes. (18) He said, Bring them hither to me. (19) And he commanded the multitude to sit down on the grass, and took the five loaves, and the two fishes, and looking up to heaven, he blessed, and brake, and gave the loaves to his disciples, and the disciples to the multitude. (20) And they did all eat, and were filled: and they took up of the fragments that remained twelve baskets full. (21) And they that had eaten were about five thousand men, beside women and children.

(22) And straightway Jesus constrained his disciples to get into a ship, and to go before him unto the other side, while he sent the multitudes away. (23) And when he had sent the multitudes away, he went up into a mountain apart to pray: and when the evening was come, he was there alone. (24) But the ship was now in the midst of the sea, tossed with waves: for the wind was contrary. (25) And in the fourth watch of the night Jesus went unto them, walking on the sea. (26) And when the disciples saw him walking on the sea, they were troubled, saying, It is a spirit; and they cried out for fear. (27) But straightway Jesus spake unto them, saying, Be of good cheer; it is I; be not afraid. (28) And Peter answered him and said, Lord, if it be thou, bid me come unto thee on the water. (29) And he said, Come. And when Peter was come down out of the ship, he walked on the water, to go to Jesus. (30) But when he saw the wind boisterous, he was afraid; and beginning to sink, he

cried, saying, Lord, save me. (31) And immediately Jesus stretched forth his hand, and caught him, and said unto him, O thou of little faith, wherefore didst thou doubt? (32) And when they were come into the ship, the wind ceased. (33) Then they that were in the ship came and worshipped him, saying, Of a truth thou art the Son of God.

(34) And when they were gone over, they came into the land of Gennesaret. (35) And when the men of that place had knowledge of him, they sent out into all that country round about, and brought unto him all that were diseased; (36) And besought him that they might only touch the hem of his garment: and as many as touched were made perfectly whole.

Matthew 15

(1) Then came to Jesus scribes and Pharisees, which were of Jerusalem, saying, (2) Why do thy disciples transgress the tradition of the elders? for they wash not their hands when they eat bread. (3) But he answered and said unto them, Why do ye also transgress the commandment of God by your tradition? (4) For God commanded, saying, Honour thy father and mother: and, He that curseth father or mother, let him die the death. (5) But ye say, Whosoever shall say to his father or his mother, It is a gift, by whatsoever thou mightest be profited by me; (6) And honour not his father or his mother, he shall be free. Thus have ye made the commandment of God of none effect by your tradition. (7) Ye hypocrites, well did Esaias prophesy of you, saying,

(8) This people draweth nigh unto me with their mouth, and honoureth me with their lips;

But their heart is far from me.

(9) But in vain they do worship me,

Teaching for doctrines the commandments of men.

(10) And he called the multitude, and said unto them, Hear, and understand: (11) Not that which goeth into the mouth defileth a man; but that which cometh out of the mouth, this defileth a man. (12) Then came his disciples, and said unto him, Knowest thou that the Pharisees were offended, after they heard this saying?

(13) But he answered and said, Every plant, which my heavenly Father hath not planted, shall be rooted up. (14) Let them alone: they be blind leaders of the blind. And if the blind lead the blind, both shall fall into the ditch. (15) Then answered Peter and said unto him, Declare unto us this parable. (16) And Jesus said, Are ye also yet without understanding? (17) Do not ye yet understand, that whatsoever entereth in at the mouth goeth into the belly, and is cast out into the draught? (18) But those things which proceed out of the mouth come forth from the heart; and they defile the man. (19) For out of the heart proceed evil thoughts, murders, adulteries, fornications, thefts, false witness, blasphemies: (20) These are the things which defile a man: but to eat with unwashen hands defileth not a man.

(21) Then Jesus went thence, and departed into the coasts of Tyre and Sidon. (22) And, behold, a woman of Canaan came out of the same coasts, and cried unto him, saying, Have mercy on me, O Lord, thou Son of David; my daughter is grievously vexed with a devil. (23) But he answered her not a word. And his disciples came and besought him, saying, Send her away; for she crieth after us. (24) But he answered and said, I am not sent but unto the lost sheep of the house of Israel. (25) Then came she and worshipped him, saying, Lord, help me. (26) But he answered and said, It is not meet to take the children's bread, and to cast it to dogs. (27) And she said, Truth, Lord: yet the dogs eat of the crumbs which fall from their masters' table. (28) Then Jesus answered and said unto her, O woman, great is thy faith: be it unto thee even as thou wilt. And her daughter was made whole from that very hour.

(29) And Jesus departed from thence, and came nigh unto the sea of Galilee; and went up into a mountain, and sat down there. (30) And great multitudes came unto him, having with them those that were lame, blind, dumb, maimed, and many others, and cast them down at Jesus' feet; and he healed them: (31) Insomuch that the multitude wondered, when they saw the dumb to speak, the maimed to be whole, the lame to walk, and the blind to see: and they glorified the God of Israel.

(32) Then Jesus called his disciples unto him, and said, I have compassion on the multitude, because they

continue with me now three days, and have nothing to eat: and I will not send them away fasting, lest they faint in the way. (33) And his disciples say unto him, Whence should we have so much bread in the wilderness, as to fill so great a multitude? (34) And Jesus saith unto them, How many loaves have ye? And they said, Seven, and a few little fishes. (35) And he commanded the multitude to sit down on the ground. (36) And he took the seven loaves and the fishes, and gave thanks, and brake them, and gave to his disciples, and the disciples to the multitude. (37) And they did all eat, and were filled: and they took up of the broken meat that was left seven baskets full. (38) And they that did eat were four thousand men, beside women and children. (39) And he sent away the multitude, and took ship, and came into the coasts of Magdala.

Matthew 16

(1) The Pharisees also with the Sadducees came, and tempting desired him that he would shew them a sign from heaven. (2) He answered and said unto them, When it is evening, ye say, It will be fair weather: for the sky is red. (3) And in the morning, It will be foul weather to day: for the sky is red and lowring. O ye hypocrites, ye can discern the face of the sky; but can ye not discern the signs of the times? (4) A wicked and adulterous generation seeketh after a sign; and there shall no sign be given unto it, but the sign of the prophet Jonas. And he left them, and departed. (5) And when his disciples were come to the other side, they had forgotten to take bread.

, (6) Then Jesus said unto them, Take heed and beware of the leaven of the Pharisees and of the Sadducees. (7) And they reasoned among themselves, saying, It is because we have taken no bread. (8) Which when Jesus perceived, he said unto them, O ye of little faith, why reason ye among yourselves, because ye have brought no bread? (9) Do ye not yet understand, neither remember the five loaves of the five thousand, and how many baskets ye took up? (10) Neither the seven loaves of the four thousand, and how many baskets ye took up? (11) How is it that ye do not understand that I spake it not to you concerning bread, that ye should beware of the leaven of the Pharisees and of the Sadducees? (12) Then understood they how that he bade them not beware of the leaven of bread, but of the doctrine of the Pharisees and of the Sadducees.

(13) When Jesus came into the coasts of Caesarea Philippi, he asked his disciples, saying, Whom do men say that I the Son of man am? (14) And they said, Some say that thou art John the Baptist: some, Elias; and others, Jeremias, or one of the prophets. (15) He saith unto them, But whom say ye that I am?

(16) And Simon Peter answered and said, Thou art the Christ, the Son of the living God. (17) And Jesus answered and said unto him, Blessed art thou, Simon Barjona: for flesh and blood hath not revealed it unto thee, but my Father which is in heaven. (18) And I say also unto thee, That thou art Peter, and upon this rock I will build my church; and the gates of hell shall not prevail against it. (19) And I will give unto thee the keys of the kingdom of heaven: and whatsoever thou shalt bind on earth shall be bound in heaven: and whatsoever thou shalt loose on earth shall be loosed in heaven. (20) Then charged he his disciples that they should tell no man that he was Jesus the Christ.

(21) From that time forth began Jesus to shew unto his disciples, how that he must go unto Jerusalem, and suffer many things of the elders and chief priests and scribes, and be killed, and be raised again the third day. (22) Then Peter took him, and began to rebuke him, saying, Be it far from thee, Lord: this shall not be unto thee. (23) But he turned, and said unto Peter, Get thee behind me, Satan: thou art an offence unto me: for thou savourest not the things that be of God, but those that be of men.

(24) Then said Jesus unto his disciples, If any man will come after me, let him deny himself, and take up his cross, and follow me. (25) For whosoever will save his life shall lose it: and whosoever will lose his life for my sake shall find it. (26) For what is a man profited, if he shall gain the whole world, and lose his own soul? or what shall a man give in exchange for his soul? (27) For the Son of man shall come in the glory of his Father with his angels; and then he shall reward every man

according to his works. (28) Verily I say unto you, There be some standing here, which shall not taste of death, till they see the Son of man coming in his kingdom.

Matthew 17

(1) And after six days Jesus taketh Peter, James, and John his brother, and bringeth them up into an high mountain apart, (2) And was transfigured before them: and his face did shine as the sun, and his raiment was white as the light. (3) And, behold, there appeared unto them Moses and Elias talking with him. (4) Then answered Peter, and said unto Jesus, Lord, it is good for us to be here: if thou wilt, let us make here three tabernacles; one for thee, and one for Moses, and one for Elias. (5) While he yet spake, behold, a bright cloud overshadowed them: and behold a voice out of the cloud, which said, This is my beloved Son, in whom I am well pleased; hear ye him. (6) And when the disciples heard it, they fell on their face, and were sore afraid. (7) And Jesus came and touched them, and said, Arise, and be not afraid. (8) And when they had lifted up their eyes, they saw no man, save Jesus only.

(9) And as they came down from the mountain, Jesus charged them, saying, Tell the vision to no man, until the Son of man be risen again from the dead. (10) And his disciples asked him, saying, Why then say the scribes that Elias must first come? (11) And Jesus answered and said unto them, Elias truly shall first come, and restore all things. (12) But I say unto you, That Elias is come already, and they knew him not, but have done unto him whatsoever they listed. Likewise shall also the Son of man suffer of them. (13) Then the disciples understood that he spake unto them of John the Baptist.

(14) And when they were come to the multitude, there came to him a certain man, kneeling down to him, and saying, (15) Lord, have mercy on my son: for he is lunatick, and sore vexed: for ofttimes he falleth into the fire, and oft into the water. (16) And I brought him to thy disciples, and they could not cure him. (17) Then Jesus answered and said, O faithless and perverse generation, how long shall I be with you? how long shall I suffer you? bring him hither to me. (18) And Jesus rebuked the

devil; and he departed out of him: and the child was cured from that very hour.

(19) Then came the disciples to Jesus apart, and said, Why could not we cast him out? (20) And Jesus said unto them, Because of your unbelief: for verily I say unto you, If ye have faith as a grain of mustard seed, ye shall say unto this mountain, Remove hence to yonder place; and it shall remove; and nothing shall be impossible unto you. (21) Howbeit this kind goeth not out but by prayer and fasting.

(22) And while they abode in Galilee, Jesus said unto them, The Son of man shall be betrayed into the hands of men: (23) And they shall kill him, and the third day he shall be raised again. And they were exceeding sorry.

(24) And when they were come to Capernaum, they that received tribute money came to Peter, and said, Doth not your master pay tribute? (25) He saith, Yes. And when he was come into the house, Jesus prevented him, saying, What thinkest thou, Simon? of whom do the kings of the earth take custom or tribute? of their own children, or of strangers? (26) Peter saith unto him, Of strangers. Jesus saith unto him, Then are the children free. (27) Notwithstanding, lest we should offend them, go thou to the sea, and cast an hook, and take up the fish that first cometh up; and when thou hast opened his mouth, thou shalt find a piece of money: that take, and give unto them for me and thee.

Matthew 18

(1) At the same time came the disciples unto Jesus, saying, Who is the greatest in the kingdom of heaven? (2) And Jesus called a little child unto him, and set him in the midst of them, (3) And said, Verily I say unto you, Except ye be converted, and become as little children, ye shall not enter into the kingdom of heaven. (4) Whosoever therefore shall humble himself as this little child, the same is greatest in the kingdom of heaven. (5) And whoso shall receive one such little child in my name receiveth me. (6) But whoso shall offend one of these little ones which believe in me, it were better for him that a millstone were hanged about his neck, and

that he were drowned in the depth of the sea.

(7) Woe unto the world because of offences! for it must needs be that offences come; but woe to that man by whom the offence cometh! (8) Wherefore if thy hand or thy foot offend thee, cut them off, and cast them from thee: it is better for thee to enter into life halt or maimed, rather than having two hands or two feet to be cast into everlasting fire. (9) And if thine eye offend thee, pluck it out, and cast it from thee: it is better for thee to enter into life with one eye, rather than having two eyes to be cast into hell fire. (10) Take heed that ye despise not one of these little ones; for I say unto you, That in heaven their angels do always behold the face of my Father which is in heaven. (11) For the Son of man is come to save that which was lost. (12) How think ye? if a man have an hundred sheep, and one of them be gone astray, doth he not leave the ninety and nine, and goeth into the mountains, and seeketh that which is gone astray? (13) And if so be that he find it, verily I say unto you, he rejoiceth more of that sheep, than of the ninety and nine which went not astray. (14) Even so it is not the will of your Father which is in heaven, that one of these little ones should perish.

(15) Moreover if thy brother shall trespass against thee, go and tell him his fault between thee and him alone: if he shall hear thee, thou hast gained thy brother. (16) But if he will not hear thee, then take with thee one or two more, that in the mouth of two or three witnesses every word may be established. (17) And if he shall neglect to hear them, tell it unto the church: but if he neglect to hear the church, let him be unto thee as an heathen man and a publican. (18) Verily I say unto you, Whatsoever ye shall bind on earth shall be bound in heaven: and whatsoever ye shall loose on earth shall be loosed in heaven. (19) Again I say unto you, That if two of you shall agree on earth as touching any thing that they shall ask, it shall be done for them of my Father which is in heaven. (20) For where two or three are gathered together in my name, there am I in the midst of them.

(21) Then came Peter to him, and said, Lord, how oft shall my brother sin against me, and I forgive him? till seven times? (22) Jesus saith unto him, I say not unto

thee, Until seven times: but, Until seventy times seven. (23) Therefore is the kingdom of heaven likened unto a certain king, which would take account of his servants. (24) And when he had begun to reckon, one was brought unto him, which owed him ten thousand talents. (25) But forasmuch as he had not to pay, his lord commanded him to be sold, and his wife, and children, and all that he had, and payment to be made. (26) The servant therefore fell down, and worshipped him, saying, Lord, have patience with me, and I will pay thee all. (27) Then the lord of that servant was moved with compassion, and loosed him, and forgave him the debt. (28) But the same servant went out, and found one of his fellowservants, which owed him an hundred pence: and he laid hands on him, and took him by the throat, saying, Pay me that thou owest. (29) And his fellowservant fell down at his feet, and besought him, saying, Have patience with me, and I will pay thee all. (30) And he would not: but went and cast him into prison, till he should pay the debt. (31) So when his fellowservants saw what was done, they were very sorry, and came and told unto their lord all that was done. (32) Then his lord, after that he had called him, said unto him, O thou wicked servant, I forgave thee all that debt, because thou desiredst me: (33) Shouldest not thou also have had compassion on thy fellowservant, even as I had pity on thee? (34) And his lord was wroth, and delivered him to the tormentors, till he should pay all that was due unto him. (35) So likewise shall my heavenly Father do also unto you, if ye from your hearts forgive not every one his brother their trespasses.

Matthew 19

(1) And it came to pass, that when Jesus had finished these sayings, he departed from Galilee, and came into the coasts of Judaea beyond Jordan; (2) And great multitudes followed him; and he healed them there.

(3) The Pharisees also came unto him, tempting him, and saying unto him, Is it lawful for a man to put away his wife for every cause? (4) And he answered and said unto them, Have ye not read, that he which made

them at the beginning made them male and female, (5) And said, For this cause shall a man leave father and mother, and shall cleave to his wife: and they twain shall be one flesh? (6) Wherefore they are no more twain, but one flesh. What therefore God hath joined together, let not man put asunder. (7) They say unto him, Why did Moses then command to give a writing of divorcement, and to put her away? (8) He saith unto them, Moses because of the hardness of your hearts suffered you to put away your wives: but from the beginning it was not so. (9) And I say unto you, Whosoever shall put away his wife, except it be for fornication, and shall marry another, committeth adultery: and whoso marrieth her which is put away doth commit adultery. (10) His disciples say unto him, If the case of the man be so with his wife, it is not good to marry. (11) But he said unto them, All men cannot receive this saying, save they to whom it is given. (12) For there are some eunuchs, which were so born from their mother's womb: and there are some eunuchs, which were made eunuchs of men: and there be eunuchs, which have made themselves eunuchs for the kingdom of heaven's sake. He that is able to receive it, let him receive it.

(13) Then were there brought unto him little children, that he should put his hands on them, and pray: and the disciples rebuked them. (14) But Jesus said, Suffer little children, and forbid them not, to come unto me: for of such is the kingdom of heaven. (15) And he laid his hands on them, and departed thence.

(16) And, behold, one came and said unto him, Good Master, what good thing shall I do, that I may have eternal life? (17) And he said unto him, Why callest thou me good? there is none good but one, that is, God: but if thou wilt enter into life, keep the commandments. (18) He saith unto him, Which? Jesus said, Thou shalt do no murder, Thou shalt not commit adultery, Thou shalt not steal, Thou shalt not bear false witness, (19) Honour thy father and thy mother: and, Thou shalt love thy neighbour as thyself. (20) The young man saith unto him, All these things have I kept from my youth up: what lack I yet? (21) Jesus said unto him, If thou wilt be perfect, go and sell that thou hast, and give to the poor, and thou shalt have treasure in heaven: and come and

follow me. (22) But when the young man heard that saying, he went away sorrowful: for he had great possessions.

(23) Then said Jesus unto his disciples, Verily I say unto you, That a rich man shall hardly enter into the kingdom of heaven. (24) And again I say unto you, It is easier for a camel to go through the eye of a needle, than for a rich man to enter into the kingdom of God. (25) When his disciples heard it, they were exceedingly amazed, saying, Who then can be saved? (26) But Jesus beheld them, and said unto them, With men this is impossible; but with God all things are possible.

(27) Then answered Peter and said unto him, Behold, we have forsaken all, and followed thee; what shall we have therefore? (28) And Jesus said unto them, Verily I say unto you, That ye which have followed me, in the regeneration when the Son of man shall sit in the throne of his glory, ye also shall sit upon twelve thrones, judging the twelve tribes of Israel. (29) And every one that hath forsaken houses, or brethren, or sisters, or father, or mother, or wife, or children, or lands, for my name's sake, shall receive an hundredfold, and shall inherit everlasting life. (30) But many that are first shall be last; and the last shall be first.

Matthew 20

(1) For the kingdom of heaven is like unto a man that is an householder, which went out early in the morning to hire labourers into his vineyard. (2) And when he had agreed with the labourers for a penny a day, he sent them into his vineyard. (3) And he went out about the third hour, and saw others standing idle in the marketplace, (4) And said unto them; Go ye also into the vineyard, and whatsoever is right I will give you. And they went their way. (5) Again he went out about the sixth and ninth hour, and did likewise. (6) And about the eleventh hour he went out, and found others standing idle, and saith unto them, Why stand ye here all the day idle? (7) They say unto him, Because no man hath hired us. He saith unto them, Go ye also into the vineyard; and whatsoever is right, that shall ye receive. (8) So when even was come, the lord of the vineyard

saith unto his steward, Call the labourers, and give them their hire, beginning from the last unto the first. (9) And when they came that were hired about the eleventh hour, they received every man a penny. (10) But when the first came, they supposed that they should have received more; and they likewise received every man a penny. (11) And when they had received it, they murmured against the goodman of the house, (12) Saying, These last have wrought but one hour, and thou hast made them equal unto us, which have borne the burden and heat of the day. (13) But he answered one of them, and said, Friend, I do thee no wrong: didst not thou agree with me for a penny? (14) Take that thine is, and go thy way: I will give unto this last, even as unto thee. (15) Is it not lawful for me to do what I will with mine own? Is thine eye evil, because I am good? (16) So the last shall be first, and the first last: for many be called, but few chosen.

(17) And Jesus going up to Jerusalem took the twelve disciples apart in the way, and said unto them, (18) Behold, we go up to Jerusalem; and the Son of man shall be betrayed unto the chief priests and unto the scribes, and they shall condemn him to death, (19) And shall deliver him to the Gentiles to mock, and to scourge, and to crucify him: and the third day he shall rise again.

(20) Then came to him the mother of Zebedee's children with her sons, worshipping him, and desiring a certain thing of him. (21) And he said unto her, What wilt thou? She saith unto him, Grant that these my two sons may sit, the one on thy right hand, and the other on the left, in thy kingdom. (22) But Jesus answered and said, Ye know not what ye ask. Are ye able to drink of the cup that I shall drink of, and to be baptized with the baptism that I am baptized with? They say unto him, We are able. (23) And he saith unto them, Ye shall drink indeed of my cup, and be baptized with the baptism that I am baptized with: but to sit on my right hand, and on my left, is not mine to give, but it shall be given to them for whom it is prepared of my Father. (24) And when the ten heard it, they were moved with indignation against the two brethren. (25) But Jesus called them unto him, and said, Ye know that the princes of the Gentiles

exercise dominion over them, and they that are great exercise authority upon them. (26) But it shall not be so among you: but whosoever will be great among you, let him be your minister; (27) And whosoever will be chief among you, let him be your servant: (28) Even as the Son of man came not to be ministered unto, but to minister, and to give his life a ransom for many. (29) And as they departed from Jericho, a great multitude followed him.

(30) And, behold, two blind men sitting by the way side, when they heard that Jesus passed by, cried out, saying, Have mercy on us, O Lord, thou Son of David. (31) And the multitude rebuked them, because they should hold their peace: but they cried the more, saying, Have mercy on us, O Lord, thou Son of David. (32) And Jesus stood still, and called them, and said, What will ye that I shall do unto you? (33) They say unto him, Lord, that our eyes may be opened. (34) So Jesus had compassion on them, and touched their eyes: and immediately their eyes received sight, and they followed him.

Matthew 21

(1) And when they drew nigh unto Jerusalem, and were come to Bethphage, unto the mount of Olives, then sent Jesus two disciples, (2) Saying unto them, Go into the village over against you, and straightway ye shall find an ass tied, and a colt with her: loose them, and bring them unto me. (3) And if any man say ought unto you, ye shall say, The Lord hath need of them; and straightway he will send them. (4) All this was done, that it might be fulfilled which was spoken by the prophet, saying,

(5) Tell ye the daughter of Sion,
Behold, thy King cometh unto thee,
meek, and sitting upon an ass,
and a colt the foal of an ass.

(6) And the disciples went, and did as Jesus commanded them, (7) And brought the ass, and the colt, and put on them their clothes, and they set him thereon. (8) And a very great multitude spread their garments in the way; others cut down branches from the trees, and

strewed them in the way. (9) And the multitudes that went before, and that followed, cried, saying, Hosanna to the Son of David: Blessed is he that cometh in the name of the Lord; Hosanna in the highest. (10) And when he was come into Jerusalem, all the city was moved, saying, Who is this? (11) And the multitude said, This is Jesus the prophet of Nazareth of Galilee.

(12) And Jesus went into the temple of God, and cast out all them that sold and bought in the temple, and overthrew the tables of the moneychangers, and the seats of them that sold doves, (13) And said unto them, It is written, My house shall be called the house of prayer; but ye have made it a den of thieves. (14) And the blind and the lame came to him in the temple; and he healed them. (15) And when the chief priests and scribes saw the wonderful things that he did, and the children crying in the temple, and saying, Hosanna to the Son of David; they were sore displeased, (16) And said unto him, Hearest thou what these say? And Jesus saith unto them, Yea; have ye never read, Out of the mouth of babes and sucklings thou hast perfected praise? (17) And he left them, and went out of the city into Bethany; and he lodged there.

(18) Now in the morning as he returned into the city, he hungered. (19) And when he saw a fig tree in the way, he came to it, and found nothing thereon, but leaves only, and said unto it, Let no fruit grow on thee henceforward for ever. And presently the fig tree withered away. (20) And when the disciples saw it, they marvelled, saying, How soon is the fig tree withered away! (21) Jesus answered and said unto them, Verily I say unto you, If ye have faith, and doubt not, ye shall not only do this which is done to the fig tree, but also if ye shall say unto this mountain, Be thou removed, and be thou cast into the sea; it shall be done. (22) And all things, whatsoever ye shall ask in prayer, believing, ye shall receive.

(23) And when he was come into the temple, the chief priests and the elders of the people came unto him as he was teaching, and said, By what authority doest thou these things? and who gave thee this authority? (24) And Jesus answered and said unto them, I also will ask you one thing, which if ye tell me, I in like wise will

tell you by what authority I do these things. (25) The baptism of John, whence was it? from heaven, or of men? And they reasoned with themselves, saying, If we shall say, From heaven; he will say unto us, Why did ye not then believe him? (26) But if we shall say, Of men; we fear the people; for all hold John as a prophet. (27) And they answered Jesus, and said, We cannot tell. And he said unto them, Neither tell I you by what authority I do these things.

(28) But what think ye? A certain man had two sons; and he came to the first, and said, Son, go work to day in my vineyard. (29) He answered and said, I will not: but afterward he repented, and went. (30) And he came to the second, and said likewise. And he answered and said, I go, sir: and went not. (31) Whether of them twain did the will of his father? They say unto him, The first. Jesus saith unto them, Verily I say unto you, That the publicans and the harlots go into the kingdom of God before you. (32) For John came unto you in the way of righteousness, and ye believed him not: but the publicans and the harlots believed him: and ye, when ye had seen it, repented not afterward, that ye might believe him.

(33) Hear another parable: There was a certain householder, which planted a vineyard, and hedged it round about, and digged a winepress in it, and built a tower, and let it out to husbandmen, and went into a far country: (34) And when the time of the fruit drew near, he sent his servants to the husbandmen, that they might receive the fruits of it. (35) And the husbandmen took his servants, and beat one, and killed another, and stoned another. (36) Again, he sent other servants more than the first: and they did unto them likewise. (37) But last of all he sent unto them his son, saying, They will reverence my son. (38) But when the husbandmen saw the son, they said among themselves, This is the heir; come, let us kill him, and let us seize on his inheritance. (39) And they caught him, and cast him out of the vineyard, and slew him. (40) When the lord therefore of the vineyard cometh, what will he do unto those husbandmen? (41) They say unto him, He will miserably destroy those wicked men, and will let out his vineyard unto other husbandmen, which shall render him the

fruits in their seasons. (42) Jesus saith unto them, Did
ye never read in the scriptures,

The stone which the builders rejected,
The same is become the head of the corner:
This is the Lord's doing,
And it is marvellous in our eyes?

(43) Therefore say I unto you, The kingdom of God
shall be taken from you, and given to a nation bringing
forth the fruits thereof. (44) And whosoever shall fall on
this stone shall be broken: but on whomsoever it shall
fall, it will grind him to powder. (45) And when the chief
priests and Pharisees had heard his parables, they
perceived that he spake of them. (46) But when they
sought to lay hands on him, they feared the multitude,
because they took him for a prophet.

Matthew 22

(1) And Jesus answered and spake unto them again
by parables, and said, (2) The kingdom of heaven is like
unto a certain king, which made a marriage for his son,
(3) And sent forth his servants to call them that were
bidden to the wedding: and they would not come. (4)
Again, he sent forth other servants, saying, Tell them
which are bidden, Behold, I have prepared my dinner:
my oxen and my fatlings are killed, and all things are
ready: come unto the marriage. (5) But they made light
of it, and went their ways, one to his farm, another to his
merchandise: (6) And the remnant took his servants, and
entreated them spitefully, and slew them. (7) But when
the king heard thereof, he was wroth: and he sent forth
his armies, and destroyed those murderers, and burned
up their city. (8) Then saith he to his servants, The
wedding is ready, but they which were bidden were not
worthy. (9) Go ye therefore into the highways, and as
many as ye shall find, bid to the marriage. (10) So those
servants went out into the highways, and gathered
together all as many as they found, both bad and good:
and the wedding was furnished with guests.

(11) And when the king came in to see the guests,
he saw there a man which had not on a wedding garment:
(12) And he saith unto him, Friend, how camest thou in
hither not having a wedding garment? And he was

speechless. (13) Then said the king to the servants, Bind him hand and foot, and take him away, and cast him into outer darkness; there shall be weeping and gnashing of teeth. (14) For many are called, but few are chosen.

(15) Then went the Pharisees, and took counsel how they might entangle him in his talk. (16) And they sent out unto him their disciples with the Herodians, saying, Master, we know that thou art true, and teachest the way of God in truth, neither carest thou for any man: for thou regardest not the person of men. (17) Tell us therefore, What thinkest thou? Is it lawful to give tribute unto Caesar, or not? (18) But Jesus perceived their wickedness, and said, Why tempt ye me, ye hypocrites? (19) Shew me the tribute money. And they brought unto him a penny. (20) And he saith unto them, Whose is this image and superscription? (21) They say unto him, Caesar's. Then saith he unto them, Render therefore unto Caesar the things which are Caesar's; and unto God the things that are God's. (22) When they had heard these words, they marvelled, and left him, and went their way.

(23) The same day came to him the Sadducees, which say that there is no resurrection, and asked him, (24) Saying, Master, Moses said, If a man die, having no children, his brother shall marry his wife, and raise up seed unto his brother. (25) Now there were with us seven brethren: and the first, when he had married a wife, deceased, and, having no issue, left his wife unto his brother: (26) Likewise the second also, and the third, unto the seventh. (27) And last of all the woman died also. (28) Therefore in the resurrection whose wife shall she be of the seven? for they all had her. (29) Jesus answered and said unto them, Ye do err, not knowing the scriptures, nor the power of God. (30) For in the resurrection they neither marry, nor are given in marriage, but are as the angels of God in heaven. (31) But as touching the resurrection of the dead, have ye not read that which was spoken unto you by God, saying, (32) I am the God of Abraham, and the God of Isaac, and the God of Jacob? God is not the God of the dead, but of the living. (33) And when the multitude heard this, they were astonished at his doctrine.

(34) But when the Pharisees had heard that he had put the Sadducees to silence, they were gathered

together. (35) Then one of them, which was a lawyer, asked him a question, tempting him, and saying, (36) Master, which is the great commandment in the law? (37) Jesus said unto him, Thou shalt love the Lord thy God with all thy heart, and with all thy soul, and with all thy mind. (38) This is the first and great commandment. (39) And the second is like unto it, Thou shalt love thy neighbour as thyself. (40) On these two commandments hang all the law and the prophets.

(41) While the Pharisees were gathered together, Jesus asked them, (42) Saying, What think ye of Christ? whose son is he? They say unto him, The Son of David. (43) He saith unto them, How then doth David in spirit call him Lord, saying,

(44) The LORD said unto my Lord,

Sit thou on my right hand,

Till I make thine enemies thy footstool?

(45) If David then call him Lord, how is he his son? (46) And no man was able to answer him a word, neither durst any man from that day forth ask him any more questions.

Matthew 23

(1) Then spake Jesus to the multitude, and to his disciples, (2) Saying, The scribes and the Pharisees sit in Moses' seat: (3) All therefore whatsoever they bid you observe, that observe and do; but do not ye after their works: for they say, and do not. (4) For they bind heavy burdens and grievous to be borne, and lay them on men's shoulders; but they themselves will not move them with one of their fingers. (5) But all their works they do for to be seen of men: they make broad their phylacteries, and enlarge the borders of their garments, (6) And love the uppermost rooms at feasts, and the chief seats in the synagogues, (7) And greetings in the markets, and to be called of men, Rabbi, Rabbi. (8) But be not ye called Rabbi: for one is your Master, even Christ; and all ye are brethren. (9) And call no man your father upon the earth: for one is your Father, which is in heaven. (10) Neither be ye called masters: for one is your Master, even Christ. (11) But he that is greatest among you shall be your servant. (12) And whosoever shall

exalt himself shall be abased; and he that shall humble himself shall be exalted.

(13) But woe unto you, scribes and Pharisees, hypocrites! for ye shut up the kingdom of heaven against men: for ye neither go in yourselves, neither suffer ye them that are entering to go in. (14) Woe unto you, scribes and Pharisees, hypocrites! for ye devour widows' houses, and for a pretence make long prayer: therefore ye shall receive the greater damnation. (15) Woe unto you, scribes and Pharisees, hypocrites! for ye compass sea and land to make one proselyte, and when he is made, ye make him twofold more the child of hell than yourselves. (16) Woe unto you, ye blind guides, which say, Whosoever shall swear by the temple, it is nothing; but whosoever shall swear by the gold of the temple, he is a debtor! (17) Ye fools and blind: for whether is greater, the gold, or the temple that sanctifieth the gold? (18) And, Whosoever shall swear by the altar, it is nothing; but whosoever sweareth by the gift that is upon it, he is guilty. (19) Ye fools and blind: for whether is greater, the gift, or the altar that sanctifieth the gift? (20) Whoso therefore shall swear by the altar, sweareth by it, and by all things thereon. (21) And whoso shall swear by the temple, sweareth by it, and by him that dwelleth therein. (22) And he that shall swear by heaven, sweareth by the throne of God, and by him that sitteth thereon.

(23) Woe unto you, scribes and Pharisees, hypocrites! for ye pay tithe of mint and anise and cummin, and have omitted the weightier matters of the law, judgment, mercy, and faith: these ought ye to have done, and not to leave the other undone. (24) Ye blind guides, which strain at a gnat, and swallow a camel. (25) Woe unto you, scribes and Pharisees, hypocrites! for ye make clean the outside of the cup and of the platter, but within they are full of extortion and excess. (26) Thou blind Pharisee, cleanse first that which is within the cup and platter, that the outside of them may be clean also. (27) Woe unto you, scribes and Pharisees, hypocrites! for ye are like unto whited sepulchres, which indeed appear beautiful outward, but are within full of dead men's bones, and of all uncleanness. (28) Even so ye also outwardly appear righteous unto men, but within ye

are full of hypocrisy and iniquity. (29) Woe unto you, scribes and Pharisees, hypocrites! because ye build the tombs of the prophets, and garnish the sepulchres of the righteous, (30) And say, If we had been in the days of our fathers, we would not have been partakers with them in the blood of the prophets. (31) Wherefore ye be witnesses unto yourselves, that ye are the children of them which killed the prophets. (32) Fill ye up then the measure of your fathers. (33) Ye serpents, ye generation of vipers, how can ye escape the damnation of hell?

(34) Wherefore, behold, I send unto you prophets, and wise men, and scribes: and some of them ye shall kill and crucify; and some of them shall ye scourge in your synagogues, and persecute them from city to city: (35) That upon you may come all the righteous blood shed upon the earth, from the blood of righteous Abel unto the blood of Zacharias son of Barachias, whom ye slew between the temple and the altar. (36) Verily I say unto you, All these things shall come upon this generation.

(37) O Jerusalem, Jerusalem, thou that killest the prophets, and stonest them which are sent unto thee, how often would I have gathered thy children together, even as a hen gathereth her chickens under her wings, and ye would not! (38) Behold, your house is left unto you desolate. (39) For I say unto you, Ye shall not see me henceforth, till ye shall say, Blessed is he that cometh in the name of the Lord.

Matthew 24

(1) And Jesus went out, and departed from the temple: and his disciples came to him for to shew him the buildings of the temple. (2) And Jesus said unto them, See ye not all these things? verily I say unto you, There shall not be left here one stone upon another, that shall not be thrown down.

(3) And as he sat upon the mount of Olives, the disciples came unto him privately, saying, Tell us, when shall these things be? and what shall be the sign of thy coming, and of the end of the world? (4) And Jesus answered and said unto them, Take heed that no man deceive you. (5) For many shall come in my name,

saying, I am Christ; and shall deceive many. (6) And ye shall hear of wars and rumours of wars: see that ye be not troubled: for all these things must come to pass, but the end is not yet. (7) For nation shall rise against nation, and kingdom against kingdom: and there shall be famines, and pestilences, and earthquakes, in divers places. (8) All these are the beginning of sorrows. (9) Then shall they deliver you up to be afflicted, and shall kill you: and ye shall be hated of all nations for my name's sake. (10) And then shall many be offended, and shall betray one another, and shall hate one another. (11) And many false prophets shall rise, and shall deceive many. (12) And because iniquity shall abound, the love of many shall wax cold. (13) But he that shall endure unto the end, the same shall be saved. (14) And this gospel of the kingdom shall be preached in all the world for a witness unto all nations; and then shall the end come.

(15) When ye therefore shall see the abomination of desolation, spoken of by Daniel the prophet, stand in the holy place, (whoso readeth, let him understand:) (16) Then let them which be in Judaea flee into the mountains: (17) Let him which is on the housetop not come down to take any thing out of his house: (18) Neither let him which is in the field return back to take his clothes. (19) And woe unto them that are with child, and to them that give suck in those days! (20) But pray ye that your flight be not in the winter, neither on the sabbath day: (21) For then shall be great tribulation, such as was not since the beginning of the world to this time, no, nor ever shall be. (22) And except those days should be shortened, there should no flesh be saved: but for the elect's sake those days shall be shortened. (23) Then if any man shall say unto you, Lo, here is Christ, or there; believe it not. (24) For there shall arise false Christs, and false prophets, and shall shew great signs and wonders; insomuch that, if it were possible, they shall deceive the very elect. (25) Behold, I have told you before. (26) Wherefore if they shall say unto you, Behold, he is in the desert; go not forth: behold, he is in the secret chambers; believe it not. (27) For as the lightning cometh out of the east, and shineth even unto the west; so shall also the coming of the Son of man be.

(28) For wheresoever the carcase is, there will the eagles be gathered together.

(29) Immediately after the tribulation of those days shall the sun be darkened, and the moon shall not give her light, and the stars shall fall from heaven, and the powers of the heavens shall be shaken: (30) And then shall appear the sign of the Son of man in heaven: and then shall all the tribes of the earth mourn, and they shall see the Son of man coming in the clouds of heaven with power and great glory. (31) And he shall send his angels with a great sound of a trumpet, and they shall gather together his elect from the four winds, from one end of heaven to the other. (32) Now learn a parable of the fig tree; When his branch is yet tender, and putteth forth leaves, ye know that summer is nigh: (33) So likewise ye, when ye shall see all these things, know that it is near, even at the doors. (34) Verily I say unto you, This generation shall not pass, till all these things be fulfilled. (35) Heaven and earth shall pass away, but my words shall not pass away.

(36) But of that day and hour knoweth no man, no, not the angels of heaven, but my Father only. (37) But as the days of Noe were, so shall also the coming of the Son of man be. (38) For as in the days that were before the flood they were eating and drinking, marrying and giving in marriage, until the day that Noe entered into the ark, (39) And knew not until the flood came, and took them all away; so shall also the coming of the Son of man be. (40) Then shall two be in the field; the one shall be taken, and the other left. (41) Two women shall be grinding at the mill; the one shall be taken, and the other left.

(42) Watch therefore: for ye know not what hour your Lord doth come. (43) But know this, that if the goodman of the house had known in what watch the thief would come, he would have watched, and would not have suffered his house to be broken up. (44) Therefore be ye also ready: for in such an hour as ye think not the Son of man cometh. (45) Who then is a faithful and wise servant, whom his lord hath made ruler over his household, to give them meat in due season? (46) Blessed is that servant, whom his lord when he cometh shall find so doing. (47) Verily I say unto you,

That he shall make him ruler over all his goods. (48) But and if that evil servant shall say in his heart, My lord delayeth his coming; (49) And shall begin to smite his fellowservants, and to eat and drink with the drunken; (50) The lord of that servant shall come in a day when he looketh not for him, and in an hour that he is not aware of, (51) And shall cut him asunder, and appoint him his portion with the hypocrites: there shall be weeping and gnashing of teeth.

Matthew 25

(1) Then shall the kingdom of heaven be likened unto ten virgins, which took their lamps, and went forth to meet the bridegroom. (2) And five of them were wise, and five were foolish. (3) They that were foolish took their lamps, and took no oil with them: (4) But the wise took oil in their vessels with their lamps. (5) While the bridegroom tarried, they all slumbered and slept. (6) And at midnight there was a cry made, Behold, the bridegroom cometh; go ye out to meet him. (7) Then all those virgins arose, and trimmed their lamps. (8) And the foolish said unto the wise, Give us of your oil; for our lamps are gone out. (9) But the wise answered, saying, Not so; lest there be not enough for us and you: but go ye rather to them that sell, and buy for yourselves. (10) And while they went to buy, the bridegroom came; and they that were ready went in with him to the marriage: and the door was shut. (11) Afterward came also the other virgins, saying, Lord, Lord, open to us. (12) But he answered and said, Verily I say unto you, I know you not. (13) Watch therefore, for ye know neither the day nor the hour wherein the Son of man cometh.

(14) For the kingdom of heaven is as a man travelling into a far country, who called his own servants, and delivered unto them his goods. (15) And unto one he gave five talents, to another two, and to another one; to every man according to his several ability; and straightway took his journey. (16) Then he that had received the five talents went and traded with the same, and made them other five talents. (17) And likewise he that had received two, he also gained other

two. (18) But he that had received one went and digged in the earth, and hid his lord's money. (19) After a long time the lord of those servants cometh, and reckoneth with them. (20) And so he that had received five talents came and brought other five talents, saying, Lord, thou deliveredst unto me five talents: behold, I have gained beside them five talents more. (21) His lord said unto him, Well done, thou good and faithful servant: thou hast been faithful over a few things, I will make thee ruler over many things: enter thou into the joy of thy lord. (22) He also that had received two talents came and said, Lord, thou deliveredst unto me two talents: behold, I have gained two other talents beside them. (23) His lord said unto him, Well done, good and faithful servant; thou hast been faithful over a few things, I will make thee ruler over many things: enter thou into the joy of thy lord. (24) Then he which had received the one talent came and said, Lord, I knew thee that thou art an hard man, reaping where thou hast not sown, and gathering where thou hast not strawed: (25) And I was afraid, and went and hid thy talent in the earth: lo, there thou hast that is thine. (26) His lord answered and said unto him, Thou wicked and slothful servant, thou knewest that I reap where I sowed not, and gather where I have not strawed: (27) Thou oughtest therefore to have put my money to the exchangers, and then at my coming I should have received mine own with usury. (28) Take therefore the talent from him, and give it unto him which hath ten talents. (29) For unto every one that hath shall be given, and he shall have abundance: but from him that hath not shall be taken away even that which he hath. (30) And cast ye the unprofitable servant into outer darkness: there shall be weeping and gnashing of teeth.

(31) When the Son of man shall come in his glory, and all the holy angels with him, then shall he sit upon the throne of his glory: (32) And before him shall be gathered all nations: and he shall separate them one from another, as a shepherd divideth his sheep from the goats: (33) And he shall set the sheep on his right hand, but the goats on the left. (34) Then shall the King say unto them on his right hand, Come, ye blessed of my Father, inherit the kingdom prepared for you from the foundation of the world: (35) For I was an hungred, and

ye gave me meat: I was thirsty, and ye gave me drink: I was a stranger, and ye took me in: (36) Naked, and ye clothed me: I was sick, and ye visited me: I was in prison, and ye came unto me. (37) Then shall the righteous answer him, saying, Lord, when saw we thee an hungred, and fed thee? or thirsty, and gave thee drink? (38) When saw we thee a stranger, and took thee in? or naked, and clothed thee? (39) Or when saw we thee sick, or in prison, and came unto thee? (40) And the King shall answer and say unto them, Verily I say unto you, Inasmuch as ye have done it unto one of the least of these my brethren, ye have done it unto me. (41) Then shall he say also unto them on the left hand, Depart from me, ye cursed, into everlasting fire, prepared for the devil and his angels: (42) For I was an hungred, and ye gave me no meat: I was thirsty, and ye gave me no drink: (43) I was a stranger, and ye took me not in: naked, and ye clothed me not: sick, and in prison, and ye visited me not. (44) Then shall they also answer him, saying, Lord, when saw we thee an hungred, or athirst, or a stranger, or naked, or sick, or in prison, and did not minister unto thee? (45) Then shall he answer them, saying, Verily I say unto you, Inasmuch as ye did it not to one of the least of these, ye did it not to me. (46) And these shall go away into everlasting punishment: but the righteous into life eternal.

Matthew 26

(1) And it came to pass, when Jesus had finished all these sayings, he said unto his disciples, (2) Ye know that after two days is the feast of the passover, and the Son of man is betrayed to be crucified. (3) Then assembled together the chief priests, and the scribes, and the elders of the people, unto the palace of the high priest, who was called Caiaphas, (4) And consulted that they might take Jesus by subtilty, and kill him. (5) But they said, Not on the feast day, lest there be an uproar among the people.

(6) Now when Jesus was in Bethany, in the house of Simon the leper, (7) There came unto him a woman having an alabaster box of very precious ointment, and poured it on his head, as he sat at meat. (8) But when his

disciples saw it, they had indignation, saying, To what purpose is this waste? (9) For this ointment might have been sold for much, and given to the poor. (10) When Jesus understood it, he said unto them, Why trouble ye the woman? for she hath wrought a good work upon me. (11) For ye have the poor always with you; but me ye have not always. (12) For in that she hath poured this ointment on my body, she did it for my burial. (13) Verily I say unto you, Wheresoever this gospel shall be preached in the whole world, there shall also this, that this woman hath done, be told for a memorial of her.

(14) Then one of the twelve, called Judas Iscariot, went unto the chief priests, (15) And said unto them, What will ye give me, and I will deliver him unto you? And they covenanted with him for thirty pieces of silver. (16) And from that time he sought opportunity to betray him.

(17) Now the first day of the feast of unleavened bread the disciples came to Jesus, saying unto him, Where wilt thou that we prepare for thee to eat the passover? (18) And he said, Go into the city to such a man, and say unto him, The Master saith, My time is at hand; I will keep the passover at thy house with my disciples. (19) And the disciples did as Jesus had appointed them; and they made ready the passover.

(20) Now when the even was come, he sat down with the twelve. (21) And as they did eat, he said, Verily I say unto you, that one of you shall betray me. (22) And they were exceeding sorrowful, and began every one of them to say unto him, Lord, is it I? (23) And he answered and said, He that dippeth his hand with me in the dish, the same shall betray me. (24) The Son of man goeth as it is written of him: but woe unto that man by whom the Son of man is betrayed! it had been good for that man if he had not been born. (25) Then Judas, which betrayed him, answered and said, Master, is it I? He said unto him, Thou hast said.

(26) And as they were eating, Jesus took bread, and blessed it, and brake it, and gave it to the disciples, and said, Take, eat; this is my body. (27) And he took the cup, and gave thanks, and gave it to them, saying, Drink ye all of it; (28) For this is my blood of the new testament, which is shed for many for the remission of

sins. (29) But I say unto you, I will not drink henceforth of this fruit of the vine, until that day when I drink it new with you in my Father's kingdom.

(30) And when they had sung an hymn, they went out into the mount of Olives. (31) Then saith Jesus unto them, All ye shall be offended because of me this night: for it is written, I will smite the shepherd, and the sheep of the flock shall be scattered abroad. (32) But after I am risen again, I will go before you into Galilee. (33) Peter answered and said unto him, Though all men shall be offended because of thee, yet will I never be offended. (34) Jesus said unto him, Verily I say unto thee, That this night, before the cock crow, thou shalt deny me thrice. (35) Peter said unto him, Though I should die with thee, yet will I not deny thee. Likewise also said all the disciples.

(36) Then cometh Jesus with them unto a place called Gethsemane, and saith unto the disciples, Sit ye here, while I go and pray yonder. (37) And he took with him Peter and the two sons of Zebedee, and began to be sorrowful and very heavy. (38) Then saith he unto them, My soul is exceeding sorrowful, even unto death: tarry ye here, and watch with me. (39) And he went a little further, and fell on his face, and prayed, saying, O my Father, if it be possible, let this cup pass from me: nevertheless not as I will, but as thou wilt. (40) And he cometh unto the disciples, and findeth them asleep, and saith unto Peter, What, could ye not watch with me one hour? (41) Watch and pray, that ye enter not into temptation: the spirit indeed is willing, but the flesh is weak. (42) He went away again the second time, and prayed, saying, O my Father, if this cup may not pass away from me, except I drink it, thy will be done. (43) And he came and found them asleep again: for their eyes were heavy. (44) And he left them, and went away again, and prayed the third time, saying the same words. (45) Then cometh he to his disciples, and saith unto them, Sleep on now, and take your rest: behold, the hour is at hand, and the Son of man is betrayed into the hands of sinners. (46) Rise, let us be going: behold, he is at hand that doth betray me. (47) And while he yet spake, lo, Judas, one of the twelve, came, and with him a great multitude with swords and staves, from the chief priests

and elders of the people. (48) Now he that betrayed him gave them a sign, saying, Whomsoever I shall kiss, that same is he: hold him fast. (49) And forthwith he came to Jesus, and said, Hail, master; and kissed him. (50) And Jesus said unto him, Friend, wherefore art thou come? Then came they, and laid hands on Jesus, and took him. (51) And, behold, one of them which were with Jesus stretched out his hand, and drew his sword, and struck a servant of the high priest's, and smote off his ear. (52) Then said Jesus unto him, Put up again thy sword into his place: for all they that take the sword shall perish with the sword. (53) Thinkest thou that I cannot now pray to my Father, and he shall presently give me more than twelve legions of angels? (54) But how then shall the scriptures be fulfilled, that thus it must be? (55) In that same hour said Jesus to the multitudes, Are ye come out as against a thief with swords and staves for to take me? I sat daily with you teaching in the temple, and ye laid no hold on me. (56) But all this was done, that the scriptures of the prophets might be fulfilled. Then all the disciples forsook him, and fled.

(57) And they that had laid hold on Jesus led him away to Caiaphas the high priest, where the scribes and the elders were assembled. (58) But Peter followed him afar off unto the high priest's palace, and went in, and sat with the servants, to see the end. (59) Now the chief priests, and elders, and all the council, sought false witness against Jesus, to put him to death; (60) But found none: yea, though many false witnesses came, yet found they none. At the last came two false witnesses, (61) And said, This fellow said, I am able to destroy the temple of God, and to build it in three days. (62) And the high priest arose, and said unto him, Answerest thou nothing? what is it which these witness against thee? (63) But Jesus held his peace. And the high priest answered and said unto him, I adjure thee by the living God, that thou tell us whether thou be the Christ, the Son of God. (64) Jesus saith unto him, Thou hast said: nevertheless I say unto you, Hereafter shall ye see the Son of man sitting on the right hand of power, and coming in the clouds of heaven. (65) Then the high priest rent his clothes, saying, He hath spoken blasphemy; what further need have we of witnesses?

behold, now ye have heard his blasphemy. (66) What think ye? They answered and said, He is guilty of death. (67) Then did they spit in his face, and buffeted him; and others smote him with the palms of their hands, (68) Saying, Prophesy unto us, thou Christ, Who is he that smote thee? (69) Now Peter sat without in the palace: and a damsel came unto him, saying, Thou also wast with Jesus of Galilee. (70) But he denied before them all, saying, I know not what thou sayest. (71) And when he was gone out into the porch, another maid saw him, and said unto them that were there, This fellow was also with Jesus of Nazareth. (72) And again he denied with an oath, I do not know the man. (73) And after a while came unto him they that stood by, and said to Peter, Surely thou also art one of them; for thy speech bewrayeth thee. (74) Then began he to curse and to swear, saying, I know not the man. And immediately the cock crew. (75) And Peter remembered the word of Jesus, which said unto him, Before the cock crow, thou shalt deny me thrice. And he went out, and wept bitterly.

Matthew 27

(1) When the morning was come, all the chief priests and elders of the people took counsel against Jesus to put him to death: (2) And when they had bound him, they led him away, and delivered him to Pontius Pilate the governor.

(3) Then Judas, which had betrayed him, when he saw that he was condemned, repented himself, and brought again the thirty pieces of silver to the chief priests and elders, (4) Saying, I have sinned in that I have betrayed the innocent blood. And they said, What is that to us? see thou to that. (5) And he cast down the pieces of silver in the temple, and departed, and went and hanged himself. (6) And the chief priests took the silver pieces, and said, It is not lawful for to put them into the treasury, because it is the price of blood. (7) And they took counsel, and bought with them the potter's field, to bury strangers in. (8) Wherefore that field was called, The field of blood, unto this day. (9) Then was fulfilled that which was spoken by Jeremy the prophet, saying, And they took the thirty pieces of

silver, the price of him that was valued, whom they of the children of Israel did value; (10) And gave them for the potter's field, as the Lord appointed me.

(11) And Jesus stood before the governor: and the governor asked him, saying, Art thou the King of the Jews? And Jesus said unto him, Thou sayest. (12) And when he was accused of the chief priests and elders, he answered nothing. (13) Then said Pilate unto him, Hearest thou not how many things they witness against thee? (14) And he answered him to never a word; insomuch that the governor marvelled greatly. (15) Now at that feast the governor was wont to release unto the people a prisoner, whom they would. (16) And they had then a notable prisoner, called Barabbas. (17) Therefore when they were gathered together, Pilate said unto them, Whom will ye that I release unto you? Barabbas, or Jesus which is called Christ? (18) For he knew that for envy they had delivered him.

(19) When he was set down on the judgment seat, his wife sent unto him, saying, Have thou nothing to do with that just man: for I have suffered many things this day in a dream because of him. (20) But the chief priests and elders persuaded the multitude that they should ask Barabbas, and destroy Jesus. (21) The governor answered and said unto them, Whether of the twain will ye that I release unto you? They said, Barabbas. (22) Pilate saith unto them, What shall I do then with Jesus which is called Christ? They all say unto him, Let him be crucified. (23) And the governor said, Why, what evil hath he done? But they cried out the more, saying, Let him be crucified.

(24) When Pilate saw that he could prevail nothing, but that rather a tumult was made, he took water, and washed his hands before the multitude, saying, I am innocent of the blood of this just person: see ye to it. (25) Then answered all the people, and said, His blood be on us, and on our children.

(26) Then released he Barabbas unto them: and when he had scourged Jesus, he delivered him to be crucified. (27) Then the soldiers of the governor took Jesus into the common hall, and gathered unto him the whole band of soldiers. (28) And they stripped him, and put on him a scarlet robe.

(29) And when they had platted a crown of thorns, they put it upon his head, and a reed in his right hand: and they bowed the knee before him, and mocked him, saying, Hail, King of the Jews! (30) And they spit upon him, and took the reed, and smote him on the head. (31) And after that they had mocked him, they took the robe off from him, and put his own raiment on him, and led him away to crucify him. (32) And as they came out, they found a man of Cyrene, Simon by name: him they compelled to bear his cross.

(33) And when they were come unto a place called Golgotha, that is to say, a place of a skull, (34) They gave him vinegar to drink mingled with gall: and when he had tasted thereof, he would not drink. (35) And they crucified him, and parted his garments, casting lots: that it might be fulfilled which was spoken by the prophet, They parted my garments among them, and upon my vesture did they cast lots. (36) And sitting down they watched him there; (37) And set up over his head his accusation written, THIS IS JESUS THE KING OF THE JEWS. (38) Then were there two thieves crucified with him, one on the right hand, and another on the left.

(39) And they that passed by reviled him, wagging their heads, (40) And saying, Thou that destroyest the temple, and buildest it in three days, save thyself. If thou be the Son of God, come down from the cross. (41) Likewise also the chief priests mocking him, with the scribes and elders, said, (42) He saved others; himself he cannot save. If he be the King of Israel, let him now come down from the cross, and we will believe him. (43) He trusted in God; let him deliver him now, if he will have him: for he said, I am the Son of God. (44) The thieves also, which were crucified with him, cast the same in his teeth. (45) Now from the sixth hour there was darkness over all the land unto the ninth hour. (46) And about the ninth hour Jesus cried with a loud voice, saying, Eli, Eli, lama sabachthani? that is to say, My God, my God, why hast thou forsaken me? (47) Some of them that stood there, when they heard that, said, This man calleth for Elias. (48) And straightway one of them ran, and took a spunge, and filled it with vinegar, and put it on a reed, and gave him to drink. (49) The rest said, Let be, let us see whether Elias will come to save him.

(50) Jesus, when he had cried again with a loud voice, yielded up the ghost. (51) And, behold, the veil of the temple was rent in twain from the top to the bottom; and the earth did quake, and the rocks rent; (52) And the graves were opened; and many bodies of the saints which slept arose, (53) And came out of the graves after his resurrection, and went into the holy city, and appeared unto many.

(54) Now when the centurion, and they that were with him, watching Jesus, saw the earthquake, and those things that were done, they feared greatly, saying, Truly this was the Son of God. (55) And many women were there beholding afar off, which followed Jesus from Galilee, ministering unto him: (56) Among which was Mary Magdalene, and Mary the mother of James and Joses, and the mother of Zebedee's children.

(57) When the even was come, there came a rich man of Arimathaea, named Joseph, who also himself was Jesus' disciple: (58) He went to Pilate, and begged the body of Jesus. Then Pilate commanded the body to be delivered. (59) And when Joseph had taken the body, he wrapped it in a clean linen cloth, (60) And laid it in his own new tomb, which he had hewn out in the rock: and he rolled a great stone to the door of the sepulchre, and departed. (61) And there was Mary Magdalene, and the other Mary, sitting over against the sepulchre.

(62) Now the next day, that followed the day of the preparation, the chief priests and Pharisees came together unto Pilate, (63) Saying, Sir, we remember that that deceiver said, while he was yet alive, After three days I will rise again. (64) Command therefore that the sepulchre be made sure until the third day, lest his disciples come by night, and steal him away, and say unto the people, He is risen from the dead: so the last error shall be worse than the first. (65) Pilate said unto them, Ye have a watch: go your way, make it as sure as ye can. (66) So they went, and made the sepulchre sure, sealing the stone, and setting a watch.

Matthew 28

(1) In the end of the sabbath, as it began to dawn toward the first day of the week, came Mary Magdalene

and the other Mary to see the sepulchre. (2) And, behold, there was a great earthquake: for the angel of the Lord descended from heaven, and came and rolled back the stone from the door, and sat upon it. (3) His countenance was like lightning, and his raiment white as snow: (4) And for fear of him the keepers did shake, and became as dead men. (5) And the angel answered and said unto the women, Fear not ye: for I know that ye seek Jesus, which was crucified. (6) He is not here: for he is risen, as he said. Come, see the place where the Lord lay. (7) And go quickly, and tell his disciples that he is risen from the dead; and, behold, he goeth before you into Galilee; there shall ye see him: lo, I have told you. (8) And they departed quickly from the sepulchre with fear and great joy; and did run to bring his disciples word.

(9) And as they went to tell his disciples, behold, Jesus met them, saying, All hail. And they came and held him by the feet, and worshipped him. (10) Then said Jesus unto them, Be not afraid: go tell my brethren that they go into Galilee, and there shall they see me.

(11) Now when they were going, behold, some of the watch came into the city, and shewed unto the chief priests all the things that were done. (12) And when they were assembled with the elders, and had taken counsel, they gave large money unto the soldiers, (13) Saying, Say ye, His disciples came by night, and stole him away while we slept. (14) And if this come to the governor's ears, we will persuade him, and secure you. (15) So they took the money, and did as they were taught: and this saying is commonly reported among the Jews until this day.

(16) Then the eleven disciples went away into Galilee, into a mountain where Jesus had appointed them. (17) And when they saw him, they worshipped him: but some doubted. (18) And Jesus came and spake unto them, saying, All power is given unto me in heaven and in earth. (19) Go ye therefore, and teach all nations, baptizing them in the name of the Father, and of the Son, and of the Holy Ghost: (20) Teaching them to observe all things whatsoever I have commanded you: and, lo, I am with you alway, even unto the end of the world. Amen.

Pier Paolo Pasolini in Rome, 1967 (by Franco Vitale).

APPENDICES

QUOTES BY
PIER PAOLO PASOLINI

I love life fiercely, desperately. And I believe that this fierceness, this desperation will carry me to the end... Love of life for me has become a more tenacious vice than cocaine. I devour my existence with an insatiable appetite. (1970)

•

...cinema is already a dream

•

...to make films is to be a poet

•

One can cheat in everything except style.

•

Even a sound image, say thunder booming in a clouded sky, is somehow infinitely more mysterious than even the most poetic description a writer could give of it. A writer has to find oniricity through a highly refined linguistic operation, while the cinema is much nearer to sounds physically, it doesn't need any elaboration. All it needs is to produce a clouded sky with thunder and straight away you are close to the mystery and ambiguity of reality.

•

...a tree photographed is poetic, a human face photographed is poetic because physicity is poetic in itself, because it is an apparition, because it is full of mystery, because it is full of ambiguity, because it is full of polyvalent meaning, because even a tree is a sign of a linguistic system. But who talks through a tree? God, or reality itself. Therefore the tree as a sign puts us in communication with a mysterious speaker.

•

When I make a film I'm always in reality, among the trees and among the people; there's no symbolic or conventional filter between me and reality as there's in literature. The cinema is an explosion of my love for reality. I have never conceived of making a film that would be a work of a group, I've always thought of a film as a work of an author, not only the script and the direction but the choices of sets and locations, the characters, even the clothes. I choose everything, not to mention the music. (1971)

•

The cinema is a language which expresses reality with reality. So the question is: what is the difference between the cinema and reality? Practically none.

•

Reality is divine. That is why my films are never naturalistic. The motivation that unites all of my films is to give back to reality its original sacred significance. (1968)

•

I avoid fiction in my films. I do nothing to console, nothing to embellish reality, nothing to sell the goods. (1973)

•

I've never wanted to make a conclusive statement. I've always posed various problems and left them open to consideration. (1971)

CRITICS ON *THE GOSPEL ACCORDING TO MATTHEW*

Pasolini's is one of the most effective films on a religious theme I have ever seen, perhaps because it was made by a nonbeliever who did not preach, glorify, underline, sentimentalize or romanticize his famous story, but tried his best to simply record it.

Roger Ebert, *Great Movies*

•

[The film] turns out to be more exciting than even the first flash reports on it were and more rewarding in its surge of human drama and spiritual power than one had hoped it might be. For this time the story of Jesus is told in the simple and naturalistic terms of a plain, humble man of the people conducting a spiritual salvation campaign in an environment and among a population that are rough, unadorned and real. [...] The viewer, taking in these freighted gatherings, has the mystical sense of being there.

Bosley Crowther (*New York Times*, 1966)

•

Watching Jesus wander the deserts, meeting the poor and delivering defiant speeches (with one famous Christ quote after another), there is a strange feeling of authenticity, as if somehow news cameras were on the scene.

Danny Peary, *Guide for the Film Fanatic* (1986)

•

Can you imagine a less likely candidate to make

what many people still consider, after more than forty years, the greatest and most moving film about Jesus Christ?

Jim's Reviews

NOTES ON
RENAISSANCE ARTISTS

MASACCIO.

Pier Paolo Pasolini responded to the flattened perspectives of Early Renaissance art, to the *tableau*
approach to grouping figures, and to the separation of
foreground and background. Pasolini didn't need to
'quote' particular painters of the Renaissance, or
individual paintings, because his visual approach in
cinema is already informed by a frontal perspective,
which arranges the action (the figures) at right angles to
the camera lens.

Each painter in the Renaissance re-shaped space to
his/ her own liking. Art historians dutifully record the
development of illusionistic space in a progression of
artists – from Cimabue and Giotto di Bondone to
Masaccio, Domenico Veneziano and Masolino da
Panicale, from Fra Filippo Lippi and Fra Angelico
through Sandro Botticelli and Filippino Lippi,
Giovanni Bellini and Raphael de Sanzio, finding an
apotheosis of depth and *sfumato* in Leonardo da Vinci,
but deepening in darkness still further with Michelangelo di Caravaggio, and, later, Rembrandt van Rijn.

In the art of Masaccio (1401-28), space begins to
open up from the spaceless, golden backgrounds of
Byzantine art. The *Crucifixion* from Masaccio's *Pisa
Altarpiece* (in Naples) depicts four figures (Jesus and the
'three Marys') against a gold background which

suggests, as gold always does in Renaissance painting, power and divinity. With the *Trinity* (in Santa Maria Novella, Florence), Masaccio's space deepens. The evocation of the architecture in Masaccio's *Trinity* is very powerful. He creates a barrel vault between two pilasters, seen from a low viewpoint. The architectonics of the *Trinity* are showy, theatrical, like a stage set. Masaccio monumentalizes his subjects, making God the apex of that strongest of all geometric shapes, the triangle or pyramid.

GIOTTO.

Giotto di Bondone (*c.* 1267-1337) was one of the premier artists in Italy of the 14th century, celebrated by Dante Alighieri, and seen today as one of the key architects of the focus in Early Renaissance art on the human figure. Giotto created works in Naples, Assisi, Padua, Florence and Rome; however, only the famous frescos in Padua (in the Arena Chapel) are recognized as definitely authored by Giotto.

In the art of Giotto, the landscape is still very much a *background*, flattened spatially, so the action in the foreground is not connected with it. Early Renaissance landscape is full of marvellous passages of detail and light, but it is flat and relatively undynamic. In the background of Giotto's *Lamentation*, one of the chief works by Giotto, where the weeping angels swarm like crazed birds in the sky, the landscape is hardly painted in: the suggestions of rocks, a tree, and not much more.

In *The Decameron*, Pasolini cast himself as Giotto (as the artist appeared in the fiction of Giovanni Boccaccio). The Giottoan set-piece in *The Decameron* was a quasi-historical representation of the artist painting a fresco commission in a church (alluding to the Paduan fresco cycle).

PIERO DELL A FRANCESCA.

Piero della Francesca (*c.* 1410/ 20-92) has one of the most special and distinctive forms of space in painting. Piero's sense of space stands out from other painters, as with Paul Cézanne, Rembrandt van Rijn and Mark Rothko. The bright, timeless spaces of Piero are instantly recognizable, and critics sometimes evoke Greek sculpture in connection with Piero's paintings.[1] One might also see in Piero's hermetic, ritualized, timeless paintings the art of Chinese landscape painting, with its evocations of emptiness, which hints at the radical void of Eastern mysticism (in Zen Buddhism and Taoism). Piero's hypnotic art coolly melds science with art, space with spirit, the personal with the cosmic, and history, myth and religion with time.

For Piero della Francesca, geometry, proportion, perspective and mathematics had a magical quality. His art exalts, on one level, a *jouissance* of mathematics and measurement, in which the 'science' of Renaissance perspective is joyously explored. Piero seemed to lean towards the cool, impersonal, impassive scientific inquiry of Aristotlean philosophy, rather than the more sensuous, more obviously mystical aspects of Platonic philosophy: he is regarded by Bernhard Berenson as 'impersonal' (1960, 136). Not a few critics have noted the cool, detached, 'impersonal' approach of Piero's art. R. Vischer calls Piero a 'realist': 'above all he wishes to be a realist, to draw in a realist manner'.[2] A. Stokes regards Piero as the first Cubist, a common view of Piero;[3] while for Kenneth Clark, Piero was a fully 'classic artist'.[4] In his *Tratto della Nabilta della Pittura*, Alberti called Piero 'the greatest geometrician of his age.'[5] F.M. Godfrey was equally breathless,

[1] Like the art of Ancient Greece, Piero della Francesca's paintings rejoice in eternal brilliance, an architectonic precision, and a 'Classical' sense of proportion and harmony. In Piero's epoch, perspective, proportion and geometry attained a fetishistic quality.

[2] R. Vischer: *Luca Signorelli and the Italian Renaissance*, 1879.

[3] A. Stokes: *The Stones of Rimini*, 1929.

[4] Kenneth Clark: *Piero della Francesca*, Phaidon, 1969.

[5] Alberti: *Tratto della Nabilta della Pittura*, 1585.

claiming that '[n]ever before has art blended so nobly with a mathematical purity of space-construction'.[6] Other art critics, though, have not been so convinced of Piero's talents. Lawrence Wright pointed out that 'his geometry is by our standards involved and laborious.[7]

MICHELANGELO MERISI DA CARAVAGGIO.

Of the many Renaissance and post-Renaissance painters, including those of the Baroque and Mannerist eras, the art of Michelangelo Merisi da Caravaggio (1573-1610) stands out as having marked affinities with the æsthetics of Pier Paolo Pasolini. Not, in contrast to the Early Renaissance artists, in the sense of space and visuals, but in subject matter, and in a tragic view of life. And Carvaggio's own life: he was a homosexual with a penchant for the rough trade of the streets (which he famously painted); his career was filled with controversy (and occasional violence); he had a troubled relationship with the authorities; he lived much of the time, like Pasolini, in Roma; and he died, like Pasolini, in mysterious circumstances, way before his time. Caravaggio is a Pasolinian personality, ideal for the subject of a biopic (altho' Pasolini much preferred the Early Italian Renaissance artists, like Masaccio and Giotto, to the Mannerists and Baroque artists).[8]

6 F.M. Godfrey: *A Student's Guide to Italian Paintings 1250-1800*, Alec Tiranti 1965, 88.
7 Lawrence Wright: *Perspective in Perspective*, Routledge 1983, 75.
8 The Pasolinian devotee, Derek Jarman, produced a very disappointing biographical movie about Caravaggio in the 1980s.

Piero, Madonna del Parto

Giotto, The Dream of St Gregory, The Legend of St Francis

Michelangelo da Caravaggio, The Lute Player, Hermitage Museum

CARL-THEODOR DREYER AND
THE PASSION OF JOAN OF ARC

One of Pier Paolo Pasolini's favourite film directors was Carl-Theodor Dreyer (Feb 3, 1889 - March 20, 1968), and his masterpiece *The Passion of Joan of Arc* is a direct influence on *The Gospel According To Matthew*, as well as Pasolini's cinema (many filmmakers have cited Dreyer as a key inspiration, including Jean-Luc Godard, Atom Egoyan and Paul Schrader).

Carl-Theodor Dreyer's reputation rests primarily on only five films: *The Passion of Joan of Arc*, *Vampyr*, *Day of Wrath*, *Ordet* and *Gertrud*. These five movies are masterpieces, with one, *The Passion of Joan of Arc* regularly included in Top 100 Film lists.

Early in his career, C.-T. Dreyer worked for the film company Nordisk. He produced 9 silent features in Scandinavia, France and Germany (including the 'gay' film, *Mikaél* in 1924).

However, the rate of production slowed considerably: after *Vampyr* (1932), Carl-Theodor Dreyer helmed only three pictures, one per decade, with roughly ten years between each one: *Day of Wrath* (1943), *Ordet* (*The Word,* 1954) and *Gertrud* (1964). Four flims in forty years. On the one hand, one mourns the lack of production; on the other, the films are of such high quality, it seems foolish and selfish to complain. Dreyer had been working on a picture about Christ for the last 20 years of his life. He was also planning a movie version of *Medea*. He made many plans for films which never materialized (as with so many filmmakers). From 1952 until his death in 1968, Dreyer ran a cinema in Copenhagen. But you have to wish for those unmade movies, in particular the life of Christ and the interpretation of *Medea*.

Carl-Theodor Dreyer's films are characterized by long takes, glowing, shadowy photography, ensemble pieces in dim interiors, close-knit rural communities, intense personal relationships, sudden flights of poetry or miracle, and a concentration on religious repression, female characters and women's issues.

THE PASSION OF JOAN OF ARC

The Passion of Joan of Arc (*La Passion de Jeanne d'Arc*, 1928) established Carl-Theodor Dreyer as a world class director: of all of his movies as director, *The Passion of Joan of Arc* is the one that is cited more than any other. It regularly crops up in Top 100 Film lists from critics, fans and filmmakers. It's easy to see why: on every level, *The Passion of Joan of Arc* is an extraordinary production.

Where to begin? Everything has probably already been said about *La Passion de Jeanne d'Arc*. Certainly it is a landmark movie, one of those films which you simply *must* see. (Some movies that're regarded as 'classics' don't always live up to their hype and legend: *Pather Panchali* is one, and also *Atalante, The Damned, Celine and Julie Go Boating, Journey To Italy* and *Last Year In Marienbad*).

✢

The script for *The Passion of Joan of Arc* was by Carl-Theodor Dreyer and Joseph Delteil; it was produced by Société Générale des Films in 1927-28. *The Passion of Joan of Arc* was photographed by Rudolph Maté and Goestula Kottula; the art directors were Jean-Victor

Hugo and Hermann Warm; Dreyer also has editor credit. *The Passion of Joan of Arc* is 7,251 feet long (and is projected at both 24 frames per second and 20 f.p.s. – silent cinema speeds being somewhat variable).[1] 82 mins (at 24 f.p.s.).

The cast included Eugene Silvain (Cauchon), Maurice Schiulta (Loyseleur), Michel Simon (Lemaître) and Antonin Artaud (Massieu), with Renée Jeanne (Maria) Falconetti in the star role. The urge towards historical accuracy (the script was based on transcripts of the trial of Joan of Arc, and the architecture and wardrobe was based on research), was off-set by an emphasis on drama and spirituality.

✦

LEGENDS ABOUT *THE PASSION OF JOAN OF ARC.*

The stories of the production of *The Passion of Joan of Arc* are well-known:

• That Carl-Theodor Dreyer and the filmmakers had a huge set constructed (of interconnecting spaces), but the producers complained that the movie didn't really show it off fully (actually, it did – you can glimpse the giant set in numerous shots).

• That Dreyer forbade the use of make-up, in the pursuit of spiritual realism.

• That *La Passion de Jeanne d'Arc* was composed largely as a series of close-ups. The camera is right in the faces of the actors – their noses are inches from the lens.

• That Carl-Theodor Dreyer was tough[2] on actress Renée Jeanne Falconetti in persuading her to deliver the performance of a lifetime (the experience of filming *La Passion* was so traumatic for Falconetti that she didn't make another movie (*Passion* wasn't her only movie, as many film critics assert – Falconetti had appeared in a couple of minor outings. But *Passion was* her last movie. If you're only going to make one major movie, tho', *The Passion of Joan of Arc* isn't bad!). Altho', talking to other actors, including many on the set, she might've found out that not all films are like *The*

1 A DVD release by Eureka has both film speeds.
2 Some reckon that the stories of Dreyer's harsh behaviour towards Falconetti have been over-done, and there was no evidence for it.

Passion of Joan of Arc, and not all film directors are like Carl-Theodor Dreyer!).

RENÉE JEANNE FALCONETTI.

Renée Jeanne[3] Falconetti (1892-1946) has rightly been praised to the skies for her performance in *The Passion of Joan of Arc*. Even curmudgeonly (impossible-to-please) film critic Pauline Kael acknowledged that Falconetti's performance may be the finest ever recorded on film.

It is, though, a self-consciously stylized and exaggerated piece of acting, as if Renée Jeanne Falconetti was being coached before every take to open her eyes as wide as possible, and to emote to the max. It's hysterical, it's over-the-top, it's on the edge of sanity. (Falconetti was troubled by mental illness, and took her life in Buenos Aires in 1946).

Pretty much every feeling that an actor can express or embody or communicate is present in Renée Jeanne Falconetti's performance in *La Passion de Jeanne d'Arc*. Wistfulness, sadness, fear, terror, horror, loneliness, doubt, confusion, suffering and spiritual ecstasy – Falconetti delivers it all, and more. Without the movie showing the rest of Joan of Arc's life, the events and experiences that led her to this trial in a castle, Falconetti manages to evoke it all (in this respect, the script cleverly summarizes some of the key events of La Puccelle's life). And Falconetti achieves most of the effects from a sitting position – she isn't racing about the set, using her whole body, gesturing and emoting. Certainly *The Passion of Joan of Arc* is a masterclass of acting.

Renée Jeanne Falconetti was a stage actress and wasn't sure about the value of the movie at first. Casting La Puccelle was of course absolutely vital in this production (as it is in any movie of Joan's story). And, as with most actresses cast as the Maid of Orleans, Falconetti was far too old (at 35). But you try finding a 17 year-old girl who convinces as Joan of Arc *and* can

---

3 Also known as Maria Falconetti.

deliver that range of feelings!

STYLE, DESIGN, SYMBOLS.

Close-ups – and tracking shots. These are two of Carl-Theodor Dreyer's favourite devices: *The Passion of Joan of Arc,* after all, opens with a long and elaborate crabwise dolly shot, behind the rows of authorities lining up for the trial of La Puccelle. Thus, in between the lengthy series of close-ups and medium close-ups, *The Passion of Joan of Arc* contains Dreyer's beloved device of tracking across a room with the camera pointing at a 90° angle to the actors. Many times the camera tracks across rows of faces, or just two faces (and always remaining in pin-sharp focus – the focus puller on *The Passion of Joan of Arc* deserved an Oscar!).

The camera is often low, often looking up at the judges who loom over the lens and over the viewer. Many of the compositions are off-centre, many are from unusual angles, and many subvert conventional evocations of space and time. DPs Rudolph Maté and Goestula Kottula explored every conceivable angle for photographing a face. This is expressive cinema (tho' not always Expressionist, in the historical sense of 1920s European cinema).[4]

There are self-conscious trick shots, too, in *The Passion of Joan of Arc;* like the bird's-eye-view shot in the gateway of the castle which tilts, following rushing crowds, ending the shot upside-down. Or the worm's-eye-view shot which looks up at the crowds from the ground (this angle was reprised in the famous coffin scene in *Vampyr*).

The Passion of Joan of Arc benefitted from the new

---

4 There is a German Expressionist influence on *The Passion of Joan of Arc* in the personnel: Hermann Warm, a regular Carl-Theodor Dreyer collaborator, designed *The Cabinet of Dr Caligari, Der Müde Tod,* and *The Student of Prague.* DP Rudolph Maté (1898-1964) started out as an assistant to Karl Freund (*Sunrise, Metropolis, The Last Laugh*). Following *Vampyr,* Maté functioned as DP for many renowned filmmakers including Fritz Lang, René Clair, King Vidor, Howard Hawks, William Wyler, William Dieterle, Leo McCarey, Alfred Hitchcock, Zoltan Korda and Ernst Lubitsch.

panchromatic film stock,[5] which enabled beautiful skin tones to be captured in pin-sharp close-ups. This is cinematography where every pore, wrinkle and wart on the skin can be discerned.[6]

La Passion de Jeanne d'Arc is a miracle of light, and how lighting can be employed to illuminate a face. It is not all high key lighting, however, and not all Expressionistic, or high contrast. There are many shots of flat lighting, and of reflected light.

✦

Death looms everywhere in *The Passion of Joan of Arc:* outside, St Joan looks at a skull unearthed by a gravedigger, and the worms crawling in the eye sockets; meanwhile, the authorities ranged against her in the courtroom look like decaying corpses.

The Passion of Joan of Arc wields symbols and motifs in a striking fashion: a crucifix (clutched by Joan for comfort), a skull, a pen, a confession, birds, and fire. The birds flying over the castle, which Joan looks up to see as she's tied to the stake, are the perfect symbol of freedom and innocent, uncorrupted nature.

CAPTIONS.

The Passion of Joan of Arc is filled, like many silent movies, with captions which communicate the dialogue (the production was intended to be a sound movie, but the equipment wasn't up to scratch. Carl-Theodor Dreyer later claimed, no, he didn't want to do a sound film). Being as so much of the movie really comprises question-and-answer dialogues (it is largely taken up with a trial, after all, in the usual courtroom format of accused and interrogators), a sound movie would be the way to go.

However, only the most significant aspects of the script are put into the white-letters-on-black captions. Large portions of the interactions between the Maid of

5 The silent era was mainly filmed using orthochromatic film stock. Eastman Kodak launched their marketing for panchromatic celluloid in 1925, and it became the industry standard by 1928.
6 So you need actors who're happy to be photographed that close, and without make-up. *Many* stars would not do it!

Orleans and her interlocutors are left without captions. But we don't need the inter-titles, because we can guess what the judges and authorities are saying (they rant, they spume, they yell). And when we cut back to yet another giant close-up of Jeanne d'Arc, we see her saying 'yes' (= *oui*), but we don't need to hear it.

INTENSITY.

Intense is a word often used to describe *The Passion of Joan of Arc*. Like the films of Ingmar Bergman, George Lucas and Andrei Tarkovsky, *The Passion of Joan of Arc* certainly is 'intense', and it begs to be viewed in one sitting, so the tension and emotion that builds and builds isn't allowed to dissipate.

The Passion of Joan of Arc does tell the story from the point-of-view of Joan of Arc, does symphaize chiefly with her, and does demonize the authorities. But not entirely: while the judges are cruel and unforgiving (no matter how much they spout nonsense about the 'mercy' of the Christian Church), they are not portrayed entirely as heavies. The 1928 movie is also keen to explore how the *system*, the *institution*, of the Catholic Church, of organized religion, of patriarchal society, is contaminated and vindictive. It's not a bunch of individuals that condemn Joan to death, but an organization, a Church, a law and a society.

The Passion of Joan of Arc is a courtroom drama, but with a very heightened atmosphere, and spectacular spiritual as well as political and military elements. The trial[7] is a format that cinema has exploited thousands of times, and *The Passion of Joan of Arc* is no different in ranging up the authorities and scribes on one side (there is a scribe taking all this down – which formed the historical basis of the script), and the accused on the other side. Poor St Joan, tho', has no lawyer to defend her, no followers in the room to offer support, and is allowed no witnesses (tho' what could a witness say about Joan talking to God?!). The format of the trial is

---

7 *The Passion of Joan of Arc* mirrors the story of the Passion at numerous points (as the stories of many saints do).

very much a lamb among the wolves, with the crude English soldiers hovering on the sidelines (and wandering in to make fun of her).

Until the ending of the 1928 movie, there is only one woman of any significance in *The Passion of Joan of Arc* – St Joan. She is surrounded by ageing men on all sides. Sarcastic, patronizing, stupid, cruel and weak men. It's a vicious portrait of patriarchal power in action, of male-made social institutions at their most inflexible and unforgiving. (But note, when the martyrdom finale arrives, there are many women who're prominent in the crowds witnessing the event. That they are also beaten by soldiers wielding maces is especially horrific).

RECEPTION.

At the box office, *The Passion of Joan of Arc* fared poorly. A number of versions of the print were created. The movie as Carl-Theodor Dreyer intended it was thought lost (copies had been vaporized in fires). Dreyer didn't have control over some of the prints and releases, and found some of the versions in poor taste.

There have been subsequent movies of the life of Joan of Arc, of course. But why bother? *The Passion of Joan of Arc* nails it once and for all. You could say, well, yes, stories and history need to be updated for each new generation of movie-goers. Sure! But, again, why bother? *The Passion of Joan of Arc* nails it. You might as well release a movie about Joan of Arc which comprises nothing but a caption on the screen for 90 minutes: 'GO AND SEE *THE PASSION OF JOAN ARC*'. Or maybe a new movie of Joan of Arc should simply be a re-release of *The Passion of Joan of Arc*.

The Passion of Joan of Arc (1928).

FILMOGRAPHY

THE GOSPEL ACCORDING TO MATTHEW

Released Oct 2, 1964. 142 minutes.

CAST

Enrique Irazoqui – Christ
Margherita Caruso – Mary (younger)
Susanna Pasolini – Mary (older)
Marcello Morante – Joseph
Mario Socrate – John the Baptist
Settimio Di Porto – Peter
Alfonso Gatto – Andrew
Luigi Barbini – James
Giacomo Morante – John
Giorgio Agamben – Philip
Guido Cerretani – Bartholomew
Rosario Migale – Thomas
Ferruccio Nuzzo – Matthew
Marcello Galdini – James son of Alphæus
Elio Spaziani – Thaddeus
Enzo Siciliano – Simon
Otello Sestili – Judas Iscariot
Juan Rodolfo Wilcock – Caiphas
Alessandro Clerici – Pontius Pilate

Amerigo Bevilacqua – Herod I
Francesco Leonetti – Herod II
Franca Cupane – Herodias
Paola Tedesco – Salomé
Rossana Di Rocco – Angel of the Lord
Renato Terra – The Possessed One
Eliseo Boschi – Joseph of Arimathea
Natalia Ginzburg – Mary of Bethania
Umberto Bevilacqua – Soldier
Ninetto Davoli – Shepherd

CREW

Directed and Written – Pier Paolo Pasolini
Producer – Alfredo Bini
Cinematography – Tonino Delli Colli
Film Editing – Nino Baragli
Production Design – Luigi Scaccianoce
Set Decoration – Andrea Fantacci
Costume Design – Danilo Donati
Original Music and music arranger – Luis Bacalov
Piero Cicoletti – assistant costumer
Piero Farani – wardrobe
Marcello Ceccarelli – makeup artist
Lamberto Marini – assistant makeup artist
Mimma Pomilia – hair stylist
Manolo Bolognini – production manager
Eliseo Boschi – production supervisor
Enzo Ocone – production manager
Maurizio Lucidi – assistant director
Paolo Schneider – assistant director
Elsa Morante – assistant director
Dante Ferretti – assistant production designer
Fausto Ancillai – sound mixer
Mario Del Pozzo – sound
Giovanni Canfarelli Modica – first assistant camera
Vittorugo Contino – assistant camera
Angelo Novi – set photographer

Giuseppe Ruzzolini – camera operator
Andreina Casini – assistant editor
Lina D'Amico – script supervisor
Bruno Frascà – production secretary
Vincenzo Taito – administration inspector
Gianni Bonagura – voice dubbing: Marcello Morante
Pino Locchi – voice dubbing: Mario Socrate
Enrico Maria Salerno – voice dubbing: Enrique Irazoqui
Pope John XXIII – dedicatee

PIER PAOLO PASOLINI

FILMOGRAPHY
AND BIBLIOGRAPHY

FEATURE FILMS

Beggar (*Accattone*, 1961)
Mother Rome (*Mamma Roma*, 1962)
Love Meetings (a.k.a. *Lessons In Love*, *Comizi d'Amore*, 1964)
The Gospel According To Matthew (*Il Vangelo Secondo Matteo*, 1964)
The Hawks and the Sparrows (*Uccellacci e Uccellini*, 1966)
Oedipus Rex (*Edipo Re*, 1967)
Theorem (*Teorma*, 1968)
Pigsty (*Porcile*, 1969)
Medea (*Medea*, 1969)
The Decameron (*Il Decamerone*, 1971)
The Canterbury Tales (*I Racconti di Canterbury*, 1972)
The Arabian Nights (*Il Fiore Delle Mille e Una Notte*, 1974)
Salò, or The 120 Days of Sodom (*Salò, o le Centoventi Giornate di Sodoma*, 1975)

SHORT FILMS

The Anger (*La Rabbia*, 1963)
Curd Cheese (*La Ricotta*, episode in *RoGoPaG*, 1963)
The Earth Seen From the Moon (*La Terra Vista Dalla Luna*, episode in *The Witches* = *Le Streghe*, 1967)
What Are the Clouds? (*Che Cosa Sono le Nuvole?*, episode in *Caprice Italian Style* = *Capriccio all'Italiana*, 1968)
The Sequence of the Flower Field (*La Sequenza del Fiore di Carta*, episode in *Love and Anger* = *Vangelo '70/ Amore e Rabbia*, 1969)

DOCUMENTARIES

Location Hunting In Palestine (*Sopralluoghi in Palestina Per Il Vangelo secondo Matteo*, 1965)
Notes For a Film In India (*Appunti Per un Film Sull'India*, 1969)
Notes For a Garbage Novel (*Appunti Per un romanzo dell'immondizia*, 1970)
Notes Towards an African Oresteia (*Appunti Per un'Orestiade Africana*, 1970)
The Walls of Sana'a (*Le Mura di Sana'a*, 1971)
12 December 1972 (*12 Dicembre 1972*, 1972)
Pasolini and the Shape of the City (*Pasolini e la forma della città*, 1975)

SCRIPTS

The River Girl (1954)
Il Prigioniero della montagna (1955)
Manon: Finestra 2 (1956)
Nights of Cabiria (1956)
A Farewell To Arms (1957)
Marisa la Civetta (1957)
Giovani Mariti (1958)
Grigio (1958)
La Notte Brava (1959)
Marte di un Amico (1960)
From a Roman Balcony (1960)
Il Carro armato dell'8 settembre (1960)
I Bell'Antonio (1960)
La Lunga Notte del '43 (1960)
Accattone, F.M., Rome, 1960
La Ragazza In Vetrina (1961)
La Commare Secca (1962)
Mamma Roma, Rizzoli, Milan, 1962
Il Vangelo secondo Matteo, Garzanti, Milan, 1964
Uccellacci e uccellini, Garzanti, Milan, 1966
Oedipus Rex, Garzanti, Milan, 1967/ Lorrimer Publishing, 1984
Requiescant (1967, uncredited)
Il Ragazzo-motore (1967)
Theorem, Garzanti, Milan, 1968
Medea, Garzanti, Milan, 1970
Ostia, Garzanti, Milan, 1970
Storie Scellerate (1973)
Trilogia della vita, Cappelli, Bologna, 1975
San Paolo, Einaudi, Turin, 1977

WORKS AFTER PASOLINI'S DEATH

Laboratorio teatrale di Luca Ronconi (1977)
Mulheres... Mulheres (1981)
Calderon (1981)
Die Leiche murde nie gefunden (1985)

L'Altro enigma (1988)
Who Killed Pasolini? (1995)
Complicity (1995)
Il Pratone del casilino (1996)
Le Bassin de J.W. (1997)
Una Disperata vitalità (1999)
Orgia (2002)
Salò: Yesterday and Today (2002)
Pasolini prossimo nostro (2006)
'Na specie de cadavere lunghissimo (2006)
La Rabbia di Pasolini (2008)
Pilades (2016)

POETRY

Poesie e Casarsa, Libreroa Antiqua Mario Landi, Bologna, 1942
Poesie, Stamperia Primon, 1945
Diarii, 1945
I Pianti, Publicazioni dell-Academiuta, Casarsa, 1946
Dove la mia patria, Publicazioni dell-Academiuta, Casarsa, 1949
Poesia dialettale del Novecento, Guanda, Parma, 1952
Tal cour di un frut, Editizioni Friuli, Tricesimo, 1953/ 1974
Dal Diario, Salvatore Sciascia, Caltanisetta, 1954
Il Canto popolare, La Meridiana, Milan, 1954
La Meglio gioventu, Sansoni, Florence, 1954
Le Ceneri di Gramsci, Garzanti, Milan, 1957
L'Usignolo della Chiesa Cattolica, Loganesi, Milan, 1958/ Turin, 1976
Roma 1950, Milan, 1960
Sonetto primaverile, Milan, 1960
La Religione del mio tempo, Garzanti, Milan, 1961
Poesia in forma di rosa, Garzanti, Milan, 1964
Poesie dimenticate, Società Filologica Friulana, Udine, 1965
Potentissima Signora, Longanesi, Milan, 1965
Poesie, Garzanti, Milan, 1970/ 1999
Transumanar e organizzar, Garzanti, Milan, 1971
Le Poesie, Garzanti, Milan, 1975
La Nuova giovento, Einaudi, Turin, 1975
Poesie e pagine ritrovate, 1980
Poems, New York, 1982
Sette Poesie e due lettere, 1984
Roman Poems, City Lights, 1986
Poems, 1996
Poems Scelte, 1997
Poesie rifiutate, 2000
La Nuova gioventu, 2002
Tutte le poesie, 2003
Meditazione orale, 2005
Poeta delle ceneri, 2010

FICTION

Ragazzi di Vita, Garzanti, Milan, 1955/ London, 1989
Una Vita Violenta, Garzanti, Milan, 1959
Donne di Roma, Il Saggiatore, Milan, 1960
A Dream of Something, 1962
Roman Nights and Other Stories, 1965
La Divina Mimesis, 1975
Amado mio, Aitti impuri, 1982
Petrolio, 1992/ 2005
Stories From the City of God, 1995
Romanzi e racconti, 1998
Il re dei giapponesi, 2003

BIBLIOGRAPHY

PIER PAOLO PASOLINI

Pasolini On Pasolini, ed. Oswald Stack, Thames & Hudson, London, 1969

Entretiens avec Pier Paolo Pasolini, Belfond, Paris, 1970

Interview, *Lui*, no. 1, June, 1970

Empirismo eretico, Garzanti, Milan, 1972

Interview, *The Guardian*, Aug 13, 1973

Con Pier Paolo Pasolini, ed. E. Magrelli, Bulzoni, Rome, 1977

Il dialogo, il potere, la morte: la critica e Pasolini, ed. L. Martellini, Cappelli, Bologna, 1979

"Sopralluoghi o la ricerca dei luoghi perduti" (1973), in M. Mancini & G. Perella, 1982

Lutheran Letters, tr. S. Hood, Carcanet Press, 1987

A Future Life, Rome, 1989

"The Lost Pasolini Interview", *Celluloid Liberation Front*, 2012

OTHERS

G. Aichele. "Translation as De-canonization: Matthew's *Gospel According to Pasolini*", *Cross Currents,* 2002

T. Aitken. "The Greatest Story – Never Told", *The Tablet*, Dec 23, 1995

H. Alpert. *Fellini: A Life*, Paragon House, New York, N.Y., 1988

R. Altman, ed. *Sound Theory, Sound Practice*, Routledge, London, 1992

—. *Film/ Genre*, British Film Institute, London, 1999

D. Andrew. *The Major Film Theories*, Oxford University Press, Oxford, 1976

—. *Concepts In Film Theory*, Oxford University Press, Oxford, 1984

—. ed. *Breathless*, Rutgers University Press, New Brunswick, N.J., 1987

G. Andrew. *The Film Handbook*, Longman, London, 1989

G. Annovi. *Pier Paolo Pasolini,* Columbia University Press, 2017

S. Arecco. *Pier Paolo Pasolini,* Partisan, Rome, 1972

G. Austin. *Contemporary French Cinema,* Manchester University Press, Manchester, 1996

B. Babington. *Biblical Epic and Sacred Narrative In the*

Hollywood, Manchester University Press, Manchester, 1993

G. Bachmann. "Pasolini on de Sade", *Film Quarterly*, vol. 29, no. 2, 1975-76

—. "The 220 Days of Sodom", *Film Comment*, vol. 12, no. 2, Mch-Apl, 1976 (and in *Scraps From the Loft*, June 7, 2018)

M. Barker, ed. *The Video Nasties: Freedom and Censorship In the Media*, Pluto Press, London, 1984

—. & J. Petley, eds. *Ill Effects: The Media/ Violence Debate*, Routledge, London, 1997

R. Barthes. *S/Z*, Hill and Wang, New York, N.Y., 1974

—. *The Pleasure of the Text*, Hill and Wang, New York, N.Y., 1975

—. *Image, Music, Text*, tr. S. Heath, Fontana, London, 1984

G. Bataille. *Literature and Evil*, Calder & Boyars, London, 1973

—. *The Story of the Eye*, Penguin, London, 1982

L. Bawden, ed. *The Oxford Companion To Film*, Oxford University Press, Oxford, 1976

J. Baxter. *An Appalling Talent: Ken Russell*, M. Joseph, London, 1973

—. *Fellini*, St Martin's Press, New York, 1993

A. Bazin. *What Is Cinema?*, University of California Press, Berkeley, C.A., 1960, 2 vols

—. "Cinema and Theology", *South Atlantic Quarterly*, 91, 2, 1992

M. Beja. *Film and Literature: An Introduction*, Longman, London, 1979

—. ed. *Perspectives On Orson Welles*, G.K. Hall, Boston, M.A., 1995

D. Bellezza. *Morte di Pasolini*, Milan, 1981

R. Bellour & M. Bandy, eds. *Jean-Luc Godard*, Museum of Modern Art, N.Y., 1992

Maurizio De Benedictis. *Sergio Citti. Lo "straniero" del cinema italiano*, Lithos, 2008

Bernard Berenson: *The Italian Painters of the Renaissance*, Phaidon 1952/ Fontana 1960

A. Bergala & J. Narboni, eds. *Pasolini Cinéaste*, Paris, 1981

R. Bergan & R. Karney. *Bloomsbury Foreign Film Guide*, Bloomsbury, London, 1988

D. Bergman. *Gaiety Transfigured*, Madison, 1991

I. Bergman. *Bergman On Bergman, Interviews with Ingmar Bergman*, eds. S. Björkman *et al,* tr. P. B. Austin, Touchstone, New York, N.Y., 1986

—. *The Magic Lantern: An Autobiography*, London, 1988

—. *Images: My Life In Film,* Faber, London, 1994

A. Bertini. *Teoria e tecnica del film in Pasolini*, Rome, 1979

B. Bertolucci. *Bertolucci By Bertolucci*, with E. Ungari and D. Ranvard, Plexus, London, 1987

P. Biskind. *Easy Riders, Raging Bulls: How the Sex 'n' Drugs 'n' Rock 'n' Roll Generation Saved Hollywood*, Bloomsbury, London, 1998

V. Boarini. *Da Accattone a Salo*, Bologna, 1982

P. Bogdanovitch. *This Is Orson Welles,* Da Capo, New York, 1998

L. Bolton & C.S. Manson, eds. *Italy On Screen: National Identity and Italian Imaginary*, New Studies in European Cinema

Series, Peter Lang, 2010

J. Boorman, ed. *Projections 4*, Faber, London, 1995

—. *Projections 4 1/2*, Positif Editions/ Faber, London, 1995

D. Bordwell & K. Thompson. *Film Art: An Introduction*, McGraw-Hill Publishing Company, New York, N.Y., 1979

—. *The Films of Carl-Theodor Dreyer*, University of California, Berkeley, 1981

—. *et al*. *The Classical Hollywood Cinema: Film Style and Mode of Production To 1960*, Routledge, London, 1985

—. *Narration In the Fiction Film*, Routledge, London, 1988

—. *Ozu and the Poetics of Cinema*, British Film Institute, London, 1988

—. *Making Meaning*, Harvard University Press, Cambridge, M.A., 1989

—. & N. Caroll, eds. *Post-Theory: Reconstructing Film Studies*, University of Wisconsin Press, Madison, W.I., 1996

—. *The Way Hollywood Tells It*, University of California Press, Berkeley, C.A., 2006

—. & K. Thompson. *Film History*, McGraw-Hill, 2010

F. Brady. *Citizen Welles*, Scribner's, New York, 1989

P. Braunberger. *Pierre Braunberger*, Centre National de la Cinématographie, Paris, 1987

D. Breskin. *Inner Voices: Filmmakers In Conversation*, Da Capo, New York, 1997

R. Bresson, *Notes On the Cinematographer*, Quartet, London, 1986

F. Brevini, ed. *Pasolini*, Mondadori, Milan, 1981

R. Brody. *Everything Is Cinema: The Working Life of Jean-Luc Godard*, Faber, London, 2008

R. Brown, ed. *Focus On Godard*, Prentice-Hall, N.J., 1972

Gian Piero Brunetta. *The History of Italian Cinema*, Princeton University Press, 2009

S. Bukatman. *Terminal Identity: The Virtual Subject In Postmodern Science Fiction*, Duke University Press, Durham, N.C., 1993

P.J. Burgard, ed. *Nietzsche and the Feminine*, University Press of Virginia, Charlottesville, 1994

R. Burgoyne. *Bertolucci's 1900*, Wayne State University Press, Detroit, M.I., 1991

F. Burke and M. Waller, eds. *Federico Fellini: Contemporary Perspectives*, University of Toronto Press, 2002

I. Butler. *Religion In the Cinema*, A.S. Barnes, New York, N.Y., 1969

J. Butler. *Gender Trouble: Feminism and the Subversion of Identity*, Routledge, London, 1990

R. Butter *et al*, eds. *Displacing Homophobia: Gay Male Perspectives In Literature and Culture*, London, 1989

I. Cameron, ed. *The Films of Jean-Luc Godard*, Praeger, N.Y., 1969

A. Carotenuto. *L'Autunno della Conscienza*, Turin, 1985

N. Carroll. *Mystifying Movies: Fads and Fallacies of Contemporary Film Theory*, Columbia University Press, New York, N.Y., 1988

S. Casi. *Desiderio di Pasolini*, La Sonda, Turin, 1990

J. Caughie, ed. *Theories of Authorship: A Reader*, Routledge, London, 1988

—. & A. Kuhn, eds. *The Sexual Subject: A* Screen *Reader In Sexuality*, Routledge, London, 1992

Centro Studi sul Cinema e sulle Communicazioni di Massa. *La Giovani generazioni e il cinema di Pier Paolo Pasolini, La Scene e lo schermo*, Dec, 1989

G. Chester & J. Dickey, eds. *Feminism and Censorship: The Current Debate*, Prism Press, Bridport, Dorset, 1988

M. Ciment. *Projections 9: French Filmmakers On Filmmaking*, Faber, London, 1999

H. Cixous. *The Newly Born Woman*, tr. B. Wing, Minnesota University Press, Minneapolis, 1986

—. *The Hélène Cixous Reader*, ed. Susan Sellers, Blackwell, Oxford, 1994

D.A. Cook. *A History of Narrative Film*, W.W. Norton, New York, N.Y., 1981, 1990, 1996

P. Cook & M. Bernink, eds. *The Cinema Book*, 2nd ed., British Film Institute, London, 1999

T. Corrigan. *A Cinema Without Walls: Movies and Culture After Vietnam*, Rutgers University Press, N.J., 1991

P. Cowie. *The Cinema of Orson Welles*, Da Capo, New York, N.Y., 1973

—. *Ingmar Bergman*, Secker & Warburg, London, 1982

R. Crittenden, ed. *Fine Cuts: The Art of European Film Editing*, C.R.C. Press, 2012

M. Crosland, ed. *The Marquis de Sade Reader*, Peter Owen, 2000

J. Davidson. *The Greeks and Greek Love*, Weidenfeld & Nicholson, London, 2007

G. Day & C. Bloch, eds. *Perspectives On Pornography: Sexuality In Film and Literature*, Macmillan, London, 1988

L. De Giusti. *I Film di Pier Paolo Pasolini*, Gremese, Rome, 1990

T. de Lauretis & S. Heath, eds. *The Cinematic Apparatus*, St Martin's Press, New York, N.Y., 1980

—. *Alice Doesn't: Feminism, Semiotics, Cinema*, Indiana University Press, Bloomington, I.N., 1984

—. *Technologies of Gender*, Macmillan, London, 1987

G. Deleuze & F. Guattari. *Cinema 1: The Movement Image*, Athlone Press, London, 1989

—. *Cinema 2: The Time Image*, Athlone Press, London, 1989

—. *What Is Philosophy?*, Verso, London, 1994

J. Derrida: *Of Grammatology*, Johns Hopkins University Press, Baltimore, M.D., 1976

—. *Spurs: Nietzsche's Styles,* University of Chicago Press, Chicago, I.L., 1979

—. *Writing and Difference,* University of Chicago Press, Chicago, I.L., 1987

—. *Archive Fever,* University of Chicago Press, Chicago, I.L., 1999

G. DeSanti *et al. Perchè Pasolini*, Guaraldi, Florence, 1978

J. Distefano. "Picturing Pasolini", *Art Journal,* 1997

W.W. Dixon. *The Films of Jean-Luc Godard*, State University of

New York Press, Albany, N.Y., 1997

J. Dollimore. *Sexual Dissidence*, Oxford, 1991

J. Duflot. *Entretiens avec Pier Paolo Pasolini*, Pierre Belfond, Paris, 1970

R. Durgnat. *Films and Feelings*, Faber, London, 1967

A. Dworkin. *Pornography: Men Possessing Women*, Women's Press, London, 1984

—. *Intercourse*, Arrow, London, 1988

—. *Letters From a War Zone: Writings, 1976-1987*, Secker & Warburg, London, 1988

A. Easthope, ed. *Contemporary Film Theory*, Longman, London, 1993

M. Eliade. *Ordeal by Labyrinth*, University of Chicago Press, Chicago, I.L., 1984

—. *Symbolism, the Sacred and the Arts*, Crossroad, New York, N.Y., 1985

A. Eliot. "*Oedipus Rex* by Pier Paolo Pasolini", *Literature Film Quarterly*, 2004

T. Elsaesser. *European Cinema*, Amsterdam University Press, Amsterdam, 2005

P. Ettedgui. *Production Design & Art Direction*, RotoVision, 1999

Etudes cinématographiques, special Pasolini number, 109-111, 1976

D. Fairservice. *Film Editing*, Manchester University Press, Manchester, 2001

M. Farber. *Negative Space*, Studio Vista, London, 1971

C. Fava & Aldo Vigano. *The Films of Federico Fellini*, Citadel, New York, N.Y., 1990

F. Fellini. *Fellini On Fellini*, Delacorte, New York, N.Y., 1976

—. *Fellini On Fellini*, ed. C. Constantin, Faber, 1995

—. *I'm a Born Liar: A Fellini Lexicon*, ed. D. Pettigrew, Abrams, New York, 2003

A. Ferrero. *Il Cinema di Pier Paolo Pasolini*, Marsilio, Venice, 1977

J. Finler. *The Movie Directors Story*, Octopus Books, London, 1985

—. *The Hollywood Story*, Wallflower Press, London, 2003

John Fletcher & Andrew Benjamin, ed. *Abjection, Melancholia and Love: The Work of Julia Kristeva*, Routledge, London, 1990

K. Forni. "A "cinema of poetry": What Pasolini Did To Chaucer's *Canterbury Tales*", *Literature Film Quarterly*, 2002

G.E. Forshey. *American Religious and Biblical Spectaculars*, Praeger, Westport, CT, 1992

M. Foucault. *The History of Sexuality*, Penguin, London, 1981

—. *The Use of Pleasure: The History of Sexuality*, vol. 2, Penguin, London, 1987

—. *Politics, Philosophy, Culture: Interviews and Other Writings, 1977-1984*, ed. L.D. Kritzmon, Routledge, New York, N.Y., 1990

J. Franklin. *New German Cinema*, Columbus Books, 1986

K. French, ed. *Screen Violence*, Bloomsbury, London, 1996

P. French *et al. The Films of Jean-Luc Godard,* Blue Star House,

1967

A. Frisch. "Francesco Vezzolini: Pasolini Reloaded", interview, Rutgers University Alexander Library, New Brunswick, N.J.

Diana Fuss. *Essentially Speaking*, Routledge, New York, 1989

—. ed. *Inside/ Out: Lesbian Theories, Gay Theories*, Routledge, London, 1991

F. Gado. *The Passion of Ingmar Bergman*, Durham, N.C., 1986

J. Gallagher. *Film Directors On Directing*, Praeger, New York, N.Y., 1989

H. Geduld, ed. *Filmmakers On Filmmaking*, Indiana University Press, Bloomington, I.N., 1967

J. Geiger & R. Rutsky, eds. *Film Analysis*, Norton & Company, New York, N.Y., 2005

J. Gelmis. *The Film Director As Superstar*, Penguin, London, 1974

D. Georgakas & L. Rubenstein, eds. *Art Politics Cinema: The Cineaste Interviews*, Pluto Press, London, 1985

F. Gérard. *Pier Paolo Pasolini*, Seghers, Paris, 1973

—. *Pasolini ou le mythe de la barbarie*, Université de Bruxelles, 1981

J. Gerber. *Anatole Dauman: Pictures of a Producer*, British Film Institute, London, 1992

M. Gervais. *Pier Paolo Pasolini*, Paris, 1973

L. Gianetti: *Godard and Others*, Tantivy, 1975

—. *Understanding Movies*, Prentice-Hall, N.J., 1982

P.C. Gibson & R. Gibson, eds. *Dirty Looks: Women, Pornography, Power*, British Film Institute, London, 1993

Jean-Luc Godard. *Godard On Godard*, ed. A. Bergala, Cahiers du Cinéma, Paris, 1985

—. *Godard On Godard*, eds. J. Narobi & T. Milne, Da Capo, New York, N.Y., 1986

—. *Interviews*, ed. D. Sterritt, University of Mississippi Press, Jackson, 1998

—. *Godard On Godard 2*, ed. A. Bergala, Cahiers du Cinéma, Paris, 1998

—. *Histoire(s) du cinéma*, Gallimard-Gaumont, Paris, 1998

—. "An Audience With Uncle Jean-Luc", *The Guardian*, Feb 11, 2000

J. Gomez. *Ken Russell*, Muller, 1976

R. Gottesman, ed. *Focus On Orson Welles*, Prentice-Hall, Englewood Cliffs, N.J., 1976

P. Grace. *The Religious Film: Christianity and the Hagiopic*, Wiley-Blackwell, Sussex, 2009

D. Graham, ed. *Film and Religion*, St Mungo Press, 1997

B.K. Grant, ed. *Film Genre*, Scarecrow Press, Metuchen, N.J., 1977

—. ed. *Crisis Cinema: The Apocalyptic Idea In Postmodern Narrative Film*, Maisonneuve Press, 1993

—. *Film Genre Reader II*, University of Texas Press, Austin, T.X., 1995

J. Green. *The Encyclopedia of Censorship*, Facts on File, New York, N.Y., 1990

N. Greene. *Pier Paolo Pasolini: Cinema As Heresy*, Princeton University Press, N.J., 1990

Elizabeth Grosz. "Philosophy, Subjectivity and the Body", in C. Pateman, 1986

—. "Desire, the body and recent French feminism", *Intervention*, 21-2, 1988

—. *Sexual Subversions*, Allen & Unwin, London, 1989

—. "The Body of Signification", in J. Fletcher, 1990

—. "Fetishization", in E. Wright, 1992

—. *Volatile Bodies*, Indiana University Press, Bloomington, I.N., 1994

—. *Space, Time and Perversion*, Routledge, London, 1995

B. Groult: "Les portiers de nuit", in *Ainsi soit-elle*, Grasset, Paris, 1975, and in E. Marks, 1981

L. Hanlon. *Fragments: Bresson's Film Style*, Farleigh Dickinson University Press, Rutherford, 1986

S. Harwood. *French National Cinema*, Routledge, London, 1993

P. Hartnoll, ed. *The Oxford Companion To the Theatre*, Oxford University Press, Oxford, 1985

S. Hayward & G. Vincendeau, eds. *French Film*, Routledge, London, 1990

S. Heath. *Questions of Cinema*, Macmillan, London, 1981

—. *Cinema and Language*, University Presses of America, 1983

W. Herzog. *Herzog On Herzog*, ed. P. Cronin, Faber & Faber, London, 2002

G. Hickenlooper. *Reel Conversations: Candid Interviews With Film's Foremost Directors and Critics*, Citadel, New York, N.Y., 1991

C. Higham. *Orson Welles*, St Martin's Press, New York, N.Y., 1985

J. Hill & P.C. Gibson, eds. *The Oxford Guide To Film Studies*, Oxford University Press, Oxford, 1998

J. Hillier, ed. *Cahiers du Cinéma: The 1950s, New-Realism, Hollywood, New Wave*, Harvard University Press, Cambridge, M.A., 1985

—. *The New Hollywood*, Studio Vista, London, 1992

L.C. Hillstrom, ed. *International Dictionary of Films and Filmmakers: Directors*, St James Press, London, 1997

D. Holmes & A. Smith, eds. *100 Years of European Cinema*, Manchester University Press, Manchester, 2000

H. Hughes. *Cinema Italiano*, I.B. Tauris, London, 2011

G. Indiana. *Salò*, British Film Institute, London, 2000

—. "Pasolini, *Mamma Roma*, and *La Ricotta*", Criterion, 2004

A. Insdorf. *Indelible Shadows: Film and the Holocaust*, Cambridge University Press, Cambridge, 1989

L. Irigaray. *The Irigaray Reader*, ed. M. Whitford, Blackwell, Oxford, 1991

F. Jameson. *Signatures of the Visible*, Routledge, New York, N.Y., 1990

—. *Postmodernism, or the Cultural Logic of Late Capitalism*, Verso, London, 1991

D. Jarman. *Modern Nature*, Century, London, 1991

P. Kael. *Kiss Kiss Bang Bang*, Bantam, New York, N.Y., 1969

—. *Going Steady*, Bantam, New York, 1971

—. *Taking It All In*, Marion Boyars, 1986

—. *State of the Art*, Marion Boyars, London, 1987

—. *Movie Love*, Marion Boyars, London, 1992

A. Kaes. *From Hitler To Heimat: The Return of History As Film*, Harvard University Press, Cambridge, M.A., 1989

E. Ann Kaplan, ed. *Psychoanalysis and Cinema*, Routledge, London, 1990

B.F. Kawin. *Mindscreen: Bergman, Godard and First-Person Film*, Princeton University Press, Princeton, N.J., 1978

—. *How Movies Work*, Macmillan, New York, N.Y., 1987

P. Keough, ed. *Flesh and Blood: The National Society of Film Critics On Sex, Violence, and Censorship*, Mercury House, San Francisco, C.A., 1995

T. Kezich. *Fellini: His Life and Work*, Faber and Faber, New York, N.Y., 2006

G. Kindem. *The International Movie Industry*, Southern Illinois University Press, Carbondale, I.L., 2000

R. Kinnard & T. Davis. *Divine Images: A History of Jesus On the Screen,* Citadel Press, New York, N.Y., 1992

C. Klimke. *Kraft der Vergangenheit: Zu Motiven der Filme von Pier Paolo Pasolini,* Frankfurt, 1988

T. Jefferson Kline. *Bertolucci's Dream Loom: A Psychoanalytic Study of Cinema*, University of Massachusetts Press, Amherst, 1987

P. Kolker. *The Altering Eye: Contemporary International Cinema*, Oxford University Press, New York, N.Y., 1983

—. *Bernardo Bertolucci*, British Film Institute, London, 1985

—. *A Cinema of Loneliness: Penn, Stone, Kubrick, Scorsese, Spielberg, Altman*, Oxford University Press, New York, N.Y., 1988/ 2000

S. Kracauer. *Theory of Film*, Princeton University Press, Princeton, N.J., 1997

L. Kreitzer. *The New Testament In Fiction and Film*, J.S.O.T., 1993

—. *The Old Testament In Fiction and Film*, Sheffield Academic Press, Sheffield, 1994

J. Kristeva. *Powers of Horror: An Essay On Abjection*, tr. L.S. Roudiez, Columbia University Press, New York, 1982

—. *Desire In Language: A Semiotic Approach To Literature and Art*, ed. L.S. Roudiez, tr. Thomas Gora, Alice Jardine & L.S. Roudiez, Blackwell, Oxford, 1982

—. *Revolution In Poetic Language*, tr. Margaret Walker, Columbia University Press, New York, 1984

—. Article in *Art Press*, 4, 1984-85

—. *The Kristeva Reader*, ed. T. Moi, Blackwell, Oxford, 1986

—. *Tales of Love*, tr. L.S. Roudiez, Columbia University Press, New York, N.Y., 1987

—. *Black Sun: Depression and Melancholy,* tr. L.S. Roudiez, Columbia University Press, New York, N.Y., 1989

—. *Strangers To Ourselves*, tr. L.S. Roudiez, Harvester Wheatsheaf, Hemel Hempstead, 1991

A. Kuhn. *Women's Pictures: Feminism and the Cinema*, Routledge & Kegan Paul, London, 1982

A. Kurosawa. *Something Like an Autobiography*, Vintage, New

York, N.Y., 1983

J. Lacan. *Écrits: A Selection*, tr. Alan Sheridan, Tavistock, 1977

—. and the École Freudienne. *Feminine Sexuality*, eds. J. Mitchell and J. Rose, Macmillan, London, 1988

R. Lapsley & M. Westlake, eds. *Film Theory: An Introduction*, Manchester University Press, Manchester, 1988

A. Lawton. *The Red Screen: Politics, Society, Art In Soviet Cinema*, Routledge, London, 1992

B. Leaming. *Orson Welles*, Viking, New York, 1985

V. Lebeau. *Psychoanalysis and Cinema*, Wallflower, London, 2001

P. Leprohan. *The Italian Cinema*, tr. R. Greaves & O. Stallybrass, Secker & Warburg, London, 1972

E. Levy. *Cinema of Outsiders: The Rise of American Independent Film*, New York University Press, New York, N.Y., 1999

J. Lewis. *Whom God Wishes To Destroy: Francis Coppola and the New Hollywood*, Duke University Press, Durham, N.C., 1995

—. ed. *New American Cinema*, Duke University Press, Durham, N.C., 1998

—. *Hollywood v. Hard Core: How the Struggle Over Censorship Created the Modern Film Industry*, New York University Press, New York, N.Y., 2000

—. ed. *The End of Cinema As We Know It: American Film In the Nineties*, New York University Press, New York, N.Y., 2002

J. Leyda, ed. *Filmmakers Speak*, Da Capo, New York, 1977/ 84

—. *Kino: A History of the Russian and Soviet Cinema*, 3rd edition, Allen & Unwin, London, 1983

M. Litch. *Philosophy Through Film*, Routledge, London, 2002

P. Livington. *Ingmar Bergman and the Rituals of Art*, Cornell University Press, Ithaca, N.Y., 1982

V. LoBrutto. *Sound-On-Film*, Praeger, New York, N.Y., 1994

—. *Stanley Kubrick*, Faber, London, 1997

Y. Loshitzky. *The Radical Faces of Godard and Bertolucci*, Wayne State University Press, Detroit, M.I., 1995

L. Lourdeaux. *Italian and Irish Filmmakers In America: Ford, Capra, Coppola and Scorsese*, Temple University Press, Philadelphia, P.A., 1990

L. Lucignani & C. Molfese, eds. *Per Conoscere Pasolini*, Bulzoni, Rome, 1978

C. MacCabe. *Godard, Images, Sound, Politics*, Macmillan/ British Film Institute, London, 1980

—. *Godard: A Portrait of the Artist At 70*, Faber, London, 2003

—. *"The Decameron"*, Criterion, 2012

M. Macciocchi, ed. *Pasolini*, Grasset, Paris, 1980

A. Maggi. *The Resurrection of the Body: Pier Paolo Pasolini From St Paul To Sade*, University of Chicago Press, 2009

P. Malone. *Movie Christs and Antichrists*, Crossroad, 1990

R. Maltby. *Harmless Entertainment: Hollywood and the Ideology of Consensus*, Scarecrow Press, Metuchen, N.J., 1983

—. *Hollywood Cinema*, 2nd ed., Blackwell, Oxford, 2003

M. Mancini & G. Perella. *Pier Paolo Pasolini: corpi e luoghi*, Theorema, Bologna, 1982

Mao Tse-tung. *The Little Red Book (Quotations From Chairman*

Mao Tse-tung), Foreign Language Press, Peking, 1967

E. Marks & I. de Courtivron, eds. *New French Feminisms: an anthology*, Harvester Wheatsheaf, Hemel Hempstead, 1981

T. Martin. *Images and the Imageless: A Study In Religious Consciousness and Film*, Bucknell University Press, 1981

G. Mast *et al*, eds. *Film Theory and Criticism: Introductory Readings*, Oxford University Press, New York, N.Y., 1992a

—. & B Kawin, *A Short History of the Movies*, Macmillan, New York, N.Y., 1992b

T.D. Matthews. *Censored*, Chatto & Windus, London, 1994

J.R. May & M. Bird, eds. *Religion In Film*, University of Tennessee Press, Knoxville, 1982

—. *Image and Likeness: Religious Vision In American Film Classics*, Paulist, 1992

—. *New Image of Religious Film*, Sheed & Ward, London, 1996

J. Mayne. *The Woman At the Keyhole: Feminism and Women's Cinema*, Indiana University Press, Bloomington, I.N., 1990

M. Medved. *Hollywood vs. America*, HarperCollins, London, 1992

P. Mellencamp & P. Rosen, eds. *Cinema Histories, Cinema Practices*, University Publications of America, Frederick, M.D., 1984

—. *A Fine Romance: Five Ages of Film Feminism*, Temple University Press, Philadelphia, P.A., 1995

M. Miles. *Seeing and Believing: Religion and Values In the Movies*, Beacon, Boston, M.A., 1996

M.C. Miller. ed. *Seeing Through Movies*, Pantheon, New York, N.Y., 1990

Wu Ming. "The Police vs. Pasolini, Pasolini vs the Police", Verso Books, 2016

T. Modleski, ed. *Studies In Entertainment*, Indiana University Press, Bloomington, I.N., 1987

—. *The Women Who Knew Too Much: Hitchcock and Feminist Theory*, Methuen, London, 1988

—. *Feminism Without Women: Culture and Criticism In a 'Postfeminist' Age*, Routledge, London, 1991

T. Moi. *Sexual/ Textual Politics: Feminist Literary Theory*, Methuen, London, 1983

J. Monaco. *The New Wave: Truffaut, Godard, Chabrol, Rohmer, Rivette*, Oxford University Press, New York, N.Y., 1977

I. Moscati. *Pasolini e il teorema del sesso*, Milan, 1995

P. Mosley. *Ingmar Bergman*, Marion Boyars, London, 1981

R. Murphy, ed. *The British Cinema Book*, Palgrave/ Macmillan, London, 2nd edition, 2009

R. Murray. *Images In the Dark: An Encyclopedia of Gay and Lesbian Film and Video*, Titan Books, London, 1998

S. Murri. *Pier Paolo Pasolini*, Rome, 1984

N. Naldini. *Nei camp dei Friuli: La giovanezza di Pasolini,* Pesce d'Oro, Milan, 1984

—. *Pasolini, una vita*, Einaudi, Turin, 1989

J. Naremore. *The Magic World of Orson Welles,* Southern Methodist University Press, Dallas, T.X., 1989

J. Natoli. *Hauntings: Popular Film and American Culture 1990-*

92, State University of New York Press, Albany, N.Y., 1994

—. *Speeding To the Millennium: Film and Culture 1993-1995*, State University of New York Press, Albany, N.Y., 1998

—. *Postmodern Journeys: Film and Culture, 1996-1998*, State University of New York Press, Albany, N.Y., 2001

S. Neale. *Cinema and Technology*, Macmillan, London, 1985

—. & B. Neve. *Film and Politics In America*, Routledge, London, 1992

J. Nelmes, ed. *An Introduction To Film Studies*, Routledge, London, 1996

R. Neupert. *The End: Narration and Closure In the Cinema*, Wayne State University Press, Detroit, M.I., 1995

K. Newman & J. Marriott. *Horror! The Definitive Companion To the Most Terrifying Movies Ever Made*, Carlton Books, London, 2013

G. Nowell-Smith. *Visconti*, British Film Institute, London, 1973

—. ed. *The Oxford History of World Cinema*, Oxford University Press, Oxford, 1996

—. & S. Ricci, eds. *Hollywood and Europe*, British Film Institute, London, 1998

—. *Making Waves: New Cinemas of the 1960s*, Bloomsbury, 2013

J. Orr & C. Nicholson, eds. *Cinema and Fiction*, Edinburgh University Press, Edinburgh, 1992

—. *Cinema and Modernity*, Polity Press, Cambridge, 1993

—. *Contemporary Cinema*, Edinburgh University Press, Edinburgh, 1998

C. Ostwalt. "Religion & Popular Movies", *Journal of Religion and Film,* 2, 3, 1998

R. Palmer, ed. *The Cinematic Text*, A.M.S., New York, N.Y., 1989

A. Panicali & S. Sestini, eds. *Pier Paolo Pasolini*, Nuovo Salani, Florence, 1982

E. Passannanti. *Il Corpo & Il Potere*, Joker, 2004

—. *La Ricotta,* Mask Press, 2007

—. *Il Cristo dell'Eresia*, Joker, 2009

—. *La Nudita del Sacro nei Film di Pier Paolo Pasolini*, Brindin Press, 2019

Carole Pateman & Elizabeth Grosz, eds. *Feminist Challenges,* Allen & Unwin, Sydney, 1986

A. Pavelin. *Fifty Religious Films,* A.P. Pavelin, Chiselhurst, Kent, 1990

C. Penley, ed. *Feminism and Film Theory*, Routledge, London, 1988

—. *et al*, eds. *Close Encounters: Film, Feminism and Science Fiction*, University of Minnesota Press, Minneapolis, 1991

V.F. Perkins. *Film As Film: Understanding and Judging Movies*, Penguin, London, 1972

T. Peterson. *The Paraphrase of an Imaginary Dialogue: The Poetics and Poetry of Pier Paolo Pasolini*, New York, 1994

S. Petraglia. *Pier Paolo Pasolini,* Nuova Italia, Florence, 1974

D. Petrie. *Screening Europe: Image and Identity In Contemporary European Cinema*, British Film Institute, London, 1992

G. Phelps. *Film Censorship*, Gollancz, London, 1975

K. Phillips. *New German Filmmakers*, Ungar, New York, N.Y., 1984

L. Polezzi & C. Ross, eds. *In Corpore: Bodies In Post-Unification Italy*, Fairleigh Dickinson University Press, 2007

C. Potter. *Image, Sound and Story: The Art of Telling In Film*, Secker & Warburg, London, 1990

N. Power & G. Nowell-Smith. "Subversive Pasolini", 2012-13, ninapower.net, 2017

P. Powrie, ed. *French Cinema In the 1990s*, Oxford University Press, Oxford, 1999

R. Prendergast. *Film Music*, W.W. Norton, New York, N.Y., 1992

S. Prince. *Savage Cinema: Sam Peckinpah and the Rise of Ultraviolent Movies*, University of Texas Press, Austin, T.X., 1998

—. ed. *Screening Violence*, Athlone Press, London, 2000

—. *A New Pot of Gold: Hollywood Under the Electronic Rainbow*, Scribners, New York, N.Y., 2000

S. Projansky. *Watching Rape: Film and Television In Post-feminism Culture*, New York University Press, New York, N.Y., 2001

T. Pugh. "Chaucerian Fabliaux, Cinematic Fabliau: Pier Paolo Pasolini's *I racconti di Canterbury*", *Literature Film Quarterly*, 2004

M. Pye & Lynda Myles. *The Movie Brats: How the Film Generation Took Over Hollywood*, Faber, London, 1979

T. Rayns, ed. *Fassbinder*, British Film Institute, London, 1979

K. Reader. *Robert Bresson*, Manchester University Press, Manchester, 2000

A. Reinhartz. "Jesus in Film: Hollywood Perspectives on the Jewishness of Jesus", *Journal of Religion and Film*, 2, 2, 1998

A. Restivo. *The Cinema of Economic Miracles: Visuality and Modernization In the Italian Art Film*, Duke University Press, 2002

La Revue d'estgétique, special Pasolini number, 3, 1982

J. Rhodes. *Stupendous, Miserable City: Pasolini's Rome*, University of Minnesota Press, 2007

P. Rice & P. Waugh, eds. *Modern Literary Theory: A Reader*, Arnold, London, 1992

J. Richards, ed. *Films and British National Identity*, Manchester University Press, Manchester, 1997

M. Richardson. *Surrealism and Cinema*, Berg, New York, N.Y., 2006

D. Richie. *The Films of Akira Kurosawa*, University of California Press, Berkeley, C.A., 1965

R. Rinaldi. *Pier Paolo Pasolini*, Mursia, Milan, 1982

D. Robinson. *World Cinema*, Methuen, London, 1981

G. Rodgerson & E. Wilson, eds. *Pornography and Censorship*, Lawrence & Wishart, London, 1991

S. Rohdie. *Antonioni*, British Film Institute, London, 1990

—. *The Passion of Pier Paolo Pasolini*, British Film Institute, London, 1995

J. Romney & A. Wootton, eds. *Celluloid Jukebox: Popular Music* and the Movies Since the 50s, British Film Institute, London, 1995

P. Rosen, ed. *Narrative, Apparatus, Ideology: A Film Theory Reader*, Columbia University Press, New York, N.Y., 1986

A. Rosenstone, ed. *Revisioning History: Film and the Construction of a New Past*, Princeton University Press, Princeton, N.J., 1995

R. Roud. *Jean-Luc Godard*, Thames & Hudson, London, 1970

R. Ruiz. *The Poetics of Cinema*, Dis Voir, Paris, 1995

P. Rumble & B. Testa, eds. *Pier Paolo Pasolini*, University of Toronto Press, Toronto, 1994

—. *Allegories of Contamination: Pier Paolo Pasolini's Trilogy of Life*, University of Toronto Press, Toronto, 1996

K. Russell. *A British Picture: An Autobiography*, Heinemann, London, 1989

M. Russell & J. Young. *Film Music*, RotoVision, 2000

V. Russo. *The Celluloid Closet: Homosexuality In the Movies*, Harper & Row, New York, N.Y., 1981

M. de Sade. *The 120 Days of Sodom*, tr. A. Wainhouse & R. Seaver, Arrow, London, 1996

J. Sanford. *The New German Cinema*, Da Capo Press, New York, N.Y., 1982

A. Sarris, ed., *Interviews With Film Directors*, Avon, New York, N.Y., 1969

T. Schatz. *Hollywood Genres*, Random House, New York, N.Y., 1981

—. *Old Hollywood/ New Hollywood*, UMI Research Press, Ann Arbor, M.I., 1983

—. *The Genius of the System: Hollywood Filmmaking In the Studio Era*, Pantheon, New York, N.Y. 1988

Naomi Schor. *Breaking the Chain: Women, Theory and French Realist Fiction*, New York, 1985

—. & Elizabeth Weed, eds. *Differences: More Gender Trouble: Feminism Meets Queer Theory*, 6, 2-3, Indiana University Press, Summer, 1994

P. Schrader. *Transcendental Style In Film: Ozu, Bresson, Dreyer*, Da Capo Press, 1972

M. Schumacher. *Francis Ford Coppola*, Bloomsbury, London, 2000

B. Schwartz. *Pasolini Requiem*, Vintage Books, New York, 1995

P. Schwenger. *Phallic Critiques: Masculinity and 20th Century Literature*, London, 1984

O. Schweitzer. *Pier Paolo Pasolini*, Hamburg, 1986

Bernhart Schwenk & Michael Semff, eds. *Pier Paolo Pasolini and Death*, Ostfildern 2005

M. Scorsese. *Scorsese On Scorsese*, ed. D. Thompson & I. Christie, Faber, London, 1989, 1995

Screen Reader I: Cinema/ Ideology/ Politics, Society for Education in Film & TV, 1977

Screen Reader II: Cinema and Semiotics, British Film Institute, London, 1982

C. Sharrett, ed. *Crisis Cinema*, Maisonneuve Press, Washington, D.C., 1993

D. Shipman. *The Story of Cinema*, Hodder & Stoughton, London, 1984

—. *Caught In the Act: Sex and Eroticism In the Movies*, Hamish Hamilton, London, 1986

T. Shone. *Blockbuster: How the Jaws and Jedi Generation Turned Hollywood Into a Boom-Town*, Scribner, London, 2005

E. Showalter, ed. *The New Feminist Criticism,* Virago, London, 1986

Enzo Siciliano. *Pasolini: A Biography*, tr. John Shepley, Random House, New York, 1982

L. Sider *et al*, eds. *Soundscapes: The School of Sound Lectures 1998-2001*, Wallflower Press, London, 2003

M. Silberman. *German Cinema,* Wayne State University Press, Detroit, M.I., 1995

K. Silverman. *The Subject of Semiotics*, Oxford University Press, New York, N.Y., 1983

—. *The Acoustic Mirror: The Female Voice In Psychoanalysis and Cinema*, Indiana University Press, Bloomington, I.N., 1988

—. *Male Subjectivity At the Margins*, Routledge, London, 1992

—. & H. Farocki. *Speaking About Godard,* New York University Press, New York, N.Y., 1998

P. Adams Sitney, ed. *The Film Culture Reader*, Praeger, New York, N.Y., 1970

—. *Vital Crises In Italian Cinema*, University of Texas Press, Austin, T.X., 1995

S. Snyder. *Pier Paolo Pasolini*, Twayne, 1980

V. Sobchack, ed. *The Persistence of History: Cinema, Television, and the Modern Event*, Routledge, London, 1995

A. Solomon. *20th Century-Fox: A Corporate and Financial History*, Scarecrow Press, Metuchen, N.J., 1988

J. Solomon. *The Ancient World In the Cinema*, London, 1978

—. *The Ancient World In the Cinema*, Yale University Press, New Haven, CT, 2001

P. Sorlin. *The Film In History: Restaging the Past*, Blackwell, Oxford, 1980

S. Spignesi. *The Woody Allen Companion*, Plexus, London, 1994

George Stambolian & Elaine Marks, eds. *Homosexuality and French Literature: Cultural Contexts/ Critical Texts,* Cornell University Press, Ithaca, 1979

B. Steene. *Ingmar Bergman*, Twayne, Boston, M.A., 1968

—. *Ingmar Bergman: A Guide To References and Resources*, Boston, M.A., 1987

N. Steimatsky. "Pasolini on Terra Sancta: Towards a Theology of Film", *Yale Journal of Criticism,* 11, 1, 1998

L. Stern. *The Scorsese Connection*, British Film Institute, London, 1995

D. Sterritt. *The Films of Jean-Luc Godard*, Cambridge University Press, Cambridge, 1999

P. Steven, ed. *Jump Cut: Hollywood, Politics and Counter Cinema*, Between the Lines, Toronto, 1985

G. Stewart. *Between Film and Screen: Modernism's Photo Synthesis*, University of Chicago Press, Chicago, I.L., 1999

C. Sylvester, ed. *The Penguin Book of Hollywood*, Penguin, London, 1999

Y. Tasker. *Spectacular Bodies: Gender, Genre and the Action Cinema*, Routledge, London, 1993

M. Temple & J. Williams, eds. *The Cinema Alone: Essays On the Work of Jean-Luc Godard, 1985-2000*, Amsterdam University Press, Amsterdam, 2000

—. *et al*, eds. *Godard For Ever*, Black Dog Publishing, London, 2004

S. Teo. *Hong Kong Cinema*, British Film Institute, London, 1997

N. Thomas, ed. *International Dictionary of Films and Filmmakers: Films*, St James Press, London, 1990

K. Thompson. *Breaking the Glass Armor: Neoformalist Film Analysis*, Princeton University Press, Princeton, N.J., 1988

—. & D. Bordwell. *Film History: An Introduction*, McGraw-Hill, New York, N.Y., 1994

—. *Storytelling In the New Hollywood*, Harvard University Press, Cambridge, M.A., 1999

D. Thomson. *A Biographical Dictionary of Film*, Deutsch, London, 1995

C. Tohill & P. Tombs. *Immoral Tales: Sex and Horror Cinema In Europe 1956-1984*, Titan Books, London, 1995

Sergio Toffetti. *La Terra vista dalla luna: il cinema di Sergio Citti*, Lindau, 1993

C. Tonetti. *Luchino Visconti*, Columbus Books, 1985

—. *Bernardo Bertolucci*, Twayne, Boston, M.A., 1994

E. Törnqvist. *Between Stage and Screen: Ingmar Bergman Directs*, Amsterdam University Press, Amsterdam, 1995

J. Trevelyan. *What the Censor Saw*, Michael Joseph, London, 1973

H. Trosman. *Contemporary Psychoanalysis and Masterworks of Art and Film,* New York University Press, New York, N.Y., 2000

F. Truffaut. *The Films In My Life*, tr. L. Mayhew, Penguin, London, 1982

P. Tyler. *Sex Psyche Etcetera In the Film*, Horizon, New York, N.Y., 1969

—. *Screening the Sexes: Homosexuality In the Movies*, Doubleday, New York, N.Y., 1973

M. Valck & M. Hagener, eds. *Cinephilia: Movies, Love and Memory*, Amsterdam University Press, Amsterdam, 2005

K. Van Gunden. *Fantasy Films*, McFarland, Jefferson, NC 1989

M. Viano. *A Certain Realism: Making Use of Pasolini's Film Theory and Practice*, University of California Press, Berkeley, 1993.

G. Vincendeau, ed. *Encyclopedia of European Cinema*, British Film Institute, London, 1995

—. ed. *Film/ Literature/ Heritage: A Sight & Sound Reader*, British Film Institute, London, 2001

P. Virilio & S. Lotringer. *The Aesthetics of Disappearance*, tr. P. Beitchman, Semiotext(e), New York, N.Y., 1991

—. *The Vision Machine*, tr. J. Rose, Indiana University Press, Bloomington, I.N., 1994

J. Vizzard. *See No Evil: Life Inside a Hollywood Censor*, Simon & Schuster, New York, N.Y., 1970

A. Vogel. *Film As a Subversive Art*, Weidenfeld & Nicolson, London, 1974

A. Walker. *Sex In the Movies*, Penguin, London, 1968

—. *Hollywood, England: The British Film Industry In the Sixties*, Harrap, London, 1986

J. Wasko. *Movies and Money*, Ablex, N.J., 1982

—. *Hollywood In the Information Age*, Polity Press, Cambridge, 1994

P. Webb. *The Erotic Arts*, Secker & Warburg, London, 1975

E. Weiss. & J. Belton, eds. *Film Sound: Theory and Practice*, Columbia University Press, New York, N.Y., 1989

O. Welles. *This Is Orson Welles*, HarperCollins, London, 1992

—. *Orson Welles: Interviews*, ed. M. Estrin, University of Mississippi Press, Jackson, 2002

Helen Wilcox *et al*, eds. *The Body and the Text: Hélène Cixous, Reading and Teaching*, Harvester Wheatsheaf, Hemel Hempstead, Herts., 1990

P. Willemen, ed. *Pier Paolo Pasolini*, British Film Institute, London, 1977

L. Williams, ed. *Viewing Positions: Ways of Seeing Film*, Rutgers University Press, New Brunswick, N.J., 1995

L.R. Williams. *Critical Desire: Psychoanalysis and the Literary Subject*, Arnold, London, 1995

—. *Sex In the Head*, Harvester Wheatsheaf, Hemel Hempstead, 1995

W. Willimon. "Faithful to the Script", *Christian Century,* 2004

S. Willis. *High Contrast: Race and Gender In Contemporary Hollywood Film*, Duke University Press, Durham, N.C., 1997

R. Wilson & W. Dissanayake, eds. *Global/ Local: Cultural Production and the Transnational Imaginary*, Duke University Press, Durham, N.C., 1996

E. Wistrich. *'I Don't Mind the Sex It's the Violence': Film Censorship Explored*, Marion Boyars, London, 1978

M. Wolf. *The Entertainment Economy,* Penguin, London, 1999

P. Wollen: *Signs and Meaning In the Cinema*, Secker & Warburg, London, 1972

B. Wood. *Orson Welles*, Greenwood Press, Westport, CT, 1990

P. Wood, ed. *Scorsese: A Journey Through the American Psyche*, Plexus, London, 2005

R. Wood. *Ingmar Bergman*, Praeger, New York, N.Y., 1969

—. *Hollywood From Vietnam To Reagan... and Beyond*, Columbia University Press, New York, N.Y., 2003

T. Woods. *Beginning Postmodernism,* Manchester University Press, Manchester, 1999

Elizabeth Wright, ed. *Feminism and Psychoanalysis: A Critical Dictionary*, Blackwell, Oxford, 1992

J. Wyatt. *High Concept: Movies and Marketing In Hollywood*, University of Texas Press, Austin, T.X., 1994

E.C.M. Yau, ed. *At Full Speed: Hong Kong Cinema In a Borderless World,* University of Minnesota Press, Minneapolis, MN, 1998

J. Young, ed. *The Art of Memory: Holocaust Memorials In History*, Prestel, New York, N.Y., 1994

G. Zigaini. *Pasolini e la morte*, Marsilio, Venice, 1987

J. Zipes, ed. *The Oxford Companion To Fairy Tales*, Oxford University Press, 2000

—. *Sticks and Stones: The Troublesome Success of Children's Literature From Slovenly Peter To Harry Potter*, Routledge, London, 2002

—. *The Enchanted Screen: The Unknown History of Fairy-tale Films*, Routledge, New York, N.Y., 2011

—. *The Irresistible Fairy Tale*, Prince University Press, Princeton, N.J., 2012

S. Zizek. *Looking Awry*, Verso, London, 1991

—. *Enjoy Your Symptom: Jacques Lacan In Hollywood and Out*, Routledge, New York, N.Y., 1992

—. ed. *Everything You Always Wanted To Know About Lacan (But Were Too Afraid To Ask Hitchcock)*, Verso, London, 1992

—. *The Metastases of Enjoyment*, Verso, London, 1994

—. *The Indivisible Remainder*, Verso, London, 1996

—. *The Fright of Real Tears: The Uses and Misuses of Lacan In Film Theory*, British Film Institute, London, 1999

Websites for Pasolini-related material include:

pierpaolopasolini.com
pasoliniroma.com
jclarkmedia.com
bernardobertolucci.org

JEREMY ROBINSON has published poetry, fiction, and studies of J.R.R. Tolkien, Samuel Beckett, Thomas Hardy, André Gide and D.H. Lawrence. Robinson has edited poetry books by Novalis, Ursula Le Guin, Friedrich Hölderlin, Francesco Petrarch, Dante Alighieri, Arseny Tarkovsky, and Rainer Maria Rilke.

Books on film and animation include: *The Akira Book* • *The Art of Katsuhiro Otomo* • *The Art of Masamune Shirow* • *The Ghost In the Shell Book* • *Fullmetal Alchemist* • *Cowboy Bebop: The Anime and Movie* • *The Cinema of Hayao Miyazaki* • *Hayao Miyazaki: Pocket Guide* • *Princess Mononoke: Pocket Movie Guide* • *Spirited Away: Pocket Movie Guide* • *Blade Runner and the Cinema of Philip K. Dick* • *Blade Runner: Pocket Movie Guide* • *The Cinema of Donald Cammell* • *Performance: Donald Cammell: Nic Roeg: Pocket Movie Guide* • *Pasolini: Il Cinema di Poesia/ The Cinema of Poetry* • *Salo: Pocket Movie Guide* • *The Trilogy of Life Movies: Pocket Movie Guide* • *The Gospel According To Matthew: Pocket Movie Guide* • *The Ecstatic Cinema of Tony Ching Siu-tung* • *Tsui Hark: The Dragon Master of Chinese Cinema* • *The Swordsman: Pocket Movie Guide* • *A Chinese Ghost Story: Pocket Movie Guide* • *Ken Russell: England's Great Visionary Film Director and Music Lover* • *Tommy: Ken Russell: The Who: Pocket Movie Guide* • *Women In Love: Ken Russell: D.H. Lawrence: Pocket Movie Guide* • *The Devils: Ken Russell: Pocket Movie Guide* • *Walerian Borowczyk: Cinema of Erotic Dreams* • *The Beast: Pocket Movie Guide* • *The Lord of the Rings Movies* • *The Fellowship of the Ring: Pocket Movie Guide* • *The Two Towers: Pocket Movie Guide* • *The Return of the King: Pocket Movie Guide* • *Jean-Luc Godard: The Passion of Cinema* • *The Sacred Cinema of Andrei Tarkovsky* • *Andrei Tarkovsky: Pocket Guide.*

'It's amazing for me to see my work treated with such passion and respect. There is nothing resembling it in the U.S. in relation to my work.'
(Andrea Dworkin)

'This model monograph – it is an exemplary job, and I'm very proud that he has accorded me a couple of mentions… The subject matter of his book is beautifully organised and dead on beam.'
(Lawrence Durrell, on *The Light Eternal: A Study of J.M.W. Turner*)

'Jeremy Robinson's poetry is certainly jammed with ideas, and I find it very interesting for that reason. It's certainly a strong imprint of his personality.'
(Colin Wilson)

'*Sex-Magic-Poetry-Cornwall* is a very rich essay… It is a very good piece… vastly stimulating and insightful.'
(Peter Redgrove)

ARTS, PAINTING, SCULPTURE

web: www.crmoon.com • e-mail: cresmopub@yahoo.co.uk

The Art of Andy Goldsworthy
Andy Goldsworthy: Touching Nature
Andy Goldsworthy in Close-Up
Andy Goldsworthy: Pocket Guide
Andy Goldsworthy In America
Land Art: A Complete Guide

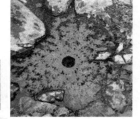

The Art of Richard Long
Richard Long: Pocket Guide
Land Art In Great Britain
Land Art in Close-Up
Land Art In the U.S.A.
Land Art: Pocket Guide
Installation Art in Close-Up

Minimal Art and Artists In the 1960s and After
Colourfield Painting
Land Art DVD, TV documentary
Andy Goldsworthy DVD, TV documentary
The Erotic Object: Sexuality in Sculpture From Prehistory to the Present Day
Sex in Art: Pornography and Pleasure in Painting and Sculpture
Postwar Art
Sacred Gardens: The Garden in Myth, Religion and Art
Glorification: Religious Abstraction in Renaissance and 20th Century Art
Early Netherlandish Painting
Jasper Johns
Brice MardenLeonardo da Vinci
Piero della Francesca
Giovanni Bellini

Fra Angelico: Art and Religion in the Renaissance
Mark Rothko: The Art of Transcendence
Frank Stella: American Abstract Artist
Alison Wilding: The Embrace of Sculpture
Vincent van Gogh: Visionary Landscapes
Eric Gill: Nuptials of God
Constantin Brancusi: Sculpting the Essence of Things

Max Beckmann
Gustave Moreau
Caravaggio
Egon Schiele: Sex and Death In Purple Stockings
Delizioso Fotografico Fervore: Works In Process I

Sacro Cuore: Works In Process 2
The Light Eternal: J.M.W. Turner
The Madonna Glorified: Karen Arthurs

LITERATURE

J.R.R. Tolkien: The Books, The Films, The Whole Cultural Phenomenon
J.R.R. Tolkien: Pocket Guide
Beauties, Beasts and Enchantment: Classic French Fairy Tales
Tolkien's Heroic Quest

Brothers Grimm: German Popular Stories
Sexing Hardy: Thomas Hardy and Feminism
Thomas Hardy's *Tess of the d'Urbervilles*
Thomas Hardy's *Jude the Obscure*
Thomas Hardy: The Tragic Novels
Love and Tragedy: Thomas Hardy
The Poetry of Landscape in Hardy

Wessex Revisited: Thomas Hardy and John Cowper Powys
Wolfgang Iser: Essays and Interviews
Petrarch, Dante and the Troubadours
Maurice Sendak and the Art of Children's Book Illustration
Andrea Dworkin
Cixous, Irigaray, Kristeva: The *Jouissance* of French Feminism
Julia Kristeva: Art, Love, Melancholy, Philosophy, Semiotics and Psychoanalysis
Hélene Cixous I Love You: The *Jouissance* of Writing
Luce Irigaray: Lips, Kissing, and the Politics of Sexual Difference
Peter Redgrove: Here Comes the Flood
Peter Redgrove: Sex-Magic-Poetry-Cornwall
Lawrence Durrell: Between Love and Death, East and West
Love, Culture & Poetry: Lawrence Durrell
Cavafy: Anatomy of a Soul

German Romantic Poetry: Goethe, Novalis, Heine, Hölderlin
Novalis: *Hymns To the Night*
Feminism and Shakespeare
Shakespeare: *The Sonnets*
Shakespeare: Love, Poetry & Magic
The Passion of D.H. Lawrence
D.H. Lawrence: Symbolic Landscapes
D.H. Lawrence: Infinite Sensual Violence

The Ecstasies of John Cowper Powys
Sensualism and Mythology: The Wessex Novels of John Cowper Powys
Amorous Life: John Cowper Powys (H.W. Fawkner)
Postmodern Powys: New Essays on John Cowper Powys (Joe Boulter)
Rethinking Powys: Critical Essays on John Cowper Powys
Paul Bowles & Bernardo Bertolucci
Rainer Maria Rilke
Joseph Conrad: *Heart of Darkness*
In the Dim Void: Samuel Beckett
Samuel Beckett Goes into the Silence
André Gide: Fiction and Fervour
Jackie Collins and the Blockbuster Novel
Blinded By Her Light: The Love-Poetry of Robert Graves

POETRY

Ursula Le Guin: *Walking In Cornwall*
Peter Redgrove: Here Comes The Flood
Peter Redgrove: Sex-Magic-Poetry-Cornwall
Dante: Selections From the *Vita Nuova*
Petrarch, Dante and the Troubadours
William Shakespeare: *The Sonnets*
William Shakespeare: Complete Poems
Blinded By Her Light: The Love-Poetry of Robert Graves
Emily Dickinson: Selected Poems
Emily Brontë: Poems
Thomas Hardy: Selected Poems
Percy Bysshe Shelley: Poems

John Keats: Selected Poems
John Keats: Poems of 1820
D.H. Lawrence: Selected Poems
Edmund Spenser: Poems
Edmund Spenser: *Amoretti*
John Donne: Poems

Henry Vaughan: Poems
Sir Thomas Wyatt: Poems
Robert Herrick: Selected Poems
Rilke: Space, Essence and Angels in the Poetry of Rainer Maria Rilke
Rainer Maria Rilke: Selected Poems
Friedrich Hölderlin: Selected Poems
Arseny Tarkovsky: Selected Poems
Paul Verlaine: Selected Poems

Novalis: *Hymns To the Night*
Arthur Rimbaud: Selected Poems
Arthur Rimbaud: *A Season in Hell*
Arthur Rimbaud and the Magic of Poetry
D.J. Enright: By-Blows

Jeremy Reed: *Brigitte's Blue Heart*
Jeremy Reed: *Claudia Schiffer's Red Shoes*
Gorgeous Little Orpheus
Radiance: New Poems
Crescent Moon Book of Nature Poetry
Crescent Moon Book of Love Poetry
Crescent Moon Book of Mystical Poetry
Crescent Moon Book of Elizabethan Love Poetry
Crescent Moon Book of Metaphysical Poetry
Crescent Moon Book of Romantic Poetry
Pagan America: New American Poetry

MEDIA, CINEMA, FEMINISM and CULTURAL STUDIES

J.R.R. Tolkien: The Books, The Films, The Whole Cultural Phenomenon
J.R.R. Tolkien: Pocket Guide
The *Lord of the Rings* Movies: Pocket Guide
The Ghost Dance: The Origins of Religion
The Cinema of Hayao Miyazaki
Hayao Miyazaki: *Princess Mononoke*: Pocket Movie Guide
Hayao Miyazaki: *Spirited Away*: Pocket Movie Guide
The Peyote Cult
HomeGround: The Kate Bush Anthology
Tim Burton : Hallowe'en For Hollywood
Ken Russell
Cixous, Irigaray, Kristeva: The *Jouissance* of French Feminism
Julia Kristeva: Art, Love, Melancholy, Philosophy, Semiotics and Psychoanalysis
Luce Irigaray: Lips, Kissing, and the Politics of Sexual Difference
Hélene Cixous I Love You: The *Jouissance* of Writing
Andrea Dworkin
'Cosmo Woman': The World of Women's Magazines
Women in Pop Music
Discovering the Goddess (Geoffrey Ashe)
The Poetry of Cinema
The Sacred Cinema of Andrei Tarkovsky
Andrei Tarkovsky: Pocket Guide
Andrei Tarkovsky: *Mirror*: Pocket Movie Guide
Walerian Borowczyk: Cinema of Erotic Dreams
Jean-Luc Godard: The Passion of Cinema
Jean-Luc Godard: Pocket Guide
John Hughes and Eighties Cinema
Ferris Buller's Day Off: Pocket Movie Guide
The Cinema of Richard Linklater
Liv Tyler: Star In Ascendance
Blade Runner and the Films of Philip K. Dick
Paul Bowles and Bernardo Bertolucci
Media Hell: Radio, TV and the Press
Detonation Britain: Nuclear War in the UK
Feminism and Shakespeare
Wild Zones: Pornography, Art and Feminism
Sex in Art: Pornography and Pleasure in Painting and Sculpture
Sexing Hardy: Thomas Hardy and Feminism

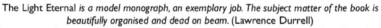

The Light Eternal *is a model monograph, an exemplary job. The subject matter of the book is
beautifully organised and dead on beam.* (Lawrence Durrell)
It is amazing for me to see my work treated with such passion and respect. (Andrea Dworkin)
Sex-Magic-Poetry-Cornwall *is a very rich essay... It is like a brightly-lighted box.* (Peter Redgrove)

CRESCENT MOON PUBLISHING P.O. Box 1312, Maidstone, Kent, ME14 5XU, Great Britain
0044-1622-729593   cresmopub@yahoo.co.uk   www.crmoon.com

Lightning Source UK Ltd.
Milton Keynes UK
UKHW020205090223
416652UK00003B/879

9 781816 718518